MW01252763

Hindu Ritual at the Margins

Studies in Comparative Religion
Frederick M. Denny, Series Editor

Hindu Ritual at the Margins

Innovations, Transformations, Reconsiderations

Edited by

LINDA PENKOWER AND TRACY PINTCHMAN

The University of South Carolina Press

GUELPH HUMBER LIBRARY
205 Humber College Blvd
Toronto, ON M9W 5L7

© 2014 University of South Carolina

Published by the University of South Carolina Press
Columbia, South Carolina 29208

www.sc.edu/uscpress

Manufactured in the United States of America

23 22 21 20 19 18 17 16 15 14 10 9 8 7 6 5 4 3 2 1

Library of Congress Cataloging-in-Publication Data

Hindu Ritual at the Margins : Innovations, Transformations, Reconsiderations / Edited by Linda Penkower and Tracy Pintchman.
pages cm. — (Studies in Comparative Religion)
Based on presentations at a conference called "Ritualizing in, on, and across the Boundaries of the Indian Subcontinent" in honor of Fred W. Clothey on the occasion of his retirement and held at the University of Pittsburgh in March 2006.
Includes bibliographical references and index.
ISBN 978-1-61117-389-5 (Hardbound : alk. paper) — ISBN 978-1-61117-390-1 (Ebook)
1. Hinduism—Rituals—Congresses. 2. Hinduism—Social aspects—Congresses.
I. Penkower, Linda L., editor of compilation. II. Pintchman, Tracy, editor of compilation.
III. Clothey, Fred W., honouree.
BL1226.2.H47 2014
294.5'38—dc23

2014004293

To Fred W. Clothey, a leader in the creation of the field of ritual studies

CONTENTS

ILLUSTRATIONS

SERIES EDITOR'S PREFACE

The editors of this pioneering volume on Hindu ritual do not intend to suggest that the contexts and practices studied are considered to be marginal as "juxtaposed against something in or about Hinduism that is normative or authoritative." They "understand ritual to be of human construct and thus fluid over time and place—neither static nor unified but rather occasioning diversity, difference, and dispute." This volume's illuminating contributions by a variety of leading contemporary scholars of Hinduism and ritual studies continue the innovative and creatively critical spirit of major theoretical studies of ritual over the past couple of decades, including Ronald Grimes's *Ritual Criticism: Case Studies in Its Practice, Essays on Its Theory,* which was published in this series in 1990.

A central goal of this collection, according to its editors, is "pushing our understanding of the complexities of religion, and Hinduism in particular, beyond the limits, boundaries, or 'margins' to which the Western scholarly community has until recently historically corralled it." As the editors declare, "We are, collectively, more interested in change, transformation, and dissonance than in stability, continuity, or consonance." The authors present diverse studies that consider Hindu ritual in traditional historical settings in South Asia, in the contemporary Hindu global diaspora, and in the contexts of contemporary ritual theory. The sophisticated, diversely fascinating, and accessible studies will reward readers—whether professors, their students, or the global market interested in Hinduism in today's world—with discourses that expand our knowledge and understanding of "popular religion" well beyond the traditional but currently declining boundaries of "official religion," whether as defined by orthodox Hindu priests or conventional Western scholars.

Frederick M. Denny

ACKNOWLEDGMENTS

Because of the efforts of scholars such as Fred W. Clothey beginning in the 1970s, the field of ritual studies has been recognized as a discrete area of scholarly pursuit within religious studies, and the study of South Asian religions, in particular, has moved out of the rarified realm of textual study to reveal vibrant and complex religious universes within diverse South and Southeast Asian and Indian diasporic communities. Clothey was a founder of the *Journal of Ritual Studies*, produced and directed six documentary films on ritual, and has written or edited eight books, including *Rhythm and Intent: Ritual Studies from South India*, *The Many Faces of Murukan*, and *Ritualizing on the Boundaries: Continuity and Innovation in the Tamil Diaspora*, which inspired the idea for this volume. We are indebted to Clothey's many contributions to the fields of ritual and South Asian studies and offer the essays that appear here with admiration, affection, and appreciation.

This volume was made possible with the help and support of many people and organizations. The essays that appear in this collection were initially prepared for a conference called "Ritualizing in, on, and across the Boundaries of the Indian Subcontinent" in honor of Clothey on the occasion of his retirement and held at the University of Pittsburgh in March 2006. The conference was convened by Linda Penkower and sponsored by the University of Pittsburgh's Office of the Provost and Dietrich School of Arts and Sciences, Asian Studies Center (ASC), and Indo-Pacific Council of the University Center of International Studies, and Department of Religious Studies. Additional support was provided by the Department of Anthropology, the Program in Cultural Studies, and the University Honors College. We are deeply grateful for the generous institutional support.

We would especially like to thank Nicole Constable, then acting director of the ASC, and Richard J. Cohen, then its associate director, for their encouragement and support of the initial conference proposal, and Jason Fuller of DePauw University for his assistance with the preorganization of the conference. The success of the conference in large part was because of the unflagging administrative and organizational skills of Judith Macey, then administrator of the Department of Religious Studies, and Dianne F. Dakis and Elizabeth Greene, formerly of the ASC. We thank them for service above and beyond the call of duty. Thanks also go to Doreen Hernández, formerly of the ASC, for her artistic and technical acumen in designing the conference website, posters, and brochure.

Our deepest appreciation is reserved for the excellent scholars whose contributions appear in this volume and to those contributors (and their friends and family) who shared their original images that grace its pages. We also wish to thank Ron L. Grimes, now professor emeritus of religion and culture at Wilfrid Laurier University and former chair of ritual studies at Radboud University (the Netherlands), who delivered the conference keynote address, Jeffrey Brackett of Ball State University, Raymond Brady Williams of Wabash College, and Katherine K. Young of McGill University. While their work does not appear in this collection, their presentations and insights during the conference both enlivened the proceedings and added to the success of the essays included here. Thanks also go to our discussants, Joseph S. Alter and Alexander Orbach of the University of Pittsburgh and Donald S. Sutton of Carnegie Mellon University, for their astute comments and critiques during the two-day conference, and to Tony Edwards, Paula M. Kane, and Adam Shear of the University of Pittsburgh for chairing the conference sessions. Thanks too to the Sri Venkateswara Temple in Penn Hills, Pennsylvania, for hosting a tour for our conference participants.

We would also wish to acknowledge two contributors to this volume who were unable to join the conference but whose excellent contributions are included in this collection: Philip Lutgendorf, who authored "The Roles of Ritual in Two 'Blockbuster' Hindi Films," and K. Ramanathan, who coauthored (with Elizabeth Fuller Collins) "The Politics of Ritual among Murukaṉ's Malaysian Devotees." We are grateful to the Rajaraja Museum and Art Gallery, Thanjavur, for permission to use two images that appear in "The Medieval Murukaṉ: The Place of a God among His Tamil Worshipers," and to the American Institute of Indian Studies for supplying those photographs. An original image by Tracy Pintchman graces the cover of this book.

We are especially indebted to Frederick M. Denny, series editor of Studies in Comparative Religion; Linda Haines Fogle, assistant director for operations; Jim Denton, acquisitions editor; Bill Adams, managing editor; Suzanne Axland, marketing director; and the editorial staff at the University of South Carolina Press for their patience and resolute support of this project and for seeing it through to publication. We also wish to express our gratitude to our two anonymous manuscript reviewers; this volume greatly benefited from their thoughtful suggestions. Finally special thanks go to Marilyn Squier of Twin Oaks Indexing, who prepared the index to the volume, with funding provided by Loyola University Chicago.

Introduction

TRACY PINTCHMAN AND LINDA PENKOWER

> Boundaries can be territorial (e.g., what space is "ours"?); more often they are boundaries of mind and spirit as people struggle for a sense of self between and within cultures, between generations, between the world of work and that of home, between the metaphors of their youth and those of their children.
>
> *Fred W. Clothey (2006, 1)*

The essays in this collection take up consideration of Hindu forms of ritual in contexts that we understand to be, generally speaking, marginal. We understand the word *marginal* in this context to be defined variously as, among other things: (1) at an edge, border, limit, or boundary, including a boundary between abstract or physical entities; (2) at an extremity or furthermost part of something, even to the point of being almost eliminated or erased; (3) at a region or point of transition in and between states, historical time periods, and so forth; or (4) at a moment in time when change or occurrence is imminent.

By using the term *marginal,* we in no way intend to suggest that the subject matter of this volume should be juxtaposed against something in or about Hinduism that is normative or authoritative. We understand ritual to be of human construct and thus fluid over time and place—neither static nor unified but rather occasioning diversity, difference, and dispute. While ritual does imply repetition, when considered as the expression of religious identity, values, myths, beliefs, even politics, it is also particularly sensitive to cultural and regional context and personal and community preferences; it can function both to reinforce existing traditions and to help create new ones. The ritual margins that we look at in this volume therefore should not be conceived as deviations from a "center" or North Star that determines orthodoxy/orthopraxy. There is nothing exceptional about Hinduism in this sense. Nor is this volume in the business of determining who should and should not sit at the table when it comes to defining what it means to be Hindu or what constitutes, or is the focus or intended outcome of, a Hindu ritual.

Rather when we speak of margins, we are much more interested in pushing our understanding of the complexities of religion, and Hinduism in particular, beyond the limits, boundaries, or "margins" to which the Western scholarly community has until recently historically corralled it. Within the last generation or so, the field of Hindu studies has moved beyond a near exclusive concern with philology, texts, and doctrine to include methodologies employed by anthropology, art history, literary criticism, sociology, and cultural, film, and gender studies, to name a few. This trend is also reflected within the field of religious studies more broadly, where "popular religion" (itself now a contested term) is no longer considered a superfluous or secondary category in contradistinction to "official religion" (see, for example, Bell 1989). And whereas training in and study of Asian religions have more often than not come to be delineated by region, language bases, and so forth, religious studies, along with cognate disciplines in the humanities and social sciences, now readily participates in discussions of a more comparative nature. The multidisciplinary study of "ritual at the margins," which may refer to geographical or spatial relations, to dynamics in and between communities and institutions, gender groups and social classes, as well as to other tangible and intangible entities, gives us just such an opportunity to engage in this discourse.

The essays in this volume all play with ritual contexts that are "marginal" in a variety of ways: for example in diaspora, that is, geographically marginalized Hindu contexts beyond the boundaries of India, traditionally understood as beyond "Hindusthan," or the place of Hindus (for example, Canada, Malaysia, Singapore, and upstate New York); in contexts scholars have not traditionally taken up in their explorations of Hindu ritual activity (such as contemporary Indian films or texts on dharma); between communities (as in rituals that are performed differently by two different gender, ethnic, social, or political groups); in settings in which either ritual itself or direct discussion of ritual is absent (as in new guru-centered movements); in contexts that create new opportunities for traditionally marginalized participants (for example, women); in contexts where the received tradition is challenged (as in the "discovery" of medieval ritual activity absent from texts but knowable through art and epigraphy); or in theoretical perspectives that have been marginalized in the academy (such as an "indigenous" perspective on ritual found in classical mythological texts). Our main goal is to understand how ritual actors in such contexts come to shape or reshape ritual activity or conceptions pertaining to ritual, adopting either ritual action or thought about ritual action to the context in which it occurs or, conversely, how exploration of some particular context requires that we reshape our understanding of that ritual activity. We are, collectively, more interested in change, transformation, and dissonance than in stability, continuity, or consonance. We embrace contexts of dynamic tension to see how both ritual and our understanding of ritual respond to and are shaped by such tension. For us, playing at the margins means recognizing that these tensions themselves underlie ritual and that ritual itself often holds incongruous or multilayered sensibilities within it. We thus bring together in this volume a group of scholars who work across geographical areas and disciplines in order to examine how diverse groups of Hindu individuals and communities have come to understand or utilize the dynamic processes through which Hindu ritual is shaped, challenged, and redefined.

We also take under consideration two related subissues: (1) how ritual or conceptions of ritual might change in response to, for example, historical transformation, globalization, or the internal diversity of ritualizing communities; and (2) how scholarly considerations of ritual or approaches to the study of ritual might fruitfully change in response to shifting hermeneutical horizons regarding what constitutes ritual and its place in the study of religion. Questions that appear at marginal locations often can be brought to bear fruitfully on notions that sit squarely at the center of our conceptual worlds and can even function to displace received truths and accepted paradigms; it is our hope that our essays will be provocative in this way.

The "Hindu" in Hindu Ritual

Before proceeding we should say a brief word about the ritual activity that we identify as "Hindu." We use the term *Hindu* in this volume descriptively and provisionally to refer to contexts that, from a contemporary perspective, belong to categories that scholarly consensus would, in our opinion, accept as Hindu, broadly speaking. We are well aware that in recent years some scholars have challenged the very legitimacy of the categories "Hindu" and "Hinduism," categories that went pretty much unquestioned by earlier generations. These scholars argue that Hinduism as a religion was essentially invented in the nineteenth century, either by British scholars and colonial administrators or by Indians responding to colonial exigencies, and has no real referent prior to that period (for example, Lorenzen 1999; Llewellyn 2005). While in some ways quite true, this argument can also be misleading. Here reasonable counterarguments have been voiced by scholars, such as David Lorenzen, who point to the emergence in the Purāṇas, as early as 300–600 C.E., of a set of beliefs and practices that, while displaying continuities with the earlier Vedic religion, nevertheless constitute something that one could justifiably call new, perhaps even Hindu (Lorenzen 1999, 655). Inasmuch as the earlier Vedic texts are claimed by later Hindu traditions, reinterpreted, and subsumed by them, we also extend our collaborative inquiry to include Vedic materials. There is a vast body of scholarship on Vedic and Hindu ritual, and it would be foolhardy to attempt to summarize it in any way or even try to highlight its major works or themes. Instead we make note of our aim to engage broader theoretical considerations of the type outlined below as the ground on which we build our exploration of ritual activity in the context of South Asian religious expression.

The Study of Ritual and the Study of Religion

While the study of ritual practice has long been a concern in the academic study of religion, the field of ritual studies as a self-consciously constructed discipline in and of itself is a relatively new phenomenon. Ronald Grimes, one of the leading contemporary scholars of ritual studies, notes that while ritual studies may include textual analysis of some kind, its primary focus is on "performance, enactment, and other forms of overt gestural activity" (Grimes 1990, 9). Ritual studies as a field considers all types of ritual, including those, such as political rituals, that one might not ordinarily think of as religious in character. But the rise in academic attention to ritual as a category of study in its own right in the last three decades has had a profound effect on religious studies scholarship, infusing the study of religious practices from diverse religious traditions with fresh energy and new forms of critical attention.

In his attempt to understand what we might mean by the term *ritual* within the larger field of religious studies, Grimes outlines what he calls a "terminological division of labor" among four terms that appear commonly in ritual studies: *rite, ritual, ritualizing,* and *ritualization.* Grimes defines *rite* as "specific enactments in concrete times and places" that can usually be named (for example, a Bar Mitzvah). They are, says Grimes, the actions enacted by ritualists and observed by "ritologists." The term *ritual,* by contrast, refers to the "general idea" of which any particular rite is a specific instance: "ritual" is a scholarly idea, what one refers to in formal definitions, while "rites are what people enact." Hence, says Grimes, ritual itself does not exist except as an idea that scholars formulate. He uses the term *ritualizing* to suggest the process of deliberately cultivating or inventing rites and *ritualization* to refer to activity that is not culturally framed as ritual (such as television watching) but that, in certain contexts, an observer (such as a scholar of religious studies) may come to interpret as though it were ritual (Grimes 1990, 9–11). *Ritualizing,* for Grimes, is a term that is meant to refer to processes that "fall below the threshold of social recognition of rites" (10).

Yet another term that has come to be important in scholarly work on ritual, including the study of ritual within the field of religious studies, is *performance.* Stanley Tambiah (1979) was one of the first influential scholars to advocate a performative approach to the study of religious ritual, but others (including Catherine Bell, Pierre Bourdieu, Ron Grimes, and Richard Schechner) have followed in his footsteps. Bell, for example, emphasizes the performance model of ritual studies in the study of religion. Bell maintains that use of the term *performance* facilitates exploration of religious activity "in terms of the qualities of human action" (Bell 1998, 205). In religious studies scholarship, *performance* may be invoked instead of the term *ritual* especially in order "to counter the scholarly tendency to approach religious activity as if it were either a type of scriptural text to be analyzed or the mere physical execution of a preexisting ideology" (206–7). The performative approach thus advocated by Bell and others begins with the question "How do participants do what they do?" rather than the earlier interpretive question about meaning. Bell observes that performance imagery uses a vocabulary that "attempts to go beyond primarily intellectual assessments of what ritual does for a better appreciation of the emotional, aesthetic, physical, and sensory aspects of religion" (209) in much the same way, for example, that music can move us whereas its score alone does not (Sharf 2005, 250, 251–52). Mary E. Hancock, similarly, in her work on women's domestic rituals in South India, treats ritual as an "aesthetic practice" that "produces complex subjectivities. . . . Rituals only superficially enact textual recipes. More fundamentally, they are performances attributed with the power to transform participants" (1999, 22).

Bell lists several basic concepts that she considers central to most performative approaches to ritual studies. She observes, for example, that "closely involved with this perspective on ritual events is an appreciation of the physical and sensual aspects of ritual activity. Some theorists appeal to kinesthesia, the sensations experienced by the body in movement. . . . Such theories attempt to grasp more of the distinctive physical reality of ritual so easily overlooked by more intellectual approaches" (1997, 74). This shift to focusing attention on the performative dimensions of ritual activity signals a shift away from what Bell and others observe to be a problematic bifurcation between action and thought, with an implicit subordination of act to thought (Bell 1998, 205; Bell 1992, 49; cf. Sered 1994, 121). The contemporary study of ritual rejects this dichotomy and its associated value hierarchy, instead highlighting the complex dynamics inherent within religious performance itself. In so doing the performative approach largely avoids essentialism by focusing on the elements (such as institutions and training) through which ritual mastery ("the ritualized body" in Bell's words; or "practical mastery" in Bourdieu's) is obtained (Bell 1992, 98–99; Bourdieu 1990, 90–91).

More specifically, in this volume we retain the term *ritual* as a hermeneutically useful term readily recognizable to both academic and general audiences to encompass *ritual, rite,* and *performance.* Differences between specific occurrences of particular enactments and the general idea that is illustrated by the rite are often not at all clear in many of the contexts explored in this book, so the distinction that Grimes draws between rite and ritual is not one to which we call attention in our collaborative work. Furthermore while some of our chapters do emphasize the performative dimensions of ritual, others do not. Hence we use *ritual* as an encompassing term that can incorporate the concerns that we highlight collectively in all our essays.

This volume does not aim to advance new definitions of ritual, and the essays presented here, for the most part, do not set out to engage directly in ritual theory; nonetheless the above overview does lead to a question that is fundamental to our collective enterprise.

What Is Ritual?

Numerous definitions of the term *ritual* exist. They are, however, limited in usefulness at best and misleading at worst. Bell observes that definitions of *ritual* presume, "however provisionally, that there is something we can generally call ritual and whenever or wherever it occurs it has certain distinctive features" (1992, 69). Contemporary scholars of ritual have called such a presumption into question. In this regard many have argued that ritual may be more properly thought of as an aspect of human activity or way of performing an activity rather than a specific type of activity. Grimes, for example, emphasizes the importance of viewing ritual as "not a 'what,' not a thing,'" but "a 'how,' a quality, and there are 'degrees' of it. Any action can be ritualized, though not every action is a rite" (1990, 13). Bell adopts the term *ritualization* in a way that is distinct from that of Grimes to refer to "the way in which certain social actions distinguish themselves in relation to other actions. . . . Ritualization is a way of acting that is designed and orchestrated to distinguish and privilege what is being done in comparison to other, usually more quotidian, activities" (1992, 74).

Grimes also steers away from defining ritual as such, preferring instead to identify the "family characteristics" by which we come to think of particular activities as ritual. The benefit of such an approach, he suggests, is twofold. First, it prevents us from thinking of actions in a binary way, as either ritual or not ritual, as many activities may be ritualistic in at least some aspects. Second, it enables us to think of ritual not as a "thing" but as a quality, a way of acting, which, as noted above, is what he advocates (1990, 13). Grimes identifies fifteen characteristics of ritual (1990, 14), which we list here. For him ritual is activity that is characterized by some or all of these qualities, although none of them is either definitive or unique to ritual. Ritual may be

1. Performed, enacted gestural (not merely thought or said);
2. Formalized, elevated, stylized, differentiated (not ordinary, unadorned, or undifferentiated);
3. Repetitive, redundant, rhythmic (not singular or once-for-all);
4. Collective, institutionalized, consensual (not personal or private);

5. Patterned, invariant, standardized, stereotyped, ordered, rehearsed (not improvised, idiosyncratic, or spontaneous);
6. Traditional, archaic, primordial (not invented or recent);
7. Valued highly or ultimately, deeply felt, sentiment-laden, meaningful, serious (not trivial or shallow);
8. Condensed, multilayered (not obvious; requiring interpretation);
9. Symbolic, referential (not merely technological or primarily means-end oriented);
10. Perfected, idealized, pure, ideal (not conflictual or subject to criticism and failure);
11. Dramatic, ludic (not primarily discursive or explanatory);
12. Paradigmatic (not ineffectual in modeling either other rites or nonritualized action);
13. Mystical, transcendent, religious, cosmic (not secular or merely empirical);
14. Adaptive, functional (not obsessional, neurotic, dysfunctional);
15. Conscious, deliberate (not unconscious or preconscious).

Jonathan Z. Smith similarly describes ritual not as a particular type of activity but instead as "a mode of paying attention" (1987, 104). He continues: "A ritual object or action becomes sacred by having attention focused on it in a highly marked way. From such a point of view, there is nothing that is inherently sacred or profane. These are not substantive categories, but rather situational ones" (105). Hence for Smith, too, ritual is a way of acting rather than a specific type of action. He emphasizes in his understanding of ritual the difference between ordinary, mundane activity and activity that is set apart as ritual. He asserts, "Ritual represents the creation of a controlled environment where the variables (the accidents) of ordinary life may be displaced precisely because they are felt to be so overwhelmingly present and powerful. Ritual is a means of performing the way things ought to be in conscious tension to the way things are" (109).

Elizabeth Fuller Collins articulates two distinctive approaches to the contemporary study of ritual: one that emphasizes what ritual does to people and another that emphasizes what people do with ritual (1997, 17). The first approach elicits a hermeneutics of suspicion, seeking to elucidate ways that ritual practices affirm and reproduce larger relations of social power, often without the conscious assent of ritual actors. The second approach emphasizes instead the ways people use ritual forms to pursue their own individual and collective interests, appropriating and sometimes modifying rituals when convenient or desirable (178). While the first approach Collins outlines stresses the nature of ritual actors as (frequently unwitting) recipients of larger ideological and hegemonic structures, the second stresses their nature as agents who may creatively deploy ritual for their own purposes. While both approaches clearly have a role to play in shedding light on the nature of ritual practice, the essays in this volume tend to emphasize the latter approach, highlighting the agency of human actors in shaping their worlds through and with ritual action.

In this regard some scholars have emphasized the nature of ritual as both constructive and strategic, producing through particular strategies specific types of meaning and values. Through practice ritual actors are, for example, able to appropriate, modify, or reshape cultural values and ideals that mold social identity (Bell 1997, 73, 82). The understanding of ritual as a type of performance becomes especially helpful here for, as Bell notes, *performance* suggests "active rather than passive roles for ritual participants who reinterpret value-laden symbols as they communicate them. . . . Ritual . . . does not simply express cultural values or enact symbolic scripts but actually effects changes in people's perceptions and interpretations" (1997, 73–74).

The active imagery of performance has also brought the possibility of a fuller analytical vocabulary with which to talk about the nonintellectual dimensions of what ritual does, that is, the emotive, physical, and even sensual aspects of ritual participation. Hence ritual as a performative medium for social change emphasizes human creativity and physicality: ritual does not mold people; people fashion rituals that mold their world (Bell 1997, 73). Collins observes that thinking of ritual as performance also requires greater sophistication in thinking through issues of agency. She notes, "The model of performance implies several different agents and different kinds of agency. There is the agency of the author of the text, but also the agency of the performers who choose to perform a particular ritual or a particular variant of a ritual text and who may even revise the text or tradition in their performance. There is the agency of those who participate as audience" (1997, 183–84).

Bell, Grimes, Smith, and Collins present ways of understanding ritual and approaches to the study of ritual that offer us complex, nuanced, and dynamic categories for thinking about human religious activity. Building on their observations, we take under consideration in this volume a range of human action that we understand to be "ritual" not as a particular type of circumscribed activity but rather as a way of performing action—religious action in particular—that sets it apart from ordinary life (Bell), draws on a shared set of formal characteristics (Grimes), focuses the attention of participants and observers in a way that sets the action in question apart from everyday life (Smith), and both shapes and is shaped by human ritual actors (Collins).

Scholarly work on ritual that contemplates human behavior at the margins is not new to the field of religious studies, connected as it is to larger issues concerning shifting senses of identity. This line of inquiry has become increasingly timely as more people in various parts of the world come to interact (sometimes through global media, sometimes quite closely) with individuals, ethnic and social groups, and whole societies that differ in orientation from their own. Marriage, death, or any of the traditional rites of passage have been prime subjects for cross-cultural investigation. Those studies have been joined by work on "center" and "periphery," ritual and diasporic and minority communities, ritual and politics, and so forth (see, for example, Clothey 2006; Harlan and Courtright 1995). When we organized the conference on Hindu rituals at the margins that subsequently led to this collection of essays, bringing together a diverse group of scholars whose independent work maintains a social or historical focus on a particular geographic area or a particular textual or visual medium, we wondered whether or not a set of patterns or thematic considerations might emerge that would allow us to initiate a more comparative dialogue that would contribute to our understanding of ritual actors within Hinduism across a broader spectrum, both premodern and modern, and which might also be of value to ritual studies more broadly. As ritual—whether designed to reinforce or to transform—has been and remains a key activity for negotiating multidimensional margins among Hindu individuals and communities, we turn next to the thematic considerations that came to inform the essays in this volume.

Organization of the Volume

This volume is organized into three sections: "Transformations: History and Identity," "Innovations: Globalization and the Hindu Diaspora," and "Reconsiderations: Context and Theory." Each section comprises three chapters. In some ways these are artificial distinctions. Each essay in this collection has its own historical or social orientation, geographical or textual referent, and thematic focus, and each addresses one or more of the marginal aspects of ritual outlined at the beginning of this introduction. Readers will no doubt uncover multiple layers of overlap and synergy and different patterns and configurations between and among essays. As a rule we do not emphasize geographical or periodization groupings. Rather we highlight three thematic considerations that are suggested by the essays collected here, which offer new ways of thinking about a wide range of ritual activity.

Transformations: History and Identity

The essays in the first section focus on ways that Hindu ritual activity performed in Indian contexts intersects with historical, contextual, and social change. These essays look at ritual transformation at the margins of text and context or between contexts. Among other concerns shared by these three essays is the overriding question of what comparing and contrasting like activities enacted by dissimilar groups might suggest about issues concerning identity, ritual performance, and religious agency. In each instance ritual activity dedicated to a deity ("The Medieval Murukaṉ: The Place of a God among His Tamil Worshipers"), festival ("A Tale of Two Weddings: Gendered Performances of Tulsī's Marriage to Kṛṣṇa"), or rite of passage ("The Roles of Ritual in Two 'Blockbuster' Hindi Films") functions as though it were itself a complementary set of opposites, its structure and identity defined and transformed by its distinct groupings of participants. Yet even in the case where one group historically captures (most of) the narrative, what we learn from each of these essays is that we should not be too quick to label one ritual set of activities—or one group of participants—as marginal and the other not; more often than not, the two coexist in tandem—sometimes playing off or in contention with one another and at other times not.

In the opening essay to this volume, Leslie C. Orr explores the worship of the god Murukaṉ, who, with his lance (*vēl*) and other attributes and associations, is virtually emblematic of Tamil South India identity today. Orr notes that an abundance of devotional literature dedicated to Murukaṉ exists dating from before the seventh century and again after the fourteenth century, when Murukaṉ became an immensely popular object of worship. Yet despite significant religious developments in South India during the intervening centuries, the received literature is silent about the role of Murukaṉ. This has led scholars to speculate that the god was "Sanskritized" into Brahmanic Hinduism and subsumed within the pantheon of the god Śiva only to enjoy a "revival" in the past several centuries. Orr employs art historical and epigraphical evidence to challenge these assumptions convincingly. Rather, through the use of temple images, architecture, and inscriptions, she exposes the variations, shifting patterns, and significance of the worship of Murukaṉ (then commonly referred to as Subrahmaṇya) within the ritual context of the medieval temple during this "gap" period. Orr traces over time the variety of forms and modes of worship of him and the different ways in which his image was placed within the ritual space of the temple, highlighting the dynamic, pluralistic, and even subversive approaches to arrangements for and practices of worship in medieval Tamilnadu. In so doing she offers a detailed picture of the complexity, variety, and fluidity of Subrahmaṇya's significance in the ritual activities and ritual spaces of the medieval South Indian temple, which differed considerably from the ritual concerns reflected in medieval Sanskrit texts and which developed at sites (some still viable today) not associated with Murukaṉ's archaic Tamil mythos.

While Orr reads at the margins of her evidence, looking for clues about religious practice in contexts outside of the ritual context, Tracy Pintchman's "A Tale of Two Weddings" confronts ritual performance head-on, looking at how two different ritual communities perform what is ostensibly the same ritual. Toward the end of the autumn month of Kārtik (October–November), many Hindus in North

India celebrate the marriage of Tulsī, the auspicious basil plant goddess, to her divine groom, usually understood to be Viṣṇu or one of his forms, most often his incarnation Kṛṣṇa. In Vārāṇasī (also called Benares), the wedding is performed ritually in numerous locations, including Hindu homes, temples, and public spaces. Pintchman examines two popular public celebrations of Tulsī's marriage—one enacted by female householders along the banks of the Ganges River, and the other performed by male renunciants in Śrī Maṭh, a Rāmānandi monastery. Here the margin of difference between the two communities becomes the focus of inquiry. Pintchman frames her argument in relation to the Hindu value of auspiciousness, a value that encompasses a concern both for fertility and for cosmic order. Not surprisingly the ritual performed by the women householders lays claim to the former concern, while the male renunciants' ritual emphasizes the latter. What Pintchman demonstrates, moreover, is that this dual interpretation of auspiciousness does not turn the ritual enactments into a duel. Rather, despite clearly drawn differences in both structure and interpretation, both sets of participants do not see their ritual in competition with the other. The lines between the this-worldly and liberative values of the ritual—and by extension between the two appropriations of Tulsī's wedding—remain fluid and permeable, resonating with the values and concerns that religious and social identity help push to the fore.

Philip Lutgendorf's essay, "The Roles of Ritual in Two 'Blockbuster' Hindi Films," completes this section on transformations. Lutgendorf challenges the conventional assumption that film viewing belongs to a "secular" sphere of human activity that is marginal to the "sacred" or "religious" sphere, taking under consideration two unusually successful film productions that were centrally structured around elaborate ritual performances. The narrative of the "mythological" film *Jai Santoshi Maa* (Hail to the Mother of Satisfaction, dir. Vijay Mishra, 1975) largely focuses on the integration of a newly married woman into an extended rural household, even as it cinematically adapts the text of a popular *vrat-kathā*, a story told to accompany the performance of a votive fast performed over sixteen successive Fridays. The film climaxes with the successful completion of this ritual, resulting in a miraculous divine intervention. The second film, *Hum Aapke Hain Koun . . . !* (Who Am I to You?, dir. Sooraj Barjatya, 1994), offers a near operatic extravaganza structured around the paradigmatic performance of an upper-class Hindu wedding, with a coda of a second marriage ceremony involving divine intervention through a family pet. Lutgendorf examines these two films through a kaleidoscope of opposites (family perceptions and gender orientation, sociopolitical contexts, ritual practice and object of devotion, and religious textual references, among others), focusing on how the ritual performances in each film function in both a narrative and perspective manner. For Lutgendorf just as the enactment of rituals is central to the unfolding of the plot and to its satisfactory resolution, in the context of the film's reception, these practices have come to be emulated, in part through "ritualized" reviewing of the films themselves. Thus in the end the films themselves become the ritual and the audience itself the ritual actors.

Innovations: Globalization and the Hindu Diaspora

The essays in the first section all take under consideration ritual and change in Indian contexts, where the issues of agency and identity, as well as points of contention, are, broadly speaking, internal affairs. Those in the second section focus on Hindu ritual practices that occur in geographically marginalized places outside of India. From this perspective each of these essays deals with the tensions and/or freedoms that underlie the adaptation and adoption of ritual activity that in large part stem from minority status in a diasporic community, shifting senses of personal and/or national identity, and the concomitant assumption of multiple orientations. These essays, moreover, all focus on the temple as the site where control of ritual activity is formed, challenged, and redefined, whether that involves the contestation for social status ("The Politics of Ritual among Murukaṉ's Malaysian Devotees"), nontraditional roles for women ("Women, Ritual, and the Ironies of Power at a North American Goddess Temple"), or negotiation and accommodation among diverse participants ("Hindu Ritual in a Canadian Context"). Thus while each of these essays shares some concerns with various essays in the first section, they stand apart in that they involve ritual change and politics: power struggles over a festival exacerbated by political events, gender politics in a Western environment, and immigration policies that initiated new ways of thinking about ritual space.

In "The Politics of Ritual among Murukaṉ's Malaysian Devotees," Elizabeth Fuller Collins and K. Ramanathan examine the politics of Hindu ritual devotion to Murukaṉ during the Tai Pūcam ritual, the major religious festival for Tamil Hindus in Malaysia, to illustrate how ritual performance gives expression to group identities and contested relations of power. They begin with a history of Tamil Hindu immigration to Malaysia in the nineteenth and twentieth centuries to show how claims to ritual authority were expressed in a community that remains deeply divided by caste and class differences. The caste-conscious Nattukottai Chettiyars worship Murukaṉ as Subrahmaṇia (Subrahmaṇya), who is associated with Brahmanic orthodoxy, and sought to reform forms of vow fulfillment that they found "primitive," including piercing the body and fire-walking. Working-class devotees of Murukaṉ, on the other hand, worship him as Taṇṭāyutapāṇi, the ascetic youth of the Palani Temple who rejects caste orthodoxy, and used various forms of bodily vow renewal rituals as a political statement. Collins and Ramanathan go on to demonstrate how the image of Murukaṉ has changed over the last thirty years, during which a transnational Hindu reform movement has promoted a vision of Hinduism as an egalitarian, inclusive, and universal religion. At the same time, in response to a transnational Islamic resurgence and violent clashes between Hindus and Muslims in India, Malaysian Hindus have adopted a defensive stance that ritually glorifies Murukaṉ as a warrior deity. Thus in Malaysia, as elsewhere, as religion becomes a political force, ritual tends to become ideological, with martial images superseding spiritual ones.

Corinne Dempsey's essay, "Women, Ritual, and the Ironies of Power at a North American Goddess Temple," explores the many-layered and specifically gendered ritual dynamics at a temple dedicated to the goddess Rājarājeśwarī in the town of Rush in upstate New York. In adherence with its Śrīvidyā Tantric tradition, this temple strictly follows orthodox ritual prescription yet departs sharply from convention when it encourages women's public participation in central priestly functions, the latter a deviation from other South Indian–style Hindu temples in the North American diaspora and elsewhere. This unusual mixing of strict orthopraxy with nonconvention in ritual contexts sets the stage for ironies that underlie power relations, both human and divine, at the temple. While ritual performances at Rush disregard traditional gender distinctions, the powerful *effects* garnered by ritual performance are understood to underscore gender distinction that in some cases curtail women's—but not men's—participation. The factors that render many women vulnerable to some of the very powers to which they have specialized ritual access have to do with the potentially damaging effects of male temple divinities on menstruating women. Dempsey explores these ritual ironies as executed by Rush temple practices and interpreted by temple theology and lore by tracing the problems that menstruation and male divine power pose for female practitioners amid a celebration of women's exceptional privilege and authority. She concludes that while the ritual ironies that affect women at Rush may be rooted in part in the community's explicit support for women's ritual participation, their flipside hinges on cosmic and theological conundrums that can be far more difficult to unravel.

While Dempsey does not find the typical diasporic preoccupations with ethnic, communal, and national identity formation widely reflected in the temple practices at Rush, Paul Younger returns us to that theme in his essay. In the final chapter in this section on innovations, "Hindu Ritual in a Canadian Context," Younger offers a comparative analysis of the issues involved in the establishment of ritual routines in a variety of Canadian Hindu temples. Among the first wave of immigrants after Canadian immigration law changed to become more inclusive in 1967 was a significant number of Hindu individuals from many different parts of the world. Without any organization representing Hinduism to greet these immigrants, their impetus for forming temple communities was the Canadian law that required legally constituted boards to appoint "clergy" to officiate at weddings. Thus began the work of setting about forming temple communities and deciding which deities to worship and what variety of ritual practices to use in that worship. Younger presents a detailed analysis of the ways in which this discussion took (and continues to take) place in six representative temples in and around Toronto. The Hindu Samaj provides the example of how this process worked in community-style temples all over the country, where "ritual" is what the board democratically determines and where there is no claim of "authenticity" or a direct link with Indian practice. Hindu leaders who pictured the immigrant situation in a more confrontational way and offered to represent the Hindu community in that cultural challenge, on the other hand, did not ultimately fare well among Canadian Hindus. More recently as the Hindu population continues to expand and ethnic communities have begun to congregate in specific suburban areas or urban enclaves, the size and demographics of temples have changed, but the pattern of allowing the worshiping community to determine ritual forms democratically remains.

Reconsiderations: Theory and Context

The final section in this collection considers ritual in and from marginalized perspectives and contexts in ways that theorize from or with absence. The first two essays reconsider what we can learn from primary Hindu sources if we take serious note of their silences or look at their margins, to what may not have been the principal concern of their authors but which is nonetheless implicit in their narrative structure. David L. Haberman's "The Accidental Ritualist" navigates the transgression of an academic boundary that divides those who promote and perform rituals from those who theorize about them to discover ritual theory embedded in ancient narrative literature; Alf Hiltebeitel's "Ritual as Dharma: The Narrowing and Widening of a Key Term" challenges the roots of a theological model that ritualizes war and violence. The final essay in this volume, Joanne Punzo Waghorne's "From Diaspora to (Global) Civil Society: Global Gurus and the Processes of De-ritualization and De-ethnization in Singapore," while sharing some of the concerns that result from globalization with essays in the previous section, considers that the absence of ritual may be the new "ritual" or antiritual and warns us, as scholars of ritual studies, to pay greater attention to new terminologies and nuance shifts in familiar terms.

In "The Accidental Ritualist" Haberman observes that theorizing about ritual has largely been assumed to be the intellectual property of Western academics. Scholars of religious studies are familiar with academic theories about the nature and function of rituals, as we ourselves have taken note earlier in this introduction. Haberman comes at ritual theory from the other end and draws our attention to the idea that there are other perspectives on ritual available to us outside the Western academy with which we can usefully think, namely, indigenous views on ritual experience to be found in nonacademic literature and even sacred texts. Such genres are usually marginalized by Western academic discourse and are in fact completely absent from serious theoretical inquiry. Haberman takes as his case study a genre of Purāṇic narratives in which a person performs a ritual accidentally and yet the ritual nonetheless has a transformative effect. Although the Purāṇas, while filled with detailed descriptions of ritual performances and accounts of benefits to be gained by performing these rituals, do not treat the subject of ritual theory explicitly, Haberman investigates this genre of story as a kind of implicit theorizing about the efficacy of the ritual experience. He proposes that by emphasizing the fortuitous, these Purāṇic accounts highlight the importance of physical performance in rituals and cause us to ponder the efficacy of bodily acts completely divorced from any intention. Accidental ritualists may be lost with regard to knowledge and intentionality, but in the Purāṇas they achieve the desired goal nonetheless and in so doing give us much to think about when considering the nature of ritual performance.

Hiltebeitel's "Ritual as Dharma" brings differential light on the roles of Brahmans, kings, and Kṣatriyas in the ritualization of war and violence. He begins with the equation often made in writings on Hinduism between dharma and karma as ritual action. The usual argument is that dharma is defined primarily by sacrificial action as a type of ritual action and therefore is a subspecies of ritual action. Hiltebeitel counters that it is misleading to derive this equation from the earliest Ṛgvedic uses of the term *dhárman*, from which the concept and word *dharma* derive. He goes on to argue that this equation, which is in fact absent from the earliest Hindu texts, persists in overgeneralized discussions that overlook three splits in the way dharma is treated in the legal and epic texts, where it is for first time made a central concept. By calling attention to how activities are ascribed to different castes and personages within them in these later texts, Hiltebeitel demonstrates that the equation between dharma and ritual action has been familiarized on a carefully hedged ideological model that ritualizes war and violence in the name of the Kṣatriya's *svadharma* ("own law" or "own job") as self-sacrificial, desireless action. Such a perspective of invoking ritual as the model for interpreting dharma, he concludes, is more marginal to the contexts he explores than scholars have previously acknowledged.

In Waghorne's essay, "From Diaspora to (Global) Civil Society," the author explores the place of ritual practice in guru-centered movements among the largely Tamil Indian diaspora in multiethnic Singapore. These formal and informal groups openly replace "religion" (and with it "ritual") with "spirituality" (and with it "yoga") and emphasize the search for widely applicable values and practices over the construction of ethno-religious identity. With their gurus based mostly in South India, these movements nonetheless remain global in outlook as they seek to move their rhetoric of inclusiveness into practice by seeking members from the more numerous Chinese among the population of Singapore. In this process of restructuring religiosity, "ritual" becomes suspect as part of the traditional Hindu world, useful for self-identifying Hindus but ineffective as a source for personal spiritual growth or the development of a multiethnic constituency. Waghorne argues that for these new movements, "ritual" is religion, but *kriya* (yoga-mediation practice) is spirituality; the former is for Hindus, the latter for the world. De-ethnization requires de-ritualization. She concludes by urging theorists of ritual studies to listen for these changing tones in terminology, signaling the rise of global secular values within which actions we would call "ritual" are understood as scientific, universal, and therefore widely applicable to daily human problems in a rapidly consumer-driven, technology-centered globalizing world.

While we draw upon a broad diversity of historical, geographical, and textual contexts, together these chapters argue for inclusion of approaches to and perspectives on the study of Hindu ritual that are attentive to difference, silence, and even absence. We contend that the new attention in ritual studies given to ritual as a "how" instead of a "what," to use Grimes's words, or as the way of acting that Bell wants to call "ritualizing," requires that we stretch our attention to the margins, as it were, and look beyond the familiar, both in terms of data and in terms of theoretical and critical approach. This volume represents one step, however incomplete, in that direction.

References

Bell, Catherine. 1989. "Religion and Chinese Culture: Towards an Assessment of 'Popular Religion.'" *History of Religions* 29, no. 1: 35–57.

——. 1992. *Ritual Theory, Ritual Practice.* New York: Oxford University Press.

——. 1997. *Ritual: Perspectives and Dimensions.* New York: Oxford University Press.

——. 1998. "Performance." In *Critical Terms for Religious Studies,* edited by Mark C. Taylor, 205–24. Chicago: University of Chicago Press.

Bourdieu, Pierre. [1980] 1990. *The Logic of Practice.* Translated by Richard Nice. Stanford, Cal.: Stanford University Press.

Clothey, Fred W. 2006. *Ritualizing on the Boundaries: Continuity and Innovation in the Tamil Diaspora.* Studies in Comparative Religion. Columbia: University of South Carolina Press.

Collins, Elizabeth Fuller. 1997. *Pierced by Murugan's Lance: Ritual, Power, and Moral Redemption among Malaysian Hindus.* DeKalb: Northern Illinois University Press.

Grimes, Ronald. 1990. *Ritual Criticism: Case Studies in Its Practice, Essays on Its Theory.* Columbia: University of South Carolina Press.

Hancock, Mary Elizabeth. 1999. *Womanhood in the Making: Domestic Ritual and Public Culture in Urban South India.* Boulder, Colo.: Westview.

Harlan, Lindsey, and Paul B. Courtright, eds. 1995. *From the Margins of Hindu Marriage: Essays on Gender, Religion, and Culture.* New York: Oxford University Press.

Llewellyn, J. E. 2005. *Defining Hinduism: A Reader.* London: Routledge.

Lorenzen, David. 1999. "Who Invented Hinduism?" *Society for the Comparative Study of Society and History:* 630–59.

Schechner, Richard. 1988. *Performance Theory.* Revised and expanded edition. New York: Routledge.

Sered, Susan Starr. 1994. *Priestess, Mother, Sacred Sister: Religions Dominated by Women.* New York: Oxford University Press.

Sharf, Robert H. 2005. "Ritual." In *Critical Term for the Study of Buddhism,* edited by Donald S. Lopez Jr., 245–70. Chicago: University of Chicago Press.

Smith, Jonathan Z. 1987. *To Take Place: Toward Theory in Ritual.* Chicago: University of Chicago Press.

Tambiah, Stanley J. 1979. "A Performative Approach to Ritual." *Proceedings of the British Academy* 65: 113–69.

PART 1

Transformations

History and Identity

The Medieval Murukaṉ

The Place of a God among His Tamil Worshipers

LESLIE C. ORR

The god Murukaṉ enjoys immense popularity in Tamilnadu today and is virtually an emblem of Tamil identity. The temple dedicated to Murukaṉ at Palani, in the hills to the northwest of Madurai, receives the largest number of pilgrims and the greatest quantity of gifts of any temple in Tamilnadu. While it is acknowledged that the pilgrimage and patronage activities focused on Murukaṉ have seen an upsurge in the last several centuries, this is often regarded as a "revival" of devotion to a god who was widely worshiped in the Tamil country in ancient times—two thousand years ago or more. There is indeed an abundance of devotional literature and textual evidence of rituals dedicated to Murukaṉ dating from before the seventh century. But in subsequent times, up until the fourteenth century, literary sources have virtually nothing to tell us about this god—variously referred to by the Tamil and Sanskrit names Murukaṉ, Skanda, and Subrahmaṇya—or about those who may have worshiped him.

This discontinuity, the gap between the seventh and fourteenth centuries, is quite puzzling. Fred Clothey has suggested that the dearth of medieval textual references to the god is a consequence of Sanskritization and of a movement toward "proliferation and concretization," in which Murukaṉ—along with other deities—was subsumed within the Śaiva pantheon (1978, 77). That such processes took place seem to be borne out by a shift between the seventh and eighth centuries and the eleventh century in the depiction and significance of Somāskanda (Śiva together with his consort, Umā, and his son Skanda). These three figures are first found sculpted on the stone walls of temples in a variety of compositions. By the eleventh century, the composition becomes fixed, and the three figures become a single icon cast in bronze; this image is taken in procession as the main festival image representing Śiva (L'Hernault 1978, 63–66). Here indeed the god Skanda/Murukaṉ/Subrahmaṇya has lost his autonomy.

But in fact the Somāskanda image is not the only image of Murukaṉ to be found. The rich architectural and artistic heritage of medieval Tamilnadu has a great deal to tell us about how Murukaṉ was regarded and how he continued to be worshiped. For if the literary sources of the seventh to fourteenth centuries are silent on these subjects, the inscriptions engraved on temple walls in this period are not. In this essay I focus on what the art historical and epigraphical evidence has to say about the variations, shifting patterns, and significance of the worship of Murukaṉ within the ritual context of the medieval temple. Indeed these sources provide us with precious on-the-ground testimony of how people actually carried out forms of ritual worship at specific sites. With a sculpture of the god before us, we get a vivid sense of the form of the divine with which the medieval worshiper was confronted; meanwhile the inscriptions provide us with details of how worship was conducted—with offerings of lamps, flowers, and food, for example—and document the image donation and temple building of various types of patrons.

Of particular interest to my inquiry is the question of where precisely the god Murukaṉ was placed within the ritual space of the temple; both the physical fabric of the extant temple and the inscriptions at the temple speak to these issues and show the variety of possible arrangements that were made. Does the material evidence from the medieval period indicate that there was a "central" deity in the temple, that therefore it was "his temple," and that he was the main object of worship—and that this "central" deity was ever Murukaṉ? Does the placement of gods (such as Murukaṉ) in smaller structures, usually referred to as "shrines," around a "central" deity suggest hierarchical theological notions or ritual protocols? What is the significance of the appearance of Murukaṉ in a rock-cut cave in the company of other deities, or of his appearance on a temple wall, or on a *śikhara* (temple tower) or *gopura* (gate tower)? And how do worshipers interact with the space of the temple once the gods are emplaced: do they acknowledge a single god's centrality? Is it possible for them to reconstruct or reinterpret the space? What scope is there for innovative or even subversive ritual performances?

My exploration of Murukaṉ's worship in the period between the seventh and fourteenth centuries—when relevant literary sources are so scarce—is thus based on two sorts of evidence, which allow me to trace chronological changes as well as geographical variations. With reference to the latter, I consider medieval Tamilnadu to be divided into four areas: a northern region (Chingleput, North Arcot, and South Arcot districts), Cholanadu or the Kaveri River zone (Thanjavur and Tiruchirappalli districts), western Tamilnadu (Coimbatore, Kolar, and Salem districts), and southern Tamilnadu (Kanyakumari, Madurai, Ramnad, and Tirunelveli districts).[1]

The first body of evidence employed in this study consists of the nearly one hundred temple inscriptions that I was able to locate that refer to the ritual worship of Murukaṉ or whose placement on a Murukaṉ shrine or temple indicates the existence of a context for this worship. One hundred inscriptions, it must be recognized, represent a very tiny fraction of the nearly twenty thousand inscriptions that have been found in the Tamil country. Although there are surely more epigraphical references to Murukaṉ than I have thus far found, it is nonetheless clear that through the whole of the period under review, Murukaṉ worship was not a prominent feature of religious life or, at any rate, the religious life centered on the temple.

The second type of evidence I employ is art and architecture. I have catalogued more than two hundred stone and bronze images or other material evidence—apart from inscriptions—of Murukaṉ worship, including in my survey only those images which are still in situ or whose provenance is known and excluding Somāskanda images. For this study of Murukaṉ's images, I drew on a variety of sources, including my own fieldwork at temples, but am especially indebted to the comprehensive and masterful work of Françoise L'Hernault, particularly her book *L'Iconographie de Subrahmaṇya au Tamilnad.*

Before and After

The material evidence of the seventh to fourteenth centuries—when there are virtually no literary references to Murukaṉ—must be placed within the chronological frame that is built in large part from just such references. I offer a brief outline of Murukaṉ worship in the historical periods that precede and follow the span of time with which I am concerned.

The earliest references to Murukaṉ occur in the so-called Caṅkam literature, the classical Tamil literature of the first few centuries of the Common Era. Here Murukaṉ is portrayed as the beautiful god of the forested hills, bearing a lance (the *vēl*); he is married to the hunter-maiden Vaḷḷi and is the enemy of the demon Cūraṉ. Ceremonies dedicated to Murukaṉ were officiated over by the *vēlaṉ*, a priest who offered the god mountain rice mixed with blood and who was sometimes called in to perform exorcisms on young women who were possessed by the god (Zvelebil 1991, 78–80). The poems *Paripāṭal* and *Tirumurukāṟṟuppaṭai*—composed in the fourth or fifth centuries or somewhat later—contain extensive descriptions of the god and his attributes, including his association with the elephant, the peacock, and the rooster. These poems also introduce us to a second wife, Devasenā (called in Tamil Tēvayāṉai), and provide an account of Murukaṉ's birth as the son of Śiva. *Paripāṭal* describes Murukaṉ's abode Tirupparankunram, a hill just outside of the city of Madurai to the southwest. *Tirumurukāṟṟuppaṭai* mentions the presence of Murukaṉ at six places; these references are, however, quite brief, being marginal to the main theme of the poem, which is the praise of the god's qualities and exploits. Only three of the six sites mentioned in *Tirumurukāṟṟuppaṭai* can be identified with any degree of certainty: Tirupparankunram near Madurai, Tiruccentur further south on the coast east of Tirunelveli, and Palani in the hills far to the northwest of Madurai (Filliozat 1973, xxxv–xxxvii; Clothey 1978, 64–69; Clothey 1983, 23–39; L'Hernault 1978, 185ff.).

Nearly a millennium passed before Murukaṉ resurfaced in Tamil literature, most famously in the poems *Tiruppukal̲*, *Kantar aṉupūti*, and *Kantar alaṅkāram* that were composed—probably in the early fifteenth century—by Aruṇakirinâta. Aruṇakirinâta is supposed to have spent a dissolute early life in the great Śaiva temple town of Tiruvannamalai; finally driven by his misery to complete despair, he resolved to end his life by leaping from the *gopura* over the northern entrance to the temple. As he was about to cast himself down, Lord Murukaṉ appeared before him in the guise of an old man, touched Aruṇakirinâta's tongue with his *vēl*, and commanded him to sing. Thus, according to legend, began Aruṇakirinâta's career as a poet and devotee of Murukaṉ (Clothey 1984, 5–9). Aruṇakirinâta's work includes praise poems dedicated to more than two hundred places where Murukaṉ is said to dwell, many of which are (or were) actually temples dedicated to Śiva.

At the same time that Aruṇakirinâta was composing his hymns, several other important works expressing devotion to Murukaṉ appeared. The Tamil Kanta Purāṇam was composed at the end of the fourteenth century or slightly later by Kacciyappa Civācāriyar of Kanchipuram (Zvelebil 1991, 15–16). Pakal̲ikkūttar's *Tiruccentūr Piḷḷaittamil̲*, which depicts Lord Murukaṉ of Tiruchchendur as a child, also probably dates from the early fifteenth century and is celebrated as the earliest example of the fully developed poetic form of *piḷḷaittamil̲*, a genre of devotional literature that images the deity being praised in the form of a child (Richman 1997, 53–80; see also Clothey 1978, 156–60). Meanwhile between the fourteenth and eighteenth centuries, we see the building of more and more temples dedicated to Murukaṉ and increasing numbers of pilgrims visiting Murukaṉ's temples (Stein 1978, 19–22; Rudner 1987, 365–69). It is not until the late nineteenth and early twentieth centuries, however, that devotion to Murukaṉ dramatically intensified with the rediscovery and popularization of Aruṇakirinâta's works, the expansion and solidification of Murukaṉ's network of temples, and the tying of Murukaṉ to Tamil national identity (Clothey 1978, 113–31; Clothey 1984, 30–37).

The Seventh and Eighth Centuries

Up until this point, I have been referring to Murukaṉ by the name by which the god is most frequently known in the Tamil literature we have just been considering and in contemporary Tamil usage. From now on, however, when I refer to this deity as he appears in the medieval temple context, I call him Subrahmaṇya, since this is by far the most common name for the god in the inscriptions. He is often referred to by other names as well, including Iḷaiya nāyaṉār, Kuṉṟamēṟinta piḷḷaiyār, and Skanda, but is called Murukaṉ only once in a thirteenth-century inscription from Tiruvannamalai (EI 27.18).

The earliest material evidence of the ritual worship of Subrahmaṇya in the "gap" period between the composition of *Tirumurukāṟṟuppaṭai* and the work of Aruṇakirināta (ca. fifth to early fifteenth centuries) comes from sculptural representations of the seventh and eighth centuries. In this period images of Somāskanda are numerous and evidently had emblematic significance for the Pallava royal family based in northern Tamilnadu,[2] but I have found only fourteen representations of Subrahmaṇya as an individual figure dating from the seventh or eighth century. These images appear as niche figures on the walls or temple towers (*śikharas*) of structural temples or as relief sculptures in rock-cut temples or on the enclosing walls (*prākāras*) of structural temples. They are concentrated around the northern towns of Kanchipuram and Mahabalipuram, on the one hand, and around Madurai and further to the south in Kalugumalai, on the other—that is, in the areas over which the rulers of the Pallava and the Pandya dynasties, respectively, laid claim.

With the possible exception of a late eighth-century cave sculpture in the village of Kalugumalai, now located deep within the interior of a relatively recent Murukaṉ temple (Soundara Rajan 1998, 99–100), none of these figures seems to have been designed as the central object of worship in a Subrahmaṇya temple. At Anaimalai, the elephant-shaped hill to the north of Madurai, there is a cave containing a worn but graceful image of Subrahmaṇya together with a consort. This is frequently cited as the earliest extant temple dedicated to this god, but L'Hernault suggests that this rock-cut cave, without any auxiliary deities, has more the character of a shrine than a temple.[3] At Anaimalai, in fact, Subrahmaṇya is one of several deities who were established on the rocky hill in the eighth century, including Viṣṇu as Narasiṃha and a group of Jain Tīrthaṅkaras and *yakṣīs* or Jain goddesses (Pattabiramin 1971–75, 2:51; Nagaswamy 1997, 51–53).

At Tirupparankunram, to the southwest of Madurai, Subrahmaṇya is again part of a constellation of deities. This site is praised in *Paripāṭal* as the abode of Murukaṉ and is today the site of an important Murukaṉ temple, constructed for the most part in the seventeenth century by the Nayakas of Madurai. Here in the rock-cut temple excavated in the eighth century, are five separate shrines: for Gaṇeśa, Durgā, and Subrahmaṇya along the back of the cave and for Śiva and Viṣṇu, who face each other from the two side walls (L'Hernault 1978, 75, 134).[4] Apart from this temple, Tirupparankunram also features shrines and relief sculptures of a number of goddesses, Śiva in various forms, and Gaṇeśa; early Jain caves; and even a Muslim tomb on the mountain's peak, built around the time of the transformation of the rock-cut temple at its foot into a major temple dedicated to Murukaṉ in the seventeenth century (Devakunjari 1979, 106–12; Branfoot 2003).

In the Pallava territory to the north, Subrahmaṇya is once again discovered in a multi-shrine context. In the so-called Trimūrti cave at Mahabalipuram,

Subrahmaṇya. Eighth-century stone relief sculpture at the Kailasanātha temple in Kanchipuram. Photograph by the author.

excavated in the seventh century, Subrahmaṇya's shrine is placed on the worshiper's left where we would expect to find Brahmā's with Śiva's in the center and Viṣṇu's on the right. The large (1.5 meters tall) sculpture of Subrahmaṇya carved on the shrine's back wall bears the attributes of Brahmā and, like Brahmā in sculptures elsewhere, is attended by ascetics (L'Hernault 1978, 98, 103–4, ph. 51). And as at Tirupparankunram in the far south, so too in northern Tamilnadu, at the Kailasanātha temple of Kanchipuram dedicated to Śiva, we find Subrahmaṇya paired with Gaṇeśa and flanking the goddess Durgā, in this case on the southern *prākāra* (enclosing wall) near the entrance to the inner courtyard of the temple. In addition to this image illustrated above (and the dozens of beautiful Somāskanda images on the *prākāra* and temple walls and within the temple itself), one of the relief panels on the *prākāra* appears to depict the birth of Subrahmaṇya, and another sculpted panel at the Kailasanātha temple represents Subrahmaṇya's marriage.[5] At two other eighth-century temples in Kanchipuram, the Mātaṅgeśvara and the Mukteśvara, Subrahmaṇya is found as a niche figure on the north wall of the central shrine in the place of the god Brahmā, bearing the attributes of Brahmā—the rosary and water pot.

The Ninth Century

Continuing into the ninth century, we find that these two attributes of Brahmā—the rosary and water pot—borne together or singly are especially characteristic of images of Subrahmaṇya in Tondaimandalam, the Pallava area in the northern part of the Tamil country (see L'Hernault 1978, carte III). But these attributes, particularly the rosary, are also featured in at least half of the ninth-century images of Subrahmaṇya outside this zone. If one of the four hands of Subrahmaṇya holds the rosary, the opposite one typically bears the *vajra*, the weapon of Indra. Also perhaps evocative of Indra—or of the Murukaṉ of the Tamil hill country—is the presence of the elephant in sculptures of the ninth century. The elephant appears either as the mount of Subrahmaṇya—for example in the niche figures at Tiruvalisvaram (Tirunelveli district), Kodumbalur (Pudukkottai/Tiruchirappalli district), and Tirukkattuppalli (Thanjavur district)—or positioned, like Nandi, facing the image, as at the Subrahmaṇya shrine at Piranmalai (Ramnad district). In some cases Subrahmaṇya bears two weapons: the *vajra* paired with what is known as his *śakti*, a leaf-shaped blade that may hark back to Murukaṉ's *vēl* but resembles a dagger more than a lance.

All of the ninth-century figures of Subrahmaṇya (I have found nearly thirty) are stone sculptures; they are almost invariably four-armed, and most are standing figures, quite rigid in form. But what they may lack in iconographic variation they make up for in their widespread geographical distribution, including a relatively large number of images spread through the Kaveri River region, and the diversity of their positioning. Subrahmaṇya continues to appear as a niche figure in the *śikhara* of temples dedicated to Śiva, but he also is found in two cases paired with Gaṇeśa as a type of door guardian at two rock-cut shrines in Pandyanadu in the far south of Tamilnadu, Kunrakkudi (Ramnad district), and Virasikhamani (Tirunelveli district).[6] In at least three temples, all located in Tiruchirappalli district—at Malaiyatippatti, Melappaluvur, and Tiruverumbur—there are ninth-century sculptures of Subrahmaṇya as one of the *parivāra devatās*, the group of Śiva's attendant deities whose shrines encircled the Śiva *liṅga* in the central shrine. At these three temples, Subrahmaṇya is found in the position where he would originally have been placed, to the west or northwest of the central shrine.

It was in the ninth century that inscriptions referring to the worship of Subrahmaṇya first appeared. Of the two such inscriptions that have survived, one indicates the god's role by listing him as one of the eight *parivāra devatās* to whom food offerings were made; the other deities are the group of seven mothers (*mātṛkās*), Gaṇeśa, Jyeṣṭhā, Durgā, Caṇḍeśvara, Sūrya, and Yama (Tirupalatturai, Tiruchirappalli district, SII 8.560, 898 C.E.). Apart from the *parivāra* images of Subrahmaṇya, we have two ninth-century images that were *mūlamūrtis*, the central objects of worship, in temples dedicated to this god at Kannanur (Tiruchirappalli district) and at Uttaramerur (Chingleput district). At the Subrahmaṇya temple at Tiruttani (Chingleput district), we also have a ninth-century image of the god, which may not itself be the *mūlamūrti* but which provides us with early evidence of the importance of the worship of Subrahmaṇya at this site. A second ninth-century inscription confirms that also at Tiruchchendur (Tirunelveli district), Subrahmaṇya was established in his temple there and received a generous gift from the Pandya king Varaguna to provide for daily and festival offerings (SII 14.16A = EI 21.17, 875 C.E.).

The Tenth Century

In the tenth century, we have more inscriptions referring to Subrahmaṇya—nine, as opposed to two in the preceding century—but the bulk of our evidence for his ritual worship continues to be images rather than inscriptions. Even in subsequent centuries, as the number of extant images produced in the eleventh and twelfth centuries diminishes, they are still more abundant than inscriptional references to Subrahmaṇya worship—until the sudden skyrocketing of such references in the thirteenth century. Meanwhile, back in the tenth century, it is clear that the inscriptions and the images provide us with different kinds of information. For one thing the images and the inscriptions come from different places. Half of the thirty or so images that we have come from the Kaveri River region—Cholanadu—while two-thirds of the inscriptions come from Chingleput district in the north. But neither the images nor the inscriptions of the tenth century provide evidence for the worship of Subrahmaṇya very much south of the Kaveri.[7]

The inscriptions give us the opportunity to learn something about the people who sponsored Subrahmaṇya worship. Although we have seen an earlier example of royal patronage in a ninth-century inscription from Tiruchchendur recording a gift by the Pandya king, none of the tenth-century inscriptions indicates such royal involvement. Instead donors were local landowners, including Brahmans, chiefs and, in one case, a merchant of Kanchipuram who gave land to support the *śrībali* drumming service at Subrahmaṇya's temple in Uttaramerur (SII 3.171, 960 C.E.). Seven of our nine inscriptions suggest that Subrahmaṇya was worshiped in a temple or shrine that was not attached to a Śiva temple. Two of the inscriptions refer to Subrahmaṇya as he "who is pleased to stand on the hill at Tiruttani" (ARE 1905/439 and 1932–33/76); another refers to a Subrahmaṇya temple at Kalakattur, elsewhere in Chingleput district (ARE 1923/117); and several of the inscriptions refer simply to "Subrahmaṇya of our village" as the recipient of offerings and services (at three sites in Chingleput district: Kuram, Uttaramerur, and Vidaiyur). On the other hand, the two remaining inscriptions identify Subrahmaṇya as an auxiliary deity—as one of the eight *parivāra devatās* in the Śiva temples at Tirupurambiyam (Thanjavur district, SII 6.21, 995 C.E.) and Erumbur (South Arcot district, ARE 1913/384, ca. 935 C.E.). The second of these inscriptions identifies Subrahmaṇya as one of the *parivāra devatās* enshrined in the temple *gopura*, which had just been built. This is an important reminder of the possibility of multiple ritual meanings of temple structures, with the *gopura* serving both as a gateway to a Śiva temple and a focus for the worship of other gods—in this case Subrahmaṇya and other *parivāra* deities.

Among the tenth-century images of Subrahmaṇya is a relief sculpture, opposite one of Gaṇeśa, at the entrance to a cave temple dedicated to Śiva (Muvaraivenran, Ramnad district; Pattabiramin 1971–75, 1:44 and fig. 119). We also have two examples of Subrahmaṇya as a *parivāra* figure and, in what is apparently the earliest depiction of Subrahmaṇya with his peacock vehicle, in a small stone relief panel on the temple wall at Punjai (Thanjavur district), where the eight-armed god is shown in combat against demons (L'Hernault 1978, 173, ph. 215). In the tenth century, we also find the first metal images of Subrahmaṇya, three of which are from Thanjavur district. Two of these processional images preserve the rigid hieratic pose of earlier and contemporary stone sculpture, but the third, from Tiruvidaikkali (L'Hernault 1978, ph. 190; Srinivasan 1963, 171–73 and fig. 106), has the graceful *tribhanga* stance (with body bent at knee, hip, and neck) and shows Subrahmaṇya's arms in the position of holding a bow and arrow—the earliest such depiction (cf. the eleventh-century example in the following section) and one that resembles the Chola-period bronze images of Tripurāntaka and of Rāma. The tenth century thus marks the beginning of the elaboration of the iconography of Subrahmaṇya as an individual figure, in both stone and bronze, and experimentation with new positions and functions for the god in sculptural and ritual programs.

The Eleventh Century

For the eleventh century, we have only fifteen images of Subrahmaṇya, or half as many as in the preceding century, and only five inscriptions referring to the worship of this god. With the exception of two figures of Subrahmaṇya found in Tirunelveli district,[8] all of the images and inscriptions come from the Kaveri River zone or further north. Two of the inscriptions are engraved on the walls of the Subrahmaṇya temple at Uttaramerur in Chingleput district, including one that records the appointment of a Śivabrāhmaṇa and his descendants to serve in the temple (SII 6.336, 1016 C.E.) and one at the Subrahmaṇya temple at nearby Tirupporur, where people of the locality made gifts to provide offerings and lamps for "Subrahmaṇya of our village" (ARE 1933–34/121, 1076 C.E.).

But there is another inscription, from the great temple at Thanjavur, which indicates the interest of a royal figure in the worship of Subrahmaṇya. This inscription records the presentation to the temple of a four-armed bronze figure of Subrahmaṇya by the Chola ruler Rajaraja I (SII 2.49, 1014 C.E.). It is noteworthy that the king, in providing for his royal temple, deemed it necessary to have a processional image of this deity. But we must acknowledge that Subrahmaṇya was far less important in this context than his older brother, Gaṇeśa, who was represented in no fewer than ten of the sixty-six bronze images donated to the temple by Rajaraja, his queens, and ministers (SII 2.84, etc.; see Dehejia 2002, 83–85 and 140–43). It was not until the seventeenth century, when the Thanjavur Nayakas constructed the beautiful Subrahmaṇya shrine to the northwest of the central shrine, that an important place was established for Subrahmaṇya at the Thanjavur temple (L'Hernault 2002, 31).

Although the bronze image of Subrahmaṇya donated by Rajaraja has not survived, we do have two other eleventh-century bronzes. Both are quite large (almost a meter in height) and have been admired for their artistic merits. Each exhibits, as well, novel features in terms of the iconography of Subrahmaṇya. A bronze image from the Chola capital, Gangaikondacholapuram, shows the god armed not only with his dagger-like *śakti* but also with sword and shield; in addition he bears his emblem, the rooster (Sivaramamurti 1963, fig. 25b; L'Hernault 1978, ph. 44). The image of Subrahmaṇya unearthed at Tiruvengadu, illustrated on the following page, is one of the earliest representations in either stone or metal of the deity flanked by his two consorts, Vaḷḷi and Devasenā (Thomas 1986, 80–87; L'Hernault 1978, ph. 191). Today this grouping of three figures constitutes the standard form of Subrahmaṇya as processional image, but Chola-period examples of such bronzes are not very common. Another eleventh-century appearance of Subrahmaṇya in the company of his two consorts is in a stone relief panel on the outer face of the *gopura* of Rajaraja's temple in Thanjavur, on the northern side of the entrance. Here at Thanjavur we do not find a figure of Gaṇeśa on the other side of the entrance to the temple paired with Subrahmaṇya, as he is in several of the early rock-cut temples we have considered. But elsewhere, at Brahmadesam in South Arcot district, Śiva's two sons flank the entrance to an eleventh-century structural temple dedicated to Śiva (Balasubrahmanyam 1975, 150), in a pattern that was to become extremely common in subsequent times (L'Hernault 1978, 157). Finally the eleventh century produced the earliest images in which Subrahmaṇya is shown bearing a staff; this attribute, on the one hand, evokes the depiction in Caṅkam literature of Murukaṉ armed with the *vēl* and, on the other, anticipates images of the fifteenth century onward in which Subrahmaṇya is portrayed as an ascetic. An eleventh-century stone *parivāra* figure from Tiruvaiyaru (Thanjavur district) depicts the

Subrahmaṇya with consorts Vaḷḷi and Devasenā. Early eleventh-century bronze sculptures from Tiruvengadu. Courtesy Rajaraja Museum and Art Gallery, Thanjavur. Photograph courtesy of the American Institute of Indian Studies.

staff among Subrahmaṇya's several weapons, as the god stands in a graceful *tribhanga* pose in front of his peacock (L'Hernault 1978, 159, ph. 189).

The Twelfth Century

We continue to be struck by the absence of images or inscriptions from southern Tamilnadu in the twelfth century, but for the first time we find evidence for the worship of Subrahmaṇya in western Tamilnadu in the form of a stone image from Kolar district and inscriptions from Coimbatore and Salem districts. We have twelfth-century inscriptions from eleven temples, most of which are in South Arcot district, although there are also several inscriptions from the Subrahmaṇya temple at Tirupporur in Chingleput district. Of the nineteen temples that yield twelfth-century images, the largest number (eight) are located in Thanjavur district. There are five twelfth-century bronzes, of which four come from Thanjavur district. Two of the bronzes (from the towns of Tiruvidaikkali and Nagapattinam) show Subrahmaṇya in the company of his two consorts, and two (from Tiruvidaimarudur in Thanjavur district and Melakkadambur in South Arcot district) portray Subrahmaṇya as a child, in the latter case as a dancing child. Among the stone sculptures of the twelfth century, we see for the first time a six-headed Subrahmaṇya, for example, at Tiruvanaikka (Tiruchirappalli district) and Darasuram (Thanjavur district). Also at Darasuram, in a temple built by the Chola king Rajaraja II in the second half of the twelfth century, figures of Subrahmaṇya appear on the outer face of the *gopura* and in a number of narrative reliefs on pillars (L'Hernault 1978, 50, 139, 164, 173–74; L'Hernault, Srinivasan, and Dumarçay 1987, 93–95, 117–22).

In the inscriptions of the twelfth century, we see more and more references to the setting up of images of Subrahmaṇya, as well as to his ritual worship. The inscriptions also provide us with a glimpse of the relationship between Śiva temples and their associated Subrahmaṇya shrines. There is, for example, the royal order engraved at Singarattoppu near Chidambaram (South Arcot district; ARE 1913/262, 1180 C.E.) declaring that the lands formerly possessed by Subrahmaṇya at the Śiva temple of this village should henceforth be considered as the property of Lord Śiva. This inscription indicates that the god Subrahmaṇya, even as an auxiliary deity, could be a property owner in his own right and, although in this case his autonomy was being undermined, that he was clearly more than a mere adjunct to the god housed at the center of the temple complex.[9] Perhaps the distinction between "shrines" and "temples" dedicated to Subrahmaṇya (or other deities) is not very meaningful in the context of twelfth-century Tamilnadu. The Tamil inscriptions use the single term *kōyil* for both "shrine" and "temple" or use no term at all, as, for example, in the numerous references to the "Subrahmaṇya of our village," which suggest that the significant point was the god's presence rather than his occupation of a certain sort of structure placed within a particular pattern. Certainly the inscriptions indicate that the status of a god vis-à-vis other deities in his locale and the relationships between shrines and temples—relationships of domination, integration, and displacement—were fluid, various, and subject to modification.

The Thirteenth Century

That there were a variety of possible outcomes of the processes of negotiation between shrines and temples is clear from the inscriptions of the thirteenth century. Here we find indications that in some cases Subrahmaṇya shrines in Śiva temples were being refurbished and enlarged, while the Śiva temple itself was neglected (L'Hernault 1978, 191; ARE 1928–29/441–43; ARE 1925/269). Meanwhile the numerous inscriptional references to Subrahmaṇya worship dating from the thirteenth century provide abundant evidence of the existence of temples exclusively dedicated to Subrahmaṇya. Of the twenty Subrahmaṇya temples attested by pre-sixteenth-century inscriptions, twelve first come into view in the thirteenth century.[10] This is not to say that these temples did not exist in an earlier era (perhaps independently, perhaps as one of a group of shrines, perhaps as shrines associated with Śiva temples), but the appearance of these inscriptions in the thirteenth century indicates, on the one hand, the construction of new buildings *as* Subrahmaṇya temples and, on the other, an increasing flow of gifts to support the worship of this deity in temples of his own. Another aspect of the position of the Subrahmaṇya temple that emerges in thirteenth-century inscriptions are the indications that they, like Śiva temples, were managed by priests known as Śivabrāhmaṇas. Already in the eleventh century, we have seen that Śivabrāhmaṇas were appointed to carry out worship in the Subrahmaṇya temple of Uttaramerur, but now we find these figures serving as temple authorities at three other Subrahmaṇya temples—two in Chingleput district (Tirupporur and Saluvankuppam) and one in Ramnad district (Enjar).

Rather surprisingly the thirteenth century marks virtually the first moment that we find inscriptions referring to Subrahmaṇya worship from the southern part of Tamilnadu. With the exception of a single inscription of the late ninth century from Tiruchchendur in Tirunelveli district, the inscriptions of Ramnad, Madurai, Tirunelveli, and Kanyakumari districts are utterly silent about Subrahmaṇya until this time. Even images of this deity provide scant evidence for his presence in the far south after the ninth century (again, with the exception of two images of the eleventh century from Tirunelveli district). But in the thirteenth century, inscriptions in the far south, particularly in Ramnad district, suggest that Subrahmaṇya was the object of considerable attention. Among those involved in sponsoring his worship was Vira Pandya, ruling from his capital in Madurai, who made a gift of land to provide for services and food offerings in the temple of Subrahmaṇya at Palani (Madurai district, SII 17.402, 1268 C.E.).

The Pandyas not only were active as temple patrons in their traditional home territory, but also sponsored religious activities and military adventures further north. As Chola rule disintegrated in the mid-thirteenth century, a new breed of ruler was emerging, one for whom temple patronage was a means of establishing political legitimacy. The kings of the Pandya and Hoysala dynasties and the Kadavarayar, Vanakovaraiyar, and Sambuvarayar chiefs—along with the fourteenth-century princes of Vijayanagara—made generous gifts at temples throughout the Tamil country, and a number of these gifts had Subrahmaṇya as the beneficiary. For example the Kadavarayar chief Kopperuncinka gave jewels and ornaments to Subrahmaṇya at Tiruvamattur in South Arcot district (SII 12.181) and presented a golden image of Subrahmaṇya, together with his two consorts and the peacock, at the great temple of Tiruvannamalai (North Arcot district; EI 27.18).[11]

Nonetheless the majority of Subrahmaṇya's patrons in the thirteenth century were not rulers or nobles but more ordinary folk—including several temple women, a group of weavers, and a merchant—and in many cases they commissioned images of the god. Twenty-two of the fifty-five thirteenth-century inscriptions relating to Subrahmaṇya worship contain references to the setting up of his image, although few of the images themselves have survived from this era. Two inscriptions specify the location of these images at the entrance or gateway to the temple: at Tirupapuliyur (South Arcot district), a man from the Pandya country made an endowment for the worship of the image of Subrahmaṇya he had set up in the temple *gopura* (ARE 1953–54/301, 1286 C.E.); and at Tirukkalukkunram (Chingleput district), a woman arranged for the installation of images of Gaṇeśa and Subrahmaṇya at the base of the walls framing the doorway to the temple (ARE 1932–33/143, 1223 C.E.).

Half of the six stone and bronze images that have survived from the thirteenth century show Subrahmaṇya bearing a bow, and he is often shown with the peacock in this era, as in the illustration on the facing page. One stone image of considerable significance is found at the Subrahmaṇya temple at Tirupporur (Chingleput district), which shows the god seated in the posture of a yogi on the back of his peacock, in the act of instructing the sage Agastya. Various interpretations are possible; Subrahmaṇya may be teaching him the Tamil language or imparting to him the meaning of the sacred syllable *OM* (L'Hernault 1978, 118, ph. 87). If this is indeed a thirteenth-century image, it is a very early example of the depiction of Subrahmaṇya as guru, an image more characteristic of later times, particularly after the fifteenth century.[12] Such images, as well as the later images of Subrahmaṇya as the ascetic found especially in the sixteenth century and onward—two-armed and bearing a staff, and often identified as the god of Palani—are today understood as representing Subrahmaṇya's role as the source of Tamil literature, his embodiment of the truths of Tamil Śaiva Siddhānta philosophy, and his connection with the Tamil *siddhas*, the mystics associated with Palani and with the more recently built Murukaṉ temples of Coimbatore district (Clothey 1978, 80, 86, 95–99, 228n7, 228n7; L'Hernault 1978, 119–27).

Conclusion

In these manifestations of the last several centuries, the "Tamilness" of Murukaṉ/Subrahmaṇya seems to be of an almost modern character, rather than reflecting his archaic persona or the modes of worship depicted in the Caṅkam literature. Is this discontinuity the consequence of the god's incorporation into the Śaiva pantheon in early medieval times, of his becoming "Sanskritized" and losing his earlier identity? The survey of the material evidence undertaken in this essay shows that even at the very beginning of the medieval period, in the seventh and eighth centuries, Subrahmaṇya was not shown with the attributes and associations that we know from the Caṅkam literature: his consort Vaḷḷi, his weapon the *vēl*, and his characteristic exploits, such as the battle with the demon, are absent from the earliest representations.[13] Nor do the early images and shrines very often appear at sites associated with Murukaṉ's archaic Tamil mythos, such as the region around Madurai, which are evoked in legends linking Murukaṉ with the Tamil Caṅkam and the royal Pandya dynasty and praised in the poems of *Paripāṭal* as Murukaṉ's abode (see Zvelebil 1991, 20–23, 28). Throughout the whole of the period that I have surveyed, Subrahmaṇya is far better represented in images and inscriptions from the northern part of Tamilnadu than in the far south. If the archaic Murukaṉ known from Tamil literature had vanished by the seventh century, is this because he had already been incorporated into Brahmanic Hinduism and subsumed within the pantheon of the great god Śiva by the time of the earliest images and inscriptions?[14]

Subrahmaṇya with peacock. Thirteenth-century bronze sculpture from Sirkali, now at the Thanjavur Royal Museum. Courtesy Rajaraja Museum and Art Gallery, Thanjavur. Photograph courtesy of the American Institute of Indian Studies.

Such a scenario is not sustained by the evidence surveyed in this essay, which points instead to the creation of ritual settings where devotees related directly to Subrahmaṇya rather than honoring him as an adjunct to their worship of Śiva. The earliest material evidence of Subrahmaṇya worship in the Tamil country is found in the context of a plurality of deities—in rock-cut shrines that preserve a ritual setting in which Subrahmaṇya coexisted with Śiva, with Viṣṇu, with Durgā, and with other gods. As increasing numbers of structural temples were built from the ninth century onward, Subrahmaṇya was installed in a range of locations as a niche figure, *parivāra devatā, gopura* figure, processional image, door guardian, and object of worship in shrines and temples dedicated to him. This variety of placement schemes points toward a context in which worshipers and temple patrons who sponsored the installation of images of Subrahmaṇya valued the multiplicity of distinct divine manifestations within the space of the temple. This seems to have sometimes been the case even while the temple priests' ritual attentions may have been focused on a god in the temple's central sanctum other than Subrahmaṇya, who was most often Śiva in the contexts where Subrahmaṇya was worshiped. If the Śaiva priests' concerns are reflected in the medieval Sanskrit texts known as the Āgamas, which outline both the architectural/iconographic and ritual arrangements that structured a worship space with Śiva as its heart and whole reason for being, the inscriptions and images found within the medieval temple as well as the proliferation and variety of images testify to a different sort of ritual space and theological sensibility created and experienced by nonpriestly worshipers (Brunner 1990, 20–21; Goodall et al. 2006, 110–12).[15]

For such worshipers Subrahmaṇya as a niche figure, a *parivāra devatā,* a *gopura* figure, a processional image, or a door guardian might be as worthy of worship as Subrahmaṇya in his own shrine or temple, regardless of whether this image was intended by its sponsor to be an object of special devotion or was simply a part of a greater (Śiva-centered) iconographic program. That ordinary devotees had the power to alter the use of temple space, and even restructure that space, in ways unforeseen by earlier builders and patrons is strikingly illustrated at Tiruvannamalai, where, in an outer enclosure of the temple compound, a pillar bearing a sculpted image of Subrahmaṇya in a *maṇḍapa* (pavilion) built for the goddess Naṉampāḷ has become a cult site with a major shrine built around it, dwarfing the goddess's *maṇḍapa* itself.[16] In this case we cannot really speak of a redefinition of the sacred space so that worshipers are now oriented toward a new "central" deity, since the Lord of Tiruvannamalai remains Śiva, but in other instances devotees' ritual attentions and sponsorship of images and buildings did indeed result in a recentering of the temple. At the Śiva temples in Pollachi in Coimbatore district and in Tiruvidaikali in Thanjavur district, we find inscriptional evidence as early as the thirteenth century that attention was being shifted away from Śiva and toward Subrahmaṇya as the main focus of worship (ARE 1928–29/441–43; ARE 1925/269). Elsewhere at Kunrakkudi just north of Madurai, there is an eighth-century rock-cut temple for Śiva at the base of the hill, which was still a focus for worship in the sixteenth century, while the earliest evidence for the existence of a Subrahmaṇya temple at the hill's peak appears in the fifteenth century. Since that time, however, Śiva has been entirely eclipsed by his popular son on the hill above, and today not one of the pilgrims who throng the stairs climbing up to Subrahmaṇya's temple stops to worship Śiva (Orr 2008). At Tiruchengodu in Salem district, on the other hand, where Śiva and Subrahmaṇya also share a hill, they coexist within the same temple compound at the top of the hill with their temples nestled side by side facing in opposite directions. Although the temples themselves were constructed no earlier than the sixteenth century, pilgrims since at least the tenth century have mounted the hill to pay their respects to both gods (Orr 2008).

The art historical and inscriptional evidence allows us to appreciate the variety of ways in which devotees have "voted with their feet" within the sacred space of the temple—halting (or not) to offer ritual worship to deities "central" or "subsidiary"—and to recognize how these devotees have made space for new objects of worship or new ritual activities. Taking these dynamics into account makes it necessary to rethink a narrative in which gods rise and fall or arrange themselves in hierarchical formations and to reconsider the notion that sectarian formulations produce ritual consequences. It seems, in fact, that the apparent submergence of Murukaṉ in the seventh century and his resurgence in the fourteenth and fifteenth centuries, in which the god seemed first to submit to and later to break free of Śiva's dominance, was more a literary event than anything else. The collection of Tamil hymns dedicated to Śiva known as *Tēvāram,* composed in the seventh to ninth centuries, depict Murukaṉ in an auxiliary role. These hymns mention Murukaṉ about forty times but almost exclusively as the son of Śiva (Zvelebil 1991, 88). In this context Murukaṉ is clearly subordinate to Śiva. But does the imaging of Śiva and Murukaṉ and their relationship in *Tēvāram* reflect ritual practices, in terms of the dominance of one or the other of these deities, or the relationships among communities or within sites dedicated to the worship of these gods? In fact the art historical and inscriptional evidence attests to the ongoing worship of Murukaṉ/Subrahmaṇya as a god independent of Śiva throughout medieval times in various temple contexts, including Śiva temples. By the fourteenth century—a century before Aruṇakirināta's encounter with Murukaṉ (at a Śiva temple) and the so-called revival of this god's worship—there were at least twenty temples dedicated to Subrahmaṇya spread throughout the Tamil landscape.

If the physical fabric of temples, the placement of images in these temples, and the uses of temple spaces can be understood as expressing something about or as informing ritual, then we must acknowledge that there was in fact a dynamic and pluralistic approach to arrangements for and practices of worship in medieval Tamilnadu. Perhaps it is not so surprising, after all, that the sectarian formulations of texts, which stressed one god's ascendency over another, were fairly remote from the devotional attitudes and ritual behaviors of the worshipers whose experiences and activities are attested in the material record. If we take this evidence seriously, we may arrive at a fuller comprehension of the complexity, variety, and fluidity of Subrahmaṇya's significance and his relationship with other gods and with his worshipers. This can only enrich our understanding of "the many faces of Murukan̠," as Clothey puts it (1978), and the place of this god among his worshipers in the ritual activities and ritual spaces of the medieval South Indian temple.

Notes

I am grateful to the editors of this volume, and to a number of others who have provided me with encouragement and assistance, including especially Michelle Bakker, Crispin Branfoot, Padma Kaimal, Lisa Nadine Owen, Tanisha Ramachandran, Charlotte Schmid, Davesh Soneji, and S. Swaminathan. As always I must offer my thanks to the Office of the Director of Epigraphy, Archaeological Survey of India, in Mysore, headed during my visits in recent years by Dr. M. D. Sampath, Dr. K. M. Bhadri, and Dr. T.S. Ravishankar. And it is with great pleasure that I acknowledge my debt to Fred Clothey, whose work has not only inspired this paper but a great deal more.

1. The definitions of district boundaries that I have adopted are based on the usages of published editions of inscriptions, often reflecting pre-Independence political divisions.

2. Charlotte Schmid (personal communication) underscores the special significance that the Somāskanda icon has for the Pallava lineage at the early eighth-century Kailasanātha temple in Kanchipuram, built by Rajasimha I, with Skanda/Subrahmaṇya representing the *yuvarāja* (crown prince) of the Pallava lineage, Rajasimha himself. See Lockwood (1974) for an early statement of this thesis. L'Hernault treats in detail the variations and distribution of the Somāskanda image in medieval Tamilnadu (1978, 49–92, carte II).

3. L'Hernault (1978, 189–90) and Zvelebil (1991, 77) further suggest that the Anaimalai image is not even a depiction of Subrahmaṇya and his consort but represents a royal couple.

4. Subrahmaṇya also appears at Tirupparankunram in a relief sculpture with one of his consorts seated at his side (Pattabiramin 1971–75, vol. 1, plate 159), but this seems to be of somewhat later date than the image sculpted on the back wall of the main temple (cf. L'Hernault 1978, 134n).

5. I am indebted to Valérie Gillet, Padma Kaimal, and Charlotte Schmid for these identifications as well as other information and insights relating to the Kailasanātha temple.

6. It seems as though in the eighth to tenth centuries, there were a number of variations and experimentations with respect to this aspect of temple layout (Pattabiramin

1971–75, 1:26, 68; Soundara Rajan 1998, 43–46; Goodall et al. 2005, 58, 186), although in later times the Gaṇeśa-Subrahmaṇya pair at the entrance to temples comes to be virtually ubiquitous in Tamilnadu.

7. Among tenth-century images, the most southerly are four from Pudukkottai and one from Ramnad district. There are no tenth-century inscriptions relating to Subrahmaṇya worship south of Tiruchirappalli on the Kaveri River.

8. The two Subrahmaṇya images from Tirunelveli district are found in the villages of Attur and Pasuvandanai. At Pasuvandanai the Śiva temple that bears an image of Subrahmaṇya on its *śikhara* was formerly paired with a Subrahmaṇya temple, which no longer survives (Balasubrahmanyam 1975, 190).

9. Subrahmaṇya's separate ownership of land and relative independence from the main deity of the temple are confirmed by at least one other twelfth-century inscription (SII 17.205, 1166 C.E.), which records the donation of land by a chief of the Sambuvaraya clan to Subrahmaṇya in the temple at Tiruvakkarai (in South Arcot district).

10. Before the thirteenth century, four Subrahmaṇya temples are mentioned in inscriptions of the ninth or tenth century—Kalakattur, Uttaramerur, and Tiruttani, all in Chingleput district, and Tiruchchendur in Tirunelveli district—and one, Tirupporur in Chingleput district, in the eleventh century.

11. This inscription from Tiruvannamalai is the only one from the early medieval period where the god is named "Murukan̲."

12. Among these later images are a bronze from the Tirupporur temple, depicting the young Subrahmaṇya (with Brahmā's attributes) instructing his father (L'Hernault 1978, 118, ph. 84), and a stone relief sculpture on a pillar in the Viṣṇu temple at Palani (Madurai district), showing a seated Subrahmaṇya, bearing *vajra* and *śakti,* expounding the significance of *OM* to a standing sage with flowing *jaṭās* (L'Hernault 1978, 118, ph. 86).

13. Zvelebil (1991, 78) suggests that Murukan̲'s earliest worship in the Tamil country may have been aniconic; thus the image in its entirety would have been an import from the north and would account for its lack of Tamil features.

14. Clothey, in his discussion of the depiction of Murukan̲ in *Paripāṭal* and *Tirumurukāṟṟupaṭai* (1978, 62–70) points to the fact that even in these texts Sanskritic elements had already been assimilated into the god's image and that he had developed into a less local and more cosmopolitan—more "universalized"—deity. Zvelebil (1991, 86–87) similarly argues that already in *Paripāṭal* and *Tirumurukāṟṟupaṭai,* Murukan̲ is a composite figure, with the Tamil imaging of the god as a hunter combining with the Sanskritic representation of him as a hero.

15. In the case of Subrahmaṇya, we find variety and deviation from textual norms not only in the placement of images but also in the continuing development of new forms of the god. While the iconography of the Somāskanda image remained relatively fixed after the ninth century, experimentations and variations in the iconography of Subrahmaṇya as an individual figure begin precisely at that moment and continue to evolve from the tenth century onward: he appears with his elephant and later with his peacock; with one, two, or no consorts; with two arms, four arms, or twelve arms; as a child; and as an ascetic.

16. Also at Tiruvannamalai devotees raised funds to erect shrines in front of the relief figures of Subrahmaṇya on two of the eastern *gopuras* (the twelfth-century Kiligopura and the fourteenth-century Vallalagopura) (L'Hernault, Pichard, and Deloche 1990, 65, 67, 74).

References

Inscriptions

ARE *Annual Reports on Indian Epigraphy.* 1905– . Delhi: Manager of Publications. Transcripts of the inscriptions abstracted in the ARE were graciously made available to me at the Office of the Chief Epigraphist, Archaeological Survey of India, Mysore.

EI *Epigraphia Indica.* 1892– . Calcutta/Delhi: Director General, Archaeological Survey of India.

SII *South Indian Inscriptions.* 1992– . Volumes 2–26. Delhi: Director-General, Archaeological Survey of India.

Other Sources

Balasubrahmanyam, S. R. 1975. *Middle Chola Temples.* New Delhi: Thomson.

——. 1979. *Later Chola Temples.* New Delhi: Mudgala Trust.

Branfoot, Crispin. 2003. "The Madurai Nayakas and the Skanda Temple at Tirupparankunram." *Ars Orientalis* 33: 147–79.

Brunner, Hélène. 1990. "L'image divine dans le culte agamique de Siva: Rapport entre l'image mentale et le support concret du culte." In *L'Image divine: Culte et médiation dans l'hindouisme,* edited by André Padoux, 9–29. Paris: Centre national de la recherche scientifique.

Clothey, Fred W. 1978. *The Many Faces of Murukan: The History and Meaning of a South Indian God.* The Hague: Mouton.

——. 1983. *Rhythm and Intent: Ritual Studies from South India.* Madras: Blackie.

——. 1984. *Quiescence and Passion: The Vision of Arunakiri, Tamil Mystic.* Madurai: Madurai Kamaraj University.

Dehejia, Vidya. 2002. *The Sensuous and the Sacred: Chola Bronzes from South India.* New York: American Federation of Arts.

Devakunjari, D. 1979. *Madurai through the Ages: From the Earliest Times to 1801 A.D.* Madras: Society for Archaeological, Historical and Epigraphical Research.

Filliozat, Jean. 1973. Introduction to *Un texte de la religion Kaumāra: Le Tirumurukāṟṟupaṭai,* edited and translated by Jean Filliozat. Pondicherry: Institut français d'Indologie.

Goodall, Dominic, N. Rout, R. Sathyanarayanan, S. A. S. Sarma, T. Ganesan, and S. Sambandhasivacarya, eds. 2005. *The Pañcāvaraṇastava of Aghoraśivācārya: A Twelfth-Century South Indian Prescription for the Visualisation of Sadāśiva and His Retinue.* Pondicherry: Institut français de Pondichéry/Ecole française d'extrême-orient.

L'Hernault, Françoise. 1978. *L'Iconographie de Subrahmaṇya au Tamilnad.* Pondicherry: Institute français d'Indologie.

——. 2002. *The Iconography of the Bṛhadīśvara Temple*. Edited by Lalit M. Gujral. New Delhi: Indira Gandhi National Centre for the Arts/Pondicherry: Ecole française d'extrême-orient/New Delhi: Aryan Books International.

L'Hernault, Françoise, with P. R. Srinivasan and Jacques Dumarçay. 1987. *Darasuram: Epigraphical Study, Etude Architecturale, Etude Iconographique*. Paris: Ecole française d'extrême-orient.

L'Hernault, Françoise, Pierre Pichard, and Jean Deloche. 1990. *L'Archéologie du site*. Vol. 2 of *Tiruvannamalai, un lieu saint Śivaïte du sud de l'Inde*. Paris: Ecole française d'extrême-orient.

Lockwood, Michael. 1974. "Pallava Somaskanda." In *Mahabalipuram Studies*, by Michael Lockwood, Gift Siromoney, and R. Dayanandan, 18–33. Madras: Christian Literary Society.

Nagaswamy, R. 1997. "Art of the Pandyas of South India." *Oriental Art* 43: 49–60.

Orr, Leslie C. 2008. "Re-imagining, Re-shaping and Re-signifying the Temple in Medieval Tamilnadu." Paper presented at the Association of Asian Studies Annual Meeting, Atlanta.

Pattabiramin, P. Z. 1971–75. *Sanctuaires Rupestres de l'Inde du Sud*. 2 vols. Pondicherry: Institute français d'Indologie.

Richman, Paula. 1997. *Extraordinary Child: Poems from a South Indian Devotional Genre*. Honolulu: University of Hawai'i Press.

Rudner, David West. 1987. "Religious Gifting and Inland Commerce in Seventeenth-Century South India." *Journal of Asian Studies* 46, no. 2: 361–79.

Sivaramamurti, C. 1963. *South Indian Bronzes*. New Delhi: Lalit Kala Akademi.

Soundara Rajan, K. V. 1998. *Rock-Cut Temple Styles: Early Pandyan Art and the Ellora Shrines*. Mumbai: Somaiya.

Srinivasan, P. R. 1963. *Bronzes of South India*. Bulletin of the Madras Government Museum, n.s., general section, vol. 8. Madras: India Press for the Controller of Stationery and Printing.

Stein, Burton. 1978. "Temples in Tamil Country, 1300–1750." In *South Indian Temples: An Analytical Reconsideration*, edited by Burton Stein, 11–45. New Delhi: Vikas.

Thomas, Job. 1986. *Tiruvengadu Bronzes*. Madras: Cre-A.

Zvelebil, Kamil V. 1991. *Tamil Traditions on Subrahmanya-Murugan*. Madras: Institute of Asian Studies.

A Tale of Two Weddings

Gendered Performances of Tulsī's Marriage to Kṛṣṇa

TRACY PINTCHMAN

Toward the end of the autumn month of Kārtik (October–November), many Hindus living in North India celebrate the marriage of Tulsī, the auspicious basil plant goddess, to her divine groom, usually understood to be the deity Viṣṇu or one of his forms, most often his incarnation (*avatāra*) Kṛṣṇa. In the city of Vārāṇasī, also called Benares, in Uttar Pradesh, the wedding is performed ritually in numerous locations, including Hindu homes, temples, and public spaces. This divine marriage takes place during the festival of Prabodhanī Ekādaśī, the eleventh day of the second fortnight of Kārtik, which also happens to be the day on which Viṣṇu is said to awaken from four months of slumber. Prabodhanī Ekādaśī also marks the end of the inauspicious four-month monsoon period, the *caturmāsa*, and ushers in the beginning of the marriage season for North Indian Hindus.

In this chapter I explore two types of ritual performance of Tulsī's wedding: one enacted by girls and women who gather in groups on the *ghāṭs*, the stepped platforms that run along the side of the Ganges River at the edge of the city; and another conducted largely by male renunciants in Śrī Maṭh, a Rāmānandi monastery located at Pañcagaṅgā Ghāṭ, which also attracts a large audience of laypersons from around the city. These are the only two groups in the city, as far as I know, that perform celebrations of Tulsī's marriage that are public and well attended by large numbers of ritual observers. I base my comments on three cycles of fieldwork conducted between 1995 and 1998. The primary focus of my research during those years was on (largely householder) women's rituals surrounding Tulsī's marriage and the month of Kārtik more generally, about which I have extensively written elsewhere.[1] As part of my research, however, I also attended three different performances of Tulsī's marriage at Śrī Maṭh by Rāmānandi monks.

The Rāmānandi order is reportedly founded on the teachings of Swami Rāmānanda, who is said to have lived between the fourteenth and fifteenth centuries C.E.; hence it is also called the Rāmānanda *sampradāya* (sect or tradition).

Ramdas Lamb observes that according to Rāmānandi tradition, Rāmānanda was originally a renunciant in the lineage of the great philosopher Rāmānuja (tenth–eleventh centuries). He became dissatisfied with what he perceived to be social discrimination in the lineage, so he started his own order, which explicitly rejected the caste system and accepted disciples from all castes, creeds, and backgrounds. For Rāmānanda and his followers, the primary emphasis of religious life is on the love of God in the form of Rām, achieved through a life of devotion and renunciation (Lamb 2006, 168). Lamb also notes that the Rāmānandi order currently has the largest number of renunciant members of any Hindu order, estimated at up to 1.5 million (ibid.). The organizational structure of the order comprises a variety of subgroups, including nomadic renouncers (*tyāgis* and *mahātyāgis*) and those who dwell in temples and ashrams, such as Śrī Maṭh, and have more contact with householders than do other Rāmānandis (Lamb 2006, 177–78).

What I found during the course of my research on the public ritual performances of Tulsī's marriage in Vārāṇasī is that female devotees at the *ghāṭs* enact and interpret Tulsī's marriage in a manner that seems to diverge significantly from the way that male renunciants do at Śrī Maṭh. The main questions I want to bring to these materials in the context of this essay are the following: What might these ritual performances share, and where do they differ? How do the actors in these ritual performances understand the nature of their performance? What role might social location (gender or householder versus renouncer status) play in shaping both formal and hermeneutical aspects of these two performances? And finally, what might this comparison suggest about issues concerning identity, ritual performance, and religious agency among ritual actors in both cases? Fred Clothey notes, "Rituals often serve to bring awareness to the participants and/or patrons of their social context" (1983, 2). In this regard we might ask how these two ritual performances embody or reflect the shared social context of the ritual performers—that is, those who are shaping and performing the ritual in particular ways.

In contemplating shared social contexts in these two ritual performances, I focus on gender and householder versus renouncer status. Among Hindu Indians other markers of status are certainly important, especially caste and class. I do not discuss those markers here, however, for two main reasons. First, in this essay I want to concentrate on identity markers that are shared by most or all ritual performers; in both cases ritual actors come from a variety of caste and class backgrounds, so these are not broadly shared. Second, in both contexts ritual participants deny the relevance of caste and class to their ritual undertaking. Rāmānandi monks, for example, are supposed to renounce possessions and leave their caste identity behind when they take up a renunciant lifestyle; female householders who perform Tulsī's marriage do so in devotional circles that draw members from all over the city, and participating women often do not even know each others' names, much less the particulars of class or caste affiliation. It is, however, true that in both cases participants would not likely include "untouchable," or Dalit, castes or members of the lowest socioeconomic strata. Among the women, for example, all of my informants (thirty-six formally interviewed women) were from high- or middle-caste families; most were broadly middle class, although some of them were from poor families. Although I did not ask the Rāmānandi monks about caste and class background (as these questions would have been viewed as inappropriate), there has been an increasing Brahmanization of the order during the last twenty years or so, with caste becoming more important to some Rāmānandi groups. This has reportedly resulted in growing discrimination in the order against the lowest castes (Ramdas Lamb, private communication, June 2006).

Tulsī, Sacred Marriage, and Auspiciousness

In Hinduism deities often marry or at least engage in sexual relationships with members of the opposite sex. William Harman has noted that one must understand marriage among Hindu deities in a broad sense to refer to numerous forms of male-female sexual union, mirroring Hindu law codes, which tend to understand most types of sexual intercourse as forms of marriage. Harman observes that male-female pairing on the divine level, often called sacred marriage or theogamy, partakes of a more pervasive preoccupation in Hindu religious narratives, images, and practices of male-female complementarity (1989, 13). Sudhir Kakar further notes the centrality in Hinduism of imagery surrounding the unified male-female pair or couple, the *joṛi*, as two persons joined together in what he describes as a harmonious, interdependent, and mutually fulfilling oneness (1990, 83–84). The quintessential representation of this ideal of a "single two-person entity," argues Kakar, is the image of Ardhanārīśvara, that is, Śiva in a half-male, half-female form. It is, however, also embodied in the numerous male-female couples that populate the Hindu pantheon.

In Western scholarship some of the earliest academic work on sacred marriage focused on ancient Near Eastern religions and tended to assume a strong relationship between sacred marriage and a concern with fertility, understood broadly but often embodied particularly in agricultural symbolism.[2] Harman, however, has contested the centrality of fertility symbolism in Hindu sacred marriages, arguing, "In India, sacred marriage does not function primarily as an agricultural metaphor in which the earth, conceived as female, is rendered fruitful by a symbolic marriage with cosmic, divine, and male elements" (1989, 3). Harman proposes instead that "sacred marriage has much to do with organizing devotees' perceptions of relationships that exist between deities and of the relationships devotees might have with their deities" and that sacred marriage may function as a way of affirming the perceived order of the cosmos while establishing it anew (3, 139). Harman makes his claims in the context of his study of the marriage of Sundareśvara (a form of Śiva) and Mīnākṣī (a form of Pārvatī) in Madurai, Tamilnadu, where fertility symbolism does indeed seem to be largely downplayed.

I here argue instead for the efficaciousness of exploring the ritual performance of Tulsī's marriage, and perhaps sacred marriages in Hindu contexts more broadly, in relation to the Hindu value of auspiciousness, a value that encompasses both a concern for fertility and for cosmic order and order in divine and human relationships. Much has been written about the auspicious (*śubh, maṅgal*) and the inauspicious (*aśubh, amaṅgal*) in Hindu culture.[3] Generally speaking auspiciousness, which is embodied especially in the goddess Lakṣmī, is a desired value that connotes well-being and happiness. Categories that exemplify worldly auspiciousness include weddings, sexuality, and progeny; wetness and rains, abundance of food, and the well-being of crops; and health, medicines, and bodily well-being (Marglin 1985a, 65–83). Kingship and lordly power also embody auspiciousness, for the strength of a king manifests itself in the production of rain and good crops. The divine prototype of earthly kings is Viṣṇu, the deity worshiped most prominently during Kārtik; as Viṣṇu's consort, Lakṣmī embodies the life-giving powers that sustain the sovereignty of kings (cf. Marglin 1985b, 181–84). Viṣṇu is also paired with other goddesses, including the goddess Earth, Bhūdevī, whom he protects from oppressive demons. In safeguarding Bhūdevī, Viṣṇu also protects auspiciousness as it is manifest in the earth's fecundity and generativity, a role that flows from the sovereign power he embodies.

While a good deal of scholarship on auspiciousness in Hindu culture has emphasized values generally associated with householdership and worldly pursuits, Vasudha Narayanan ramifies the discussion by calling for a clear recognition of two levels of auspiciousness: one that has to do with everyday life and householder values and pertains to categories such as prosperity, happiness, or the longevity of a husband, and another that encompasses the pursuit of spiritual liberation (*mokṣa*) and is allied with renunciant values (1985, 62). This second level pertains to the achievement of spiritual advancement, renunciation of the world, and pursuit of the divine. The many festivals and religious celebrations of Kārtik, including the celebration of Tulsī's marriage, exemplify auspiciousness on both these levels and can be viewed as conducive to worldly or spiritual boons, or both, depending on the devotee: the line between the two is fluid and permeable.[4]

Tulsī's nature as a sanctifying plant naturally aligns her with both worldly and spiritual forms of auspiciousness. As an herb and a divine consort or bride, for example, she tends to be associated in many contexts with householder ideals of auspiciousness exemplified especially in bodily well-being, marriage, and fecundity. *Tulsī* is considered to be a healing and life-enhancing medicinal herb. The *tulsī* plant is used in Ayurvedic medicine for all manner of illnesses and conditions. *Tulsī* is also a form of domestic medicine, and many home cures that women take or give to family members involve *tulsī*. Tulsī's marriage marks the beginning of the auspicious Hindu wedding season and a return to earthly abundance, as the end of the rainy season brings the ripening of fruits and crops in the fertile, post-monsoon soil. Hence Tulsī's marriage to Viṣṇu on Prabodhanī Ekādaśī exemplifies the reestablishment of auspiciousness, embodied in fecundity and the domestic order of marriage, following the dangerous and inauspicious *caturmāsa* period.

Yet *tulsī* is also associated with liberative values. Several different varieties of the *tulsī* plant exist; while some are small and can flourish in small pots, others can grow several feet tall. Groves of this larger *tulsī*, called *vana-tulsī* (forest *tulsī*), grow in the wild but can also be cultivated. It might be tempting to associate sacred groves with fertility imagery, but in fact Purāṇic descriptions of Tulsī groves downplay such imagery. Instead they tend to associate *Tulsī* groves primarily with spiritual benefits, especially the destruction of sin and the promotion of *mokṣa*, or spiritual liberation. The Skanda Purāṇa, for example, claims that when planted and cultivated, *tulsī* groves destroy sinful karma (2.4.23.12). The Padma Purāṇa asserts that those who plant a grove of *tulsī* escape the clutches of Yama, the Host of Death (6.106.9–10), and that cremation with *tulsī* wood brings liberation from sins and freedom from rebirth (*saṃsāra*) (6.23.3–4). Although groves and forests generally reside outside of domestic space, groves of *tulsī* have a domestic form as well. In some Hindu homes, several *tulsī* plants are cultivated and grouped together in the courtyard, constituting a miniature forest called a *tulsī-van*. Such a domestic grove infuses the home with purifying and liberative qualities. The Skanda Purāṇa, for example, declares that a house in which a grove of *tulsī* resides becomes a *tīrtha* (2.4.23.9), thereby assigning to *tulsī* the sanctifying power normally associated with pilgrimage spots. The Padma Purāṇa claims that Brahmā, Śiva, and Viṣṇu dwell in the *tulsī* plant—with Brahmā at the tip of the leaf, Viṣṇu in the middle, and Śiva at the base of the plant—along with all the wives of the gods, planets, sages, divine sages, and holy places (7.24.6–10).

A single *tulsī* plant, as well as all its various parts, may also synecdochically exemplify the purifying and liberative ideals embodied by *tulsī* groves. The *tulsī* seed, for example, is thought to quell sexual desire or *kāma* (Simoons 1998, 27), and Rāmānandi renouncers wear a *tulsī* bead around their necks. Food consumed with *tulsī* leaves is believed to be rendered pure and becomes suitable for consumption even by deities. Foods offered to Viṣṇu in particular are purified by the addition of *tulsī*; R. S. Khare describes it as the "cultural catalizer [*sic*] in Vaiṣṇavism" that helps transform mundane food into "divine code" so that the deity can accept it (1976, 102). The leaves of *tulsī* may be placed in the mouth of a dying man to ensure spiritual liberation (*mokṣa*) at the moment of death (Upadhyaya 1965, 13). The Padma Purāṇa claims that those whose dead bodies are burnt with *tulsī* wood are liberated from the effects of negative karma and praises all parts of the plant—as well as the dirt or clay in which it is rooted—as capable of purifying sins (for example, 6.23.1–4).

Tulsī, then, is auspicious in both worldly and "otherworldly," or spiritual, senses of the term as described by Narayanan. Juxtaposing performances of Tulsī's marriage by householder women with those performed by male renunciants reveals differing emphases with regard to the various forms of auspiciousness that Tulsī embodies. One might anticipate that these women, who may be looking forward to their own weddings or the weddings of their children, might have a greater tendency to emphasize worldly dimensions of auspiciousness, "humanizing" Tulsī's marriage and drawing parallels between divine marriage and human marriage. Conversely one might expect male renunciants, who have relinquished householder life, to place greater emphasis on the significance of Tulsī's marriage in relation to auspicious spiritual values. This is precisely what my own fieldwork bears out. Furthermore I found that variations in interpretive emphases are also paralleled by formal differences, which, I contend, seem also to be rooted in differing social contexts.

Women's Performance of Tulsī's Marriage

On the morning of Probhadanī Ekādaśī, many Hindu women gather together in groups along the *ghāṭs* to perform Tulsī's marriage ritually. Most participants, however, do this as part of a larger observance of Kārtik-related traditions that take place throughout the month.

Kārtik is widely celebrated among Indian Hindus as deeply sacred, and many Benarsi Hindus count it among the three or four most religiously important months of the year. The key religious injunction pertaining to Kārtik is the Kārtik *vrat*, or votive observance, which, like other *vrat*s, entails fasting practices. Even more central to this *vrat*, however, is the practice of Kārtik *snān*, ritual bathing in the Ganges River performed daily throughout the month. Such bathing is considered especially meritorious when performed very early in the morning, before sunrise.

After completing their ritual bath, many women and girls gather in groups at the river's edge every day throughout the month to perform a special devotional ritual or *pūjā* that they consider part of their observance of the *vrat*. Participants construct several icons (*mūrtis*) of Hindu deities out of Ganges mud. Forming a circle, they perform *pūjā* to the icons while singing songs that are particular to this occasion. Many deities are honored, but several of the songs focus specifically on Kṛṣṇa, and a number of informants told me the *pūjā* is largely dedicated to Kṛṣṇa with other deities called to be present largely so they, too, can participate as devotees.

More than half of the thirty-six women I formally interviewed indicated they consider Kārtik *pūjā* to be related to Kṛṣṇa's *rāsa-līlā,* the famous circle dance of Kṛṣṇa mythology, in which Kṛṣṇa danced in the middle of a circle of cowherdesses or *gopīs*, making love with each of them. Some participants maintained that Kṛṣṇa's *rāsa-līlā* took place during the month of Kārtik, describing Kārtik *pūjā* as a form of worship enacted in commemoration of the earthly *rāsa-līlā* performed long ago. Informants also tended to employ the term *rāsa-līlā* to refer not just to the circle dance, but also to Kṛṣṇa's life in Vrindavan, where he spent his childhood and youth, and in this regard they understand their role in the *pūjā* as comparable to that of the *gopīs* who cared for Kṛṣṇa during all his years as a boy in Vrindavan.[5] In Kārtik *pūjā* this role takes on a progressive character, marking Kṛṣṇa's development from infancy to adulthood and culminating in the preparation and celebration of his marriage to Tulsī.

In Kārtik *pūjā* Kṛṣṇa is considered to be in his child form for about the first twenty days of the month. At this point participants execute his *upanayana,* or *janeū,* the traditional Hindu ceremony marking a boy's investiture with the sacred thread. This ceremony designates Kṛṣṇa's transformation from child to young man. Participants begin the *janeū* ceremony by passing the brass image of Kṛṣṇa around the circle of women, smearing the image with a mixture of turmeric and mustard oil. They then bathe the brass Kṛṣṇa lovingly in Ganges water. Laying out a fresh cloth, they place Kṛṣṇa in the middle of it, dress him in finery, and prepare him for the *janeū,* placing offerings before him of betel nut, chickpeas, and *janeū* threads. A male Brahman priest is called to the circle briefly to utter the mantras appropriate to the occasion, and participants adorn the Kṛṣṇa image with the *janeū* threads, which they have smeared with the mixture of turmeric and oil. This is a day of dancing and bawdy joking, for the *janeū* signals Kṛṣṇa's impending marriage. The *janeū* ceremony is known as a "half marriage," since it marks a boy's transition from childhood to adulthood; in contemporary India if a Hindu boy who is getting married has not undergone a *janeū,* he will undergo one just before the wedding ceremony. From the day of the *janeū* until the day of the wedding itself, women sing marriage songs in the *pūjā* circle before beginning the *pūjā* itself to mark the impending marriage.[6]

When the wedding day finally arrives, after concluding the daily *pūjā,* participants clear and purify a space for the marriage platform (*maṇḍapa*), arranging bamboo branches for the wedding canopy, as in a human marriage. They draw auspicious designs (*rangoli*) on the ground with rice flour. The bride, a potted *tulsī* plant with abundant foliage, is brought into the circle, dressed in a red cloth that functions as her wedding sari, and adorned. The groom, represented by a brass image, is also brought to the *pūjā* circle, where he is passed around, massaged with mustard oil and turmeric, bathed in Ganges water, and dressed in finery. Participants proudly and conspicuously display dowry offerings they have brought, including items such as saris, pots and pans, and jewelry.

As in the *janeū* ritual, here, too, a male Brahman priest is called into the *pūjā* circle only briefly to officiate in the *phera,* the circumambulation of the wedding fire. In human weddings bride and groom perform *phera* by circumambulating a fire seven times. Male Brahman priests ordinarily preside over both *janeū* rites and weddings, both of which belong to a class of sacramental rituals known as *saṃskāras*, which is why they are invited into the women's Kārtik circles to perform these ritual services for Kṛṣṇa. Then participating women sprinkle *sindūr,* a type of vermilion powder, on the bride's "head" to mark her married status, as is commonly done among Hindu women; throw puffed rice at the newlywed couple; and offer them yogurt sweetened with brown sugar, a mixture traditionally eaten by bride and groom. They also engage in a boisterous round of *gāli,* the often sexually explicit songs of abuse that Hindu women sing at human marriages. At the end of the celebration, participants gather in a circle singing and clapping

Wedding performed at Assi Ghāṭ, 1997. Photograph by the author.

while many women dance, pulling their coworshipers into the circle to dance with them.

The atmosphere surrounding the women's performance of Tulsī's wedding on the *ghāṭs* is festive, fun, and relaxed. In both 1997 and 1998, in the ritual circles in which I participated, a food fight broke out toward the end of the performance, and women began chasing each other and smearing yogurt on one another's faces and limbs, laughing and clearly enjoying themselves a great deal.

During the last few days of Kārtik, following the marriage of Kṛṣṇa and Tulsī, women's daily worship continues, but participants no longer use clay icons. Instead they perform the *pūjā* with a plastic or metal box said to contain the religious merit participants have earned during the month. Many Kārtik *pūjā* participants maintain that Tulsī does not depart with her new husband for her new home (with her husband and in-laws) until the final night of Kārtik, the night of the full moon, when the divine bride and groom are also said to consummate their marriage.

The Performance of Tulsī's Marriage at Śrī Maṭh

The performance of Tulsī's wedding at Śrī Maṭh is rather different—and more sober—than the one performed by women. When I asked women on the *ghāṭs* how long they had been performing Kārtik *pūjā* and, along with it, Tulsī's wedding, several of them noted many years of participation. Some claimed to have learned the tradition in childhood from their own mothers or as young brides from their mothers-in-law, indicating that this *pūjā* has been going on for at least some decades, and possibly longer. This does not seem to be the case at Śrī Maṭh, where, the spiritual and organizational head of the monastery, the Rāmnareśācārya, reported to me, the monks apparently started performing Tulsī's marriage as a public ritual during the early 1990s. I was not able to pin down a precise date or clear explanation as to why Śrī Maṭh began performing Tulsī's marriage, although one prominent Benarsi not related to Śrī Maṭh or the Rāmānandi order suggested that the monastery's involvement in the rite may be related to the rise of the kind of militant Hinduism tied to the promotion of Rām worship, which was pushed to the fore by the destruction of the Babri Mosque in 1992. In any case it appears that the decision to begin performing the marriage at Śrī Maṭh caused consternation for some of the monks, but opposition soon disappeared. In describing to me the first time the marriage was performed at Śrī Maṭh under his supervision, for example, the Rāmnareśācārya emphasized his own initial discomfort and embarrassment, noting that his feeling was that renunciants should have nothing to do with rituals of marriage. Here is what he told me during an interview in 1997:

> So the first year, we started from Dasāśamedh Ghāṭ, and I was feeling ashamed, wondering what people would say about it. But when I did the *pūjā* to the Ganges River at Dasāśamedh Ghāṭ and the procession started from there, so then

> religious feeling (*bhāv*) began [to rise up in me]. The devotional singing (*kīrtan*) started, and . . . the procession proceeded. . . . When we arrived here, there were lots of people here, too. They received the procession. And when they took down Rām's palanquin, after that, no one paid any attention to me. I was just an observer. And as I saw their religious sentiment (*bhāv*) and the way they did it, it was something divine. I never forgot that experience. So gradually my *bhāv* also developed, and that is also necessary for a renunciant, as a form of worship.

Many women who participate in Kārtik *pūjā* interpret the entire month of Kārtik in relation to the marriage of Kṛṣṇa and Tulsī, which they describe as woven into the devotional fabric of Kārtik as a whole. Some, for example, interpret food restrictions associated with the Kārtik *vrat* as commemorating the fast that Tulsī undertook in ancient times to attain Kṛṣṇa as a husband or insist that Tulsī herself began the tradition of Kārtik *pūjā*. At Śrī Maṭh, on the other hand, although the monks celebrate the month of Kārtik and its festivals, the marriage of Tulsī is an affair rather isolated from other Kārtik events and is performed pretty much in straight Vedic style. It begins in the late afternoon, when a flotilla of well-decorated boats carrying Rāmānandi monks and an icon of Viṣṇu or Rām comes up from Pañcagaṅgā Ghāṭ. The boats land at Assi Ghāṭ to collect devotees before returning to Śrī Maṭh at Pañcagaṅgā Ghāṭ. The icon is then processed amid great fanfare into the *maṭh*, where the marriage rite itself is enacted.

During the three years in which I observed the *maṭh*'s performance of Tulsī's wedding, it was preceded and followed by a lengthy sermon given by the Rāmnareśācārya. While the women's performance of the marriage at the *ghāṭs* was accompanied by group singing of folk songs, popular Hindi *bhajans*, and *gāli*, the marriage at Śrī Maṭh emphasized the chanting of Sanskrit verses, as is typical of Vedic weddings. At the *ghāṭs* all participants took some part in Tulsī's marriage: gathering around the divine couple in a circle, everyone had a turn at covering the icon of Kṛṣṇa with turmeric and washing his body; everyone got a turn at putting vermilion powder on the "head" of the bride; and everyone threw garlands and puffed rice at the divine couple. At Śrī Maṭh, on the other hand, all the "guests"—laymen and women from around the city—sat at a distance from the main event, behind a platform erected for the occasion. The marriage itself was conducted only by Śrī Maṭh insiders, almost all of whom were men and most of whom were Rāmānandi renunciants, although some lay disciples of the Rāmnareśācārya, including some married couples, also participated. In 1995, for example, I was told that lay disciples played the parts of the mother and father of the bride and groom. Women sat apart from men, at a distance from the marriage platform. The division between audience and human ritual agents—almost nonexistent at the *ghāṭs*—was drawn quite clearly at Śrī Maṭh. Toward the end of the marriage ritual, as at the *ghāṭs*, there was festive dancing among the women, and—as at the *ghāṭs*—dowry

Wedding performed at Śrī Maṭh, 1997. Photograph by the author.

items were offered and displayed. The close proximity of men, however, meant that the women present were more subdued in their behavior than at the *ghāṭ*s, and there was no singing of *gāli* or raucous food fight.

Formal differences between the two performances were paralleled by differences in interpretation offered by participants. Kārtik *pūjā* participants whom I interviewed concerning the meaning of Kārtik *pūjā* and Tulsī's marriage tended to emphasize continuity between the marriage of the divine bride and groom and that of human beings. As one participant put it, "Just as God gets married, I got married in the same way. It is the same. God's *janeū* took place, and then his marriage took place. We do the same things." Another noted in relation to the ceremony of bidding farewell to Tulsī, "Just as we sometimes cry when we bid farewell to our own daughters when they marry, so we do the same thing in our homes—we cry for Tulsī." Another noted that in her home on the night of Kārtik's full moon—the night informants cited most frequently as the night of marital consummation—she takes a *tulsī* plant and a brass image of Kṛṣṇa, puts them in a cupboard, and closes the door for the night so that bride and groom can enjoy some privacy, just as a human bride and groom might do.

At Śrī Maṭh, on the other hand, Rāmānandi monks stressed what they perceived to be the discontinuity between Tulsī's marriage and human marriage. One young man I interviewed, for example, insisted that there are two kinds of marriages:

those that are worldly (*saṃsārik* or *laukik*), the category into which human marriages fall, and those that are "otherwordly" (*alaukik*) or divine. Tulsī's marriage is of the latter kind and has nothing to do with human marriage. This division is consistent with Rāmānandi theology and the common distinction in Hindu contexts between *kāma* and *prema. Kāma* is love tinged with personal desire, including the desire for family and children. *Prema,* on the other hand, is selfless, desireless love that is aimed only at pleasing a loved one, does not aim to attain anything for oneself, and is religiously prized. My informant at Śrī Maṭh emphasized the nature of the love shared by Tulsī and her groom as one characterized by *prema* rather than *kāma.* He also emphasized the need for human conjugal relations to conform more closely to this divine model by taking seriously the moral value of sexual self-restraint—a value that male renunciants are expected to esteem highly and, one hopes, exemplify through celibacy.[7] He noted, for example: "The reason we perform Tulsī's marriage is to teach people about strength of character. The main teaching is that one should control oneself, control one's character, and use it in such a way that it produces good and healthy children. If you want to plant a good tree, so the seed should be good. If the seed is good, the tree will be healthy. And if the tree is healthy, the fruit will be good. So basically, the seed needs to be good. Your children will only be as good as your sexual self-control (*brahmacārya*)." This informant also drew clear divisions between deities, human ritual actors taking part in the ritual performance, and the largely lay audience that constituted the ritual observers—divisions that were drawn much less sharply in the women's performance of the marriage at the *ghāṭs*.

In both the sermons he delivered at the performance of Tulsī's marriage and two interviews he participated in with me, the Rāmnareśācārya emphasized the central religious meaning of the marriage as the ideal of performing *sevā,* or devotional service to God (Bhagavān), through the ritual enactment of God's marriage. Women on the *ghāṭs* also stressed the performance of the marriage as a form of *sevā.* Socially, however, the Rāmnareśācārya emphasized the performance of the marriage as a symbolic form of renunciation or *tyāga* analogous to *kanyā dān,* a father's duty to give away a daughter in marriage. Hence he highlighted the devotional and renunciatory dimensions of the ritual performance. By way of contrast, not one of the thirty-six Kārtik *pūjā* participants I formally interviewed ever mentioned *kanyā dān* in relation to the performance of Tulsī's marriage.

Conclusion

What kinds of larger points might our exploration of these two performances raise in relation to ritual and identity? First, looking at these two appropriations of Tulsī's wedding demonstrates the formal flexibility of (at least) some types of Hindu devotional practice. The formal qualities of Tulsī's wedding as a ritual performance clearly are not fixed but are adaptable to context. Furthermore I suggest they reflect and embody different ways of appropriating auspiciousness. The women's performance on the *ghāṭs* emphasizes worldly auspiciousness, including human values generally associated with householdership, whereas the performance that takes place at Śrī Maṭh emphasizes renunciant values and otherworldly auspiciousness as Narayanan describes it. It certainly seems that the Śrī Maṭh's fairly recent adoption of the Tulsī' marriage ritual might well have been motivated at least in part by its established popularity among householders. But I did not discern any noticeable tension between the women and the renunciants concerning "ownership" of Tulsī's marriage rite. In fact several of the women who performed the marriage at the *ghāṭs* in the morning also went to Śrī Maṭh to observe it again in the evening.

The two types of ritual performance also embody differing constructs of ritual community. In the case of women gathering at the *ghāṭs*, caste, class, and other formal markers of hierarchy are generally downplayed (although, as far as I was able to discover, participants in the *pūjā* circles in which I took part were all from middle or upper castes). The physical construction of the worship space as a circle grants all participants equal access to the icons used in worship, and all participants function as ritual agents. As I have noted elsewhere, participants in Kārtik *pūjā* adapt the term *sakhī* or "female friend" from Kṛṣṇa mythology as the sole term of reference for one another during the course of the *pūjā,* including at the performance of Tulsī's marriage, and informants stressed to me the antihierarchical nature of the term.[8] At Śrī Maṭh, however, hierarchy among deity, renunciant, and householder is embraced in the formal aspects of the ritual performance, with householders formally separated from the icons to which only Rāmānandi renunciants and close lay disciples are granted access.

These materials also point to the role of ritual agents in interpreting this tradition of ritual performance in ways that resonate with the values and concerns that religious and social identity may help push to the fore. As noted in the introduction to this volume, in her book *Pierced by Murugan's Lance,* Elizabeth Collins notes that, within the tradition of anthropological theory about ritual, two distinctive approaches have developed: one that emphasizes what ritual does to people and another that emphasizes what people do with ritual. She observes further that the first approach underscores ways in which the behavior of people "is shaped by culture, language, and hierarchies of power," while the second stresses the conception of human beings as agents who act upon the world and try to reshape it to reflect their values and interests (Collins 1997, 17). With respect to this latter point, ritual practice facilitates the ability of ritual agents to perpetuate, appropriate, or reshape values and ideals that have to do with social identity (Bell 1997, 73, 82).

Tulsī's marriage seems to function in this way for both female householders and male renouncers. On the *ghāṭs* female participants appropriate Tulsī's marriage in ways that have deep social resonance for many householder women.[9] Marriage, of course, effects a significant transformation on the identity of a traditional Hindu bride who leaves her own home for a new one, exchanging her natal family for her husband's family. As marriage is an important focus of many Hindu women's lives, in Kārtik *pūjā* traditions, Tulsī's marriage becomes the focus of the entire month. At Śrī Maṭh, however, where male renunciants perform the marriage, the performance seems much more isolated from larger structures of religious meaning associated with the month of Kārtik. Any explicit acknowledgment of social continuity between human and divine marriage is largely overlooked, except where the role of ritual agents is likened to the role of a father (a male authority figure) giving away his daughter. Instead what is stressed is the nature of the marriage as a form of ascetic devotional service continuous with Rāmānandi devotional ideals. In both cases we find that the ritual comes to be understood largely in relation to the cherished ideals and aspirations of the individuals responsible for its performance.

Notes

1. See, for example, Pintchman 1999, 2003a, 2003b, 2005.

2. Cf. Harman 1989, 3, where he cites several of these sources.

3. See, for example, Marglin 1985b and Carman and Marglin 1985.

4. For a fuller discussion of Kārtik and the ways it exemplifies auspiciousness, see Pintchman 2005, 45–97.

5. In John S. Hawley's research on *rāsa-līlā* performances in Braj, the term *rāsa-līlā* is also used to indicate both the *rāsa-līlā* episode itself and the entire play *(līlā)* of Kṛṣṇa's life enacted in liturgical drama. See Hawley 1981 and 1983, chaps. 6 and 7.

6. For more on the women's performance of Kṛṣṇa's *janeū* and wedding, including analysis of the women's songs, see Pintchman 2005, 129–42.

7. Lamb (2006, 172) notes that, while celibacy is the ideal, not all Rāmānandi renunciants take vows of celibacy until and unless they feel they have gained the ability to fulfill the vow successfully.

8. See Pintchman 2005, 146–55. Leslie A. Northrup (1997) has noted that women's ritual performances in general tend to downplay hierarchy.

9. I have offered a great deal more by way of interpretation and analysis of women's Kārtik *pūjā* traditions in Pintchman 2005, especially chap. 4.

References

Bell, Catherine. 1997. *Ritual: Perspectives and Dimensions.* New York: Oxford University Press.

Carman, John B., and Frederique Marglin, eds. 1985. *Purity and Auspiciousness in Indian Society.* Leiden: Brill.

Clothey, Fred W. 1983. *Rhythm and Intent: Ritual Studies from South India.* Madras: Blackie.

Collins, Elizabeth Fuller. 1997. *Pierced by Murugan's Lance: Ritual, Power, and Moral Redemption among Malaysian Hindus.* DeKalb: Northern Illinois University Press.

Harman, William P. 1989. *The Sacred Marriage of a Hindu Goddess.* Delhi: Motilal Banarsidass.

Hawley, John S. 1981. *At Play with Kṛṣṇa: Pilgrimage Dramas from Brindavan.* Princeton: Princeton University Press.

——. 1983. *Kṛṣṇa, the Butter Thief.* Princeton: Princeton University Press.

Kakar, Sudhir. 1990. *Intimate Relations: Exploring Indian Sexuality.* New Delhi: Penguin Books.

Khare, R. S. 1976. *Culture and Reality: Essays on the Hindu System of Managing Foods.* Simla: Indian Institute of Advanced Study.

Lamb, Ramdas. 2006. "Monastic Vows and the Rāmānanda Sampraday." In *Dealing with Deities: the Ritual Vow in South Asia,* edited by Selva J. Raj and William P. Harman, 165–85. Albany: State University of New York Press.

Marglin, Frederique. 1985a. "Types of Oppositions in Hindu Culture." In *Purity and Auspiciousness in Indian Society,* edited by John B. Carman and Frederique Marglin, 65–83. Leiden: Brill.

——. 1985b. *Wives of the God King: The Rituals of the Devadasis of Puri.* Delhi: Oxford University Press.

Narayanan, Vasudha. 1985. "The Two Levels of Auspiciousness in Srivaisnava Ritual and Literature." In *Purity and Auspiciousness in Indian Society,* edited by John B. Carman and Frederique Marglin, 55–64. Leiden: Brill.

Northrup, Lesley A. 1997. *Ritualizing Women.* Cleveland: Pilgrim.

Pintchman, Tracy. 1999. "The Month of Karttik as a Vaisnava *Mahotsav*: Mythic Themes and the Ocean of Milk." *Journal of Vaisnava Studies* 7, no. 2: 65–92.

——. 2003a. "The Month of Kārtik and Women's Ritual Devotions to Kṛṣṇa." In *The Blackwell Companion to Hinduism,* edited by Gavin Flood, 327–42. Oxford: Blackwell.

——. 2003b. "Women's Songs for the Marriage of Tulsī and Kṛṣṇa in Benares." *Journal of Vaisnava Studies* 12, no. 1: 57–65.

——. 2005. *Guests at God's Wedding: Celebrating Kārtik among the Women of Benares.* Albany: State University of New York Press.

Simoons, Frederick J. 1998. *Plants of Life, Plants of Death.* Madison: University of Wisconsin Press, 1998.

Upadhyaya, K. D. 1965. "Indian Botanical Folklore." In *Tree Symbol Worship in India: A New Survey of a Pattern of Folk-Religion,* edited by Sankar Sen Gupta, 1–18. Calcutta: Indian Publications.

The Roles of Ritual in Two "Blockbuster" Hindi Films

PHILIP LUTGENDORF

In ritual, the world as lived and the world as imagined, fused under the agency of a single set of symbolic forms, turn out to be the same world.

Clifford Geertz (1973, 112)

Popular Hindi films—the output of an industry based in Bombay/Mumbai and lately identified worldwide by the label "Bollywood"—contain a great deal of visual, aural, and thematic content that may be termed "religious," and most often "Hindu," in character.[1] Such content dominated the narratives of this cinema from its historical inception, since films of genres variously identified as "mythologicals" (based on epic and Purāṇic scriptures) and "devotionals" (based on the hagiographies of religious exemplars) formed the bulk of productions during the first decade of India's silent era (1913–22). They were soon joined, however, by films that drew on different and ostensibly "secular" narrative sources, giving rise to genre labels—such as "historicals," "stunt films," "crime dramas," and "costume films"—that, like those of other cinemas, served a primarily heuristic function in the conception and marketing of films. These genres, which collectively exceeded "mythologicals" in output from the early 1920s onward, were themselves largely superseded in the 1940s by the genre of "social" film—designating a story set more or less in the present and often centrally concerned with a social issue such as caste or class prejudice, particularly as it influenced the choice of marital partners. Given the ubiquity of song and dance in popular cinema since the introduction of film sound in 1931, "social" films were also "melodramas" in the original sense of the term, typically incorporating an average of six to eight musical numbers. These, together with multiple subplots that often encapsulated previously autonomous genres such as "stunt films" or "comedies," resulted in the characteristic "epic" length (160 to 180 minutes) and "loose and fragmented" narrative structure of mainstream Hindi films during the post-Independence period—a feature that led, probably in the 1970s, to the coining of the term *masālā film*, suggesting a blend of savory spices.[2]

Despite changing labels, however, and the comparative rarity of "mythologicals" in post-1920s Bombay cinema, religious content—often expressed through iconography, body language, or character names and plot motifs that allude to classical myths—has remained a ubiquitous feature of popular films, a fact recently confirmed by an ambitious survey (Dwyer 2006). Another of the common ways in which religion enters Hindi cinema is through the representation of ritual. Diurnal rites—such as "taking *darśan*"; receiving *prasād* (auspicious viewing of a deity or holy person and acceptance of consecrated food or water as his or her tangible "grace"); performing *ārati* (worship with an oil lamp and other offerings, often accompanied by a devotional song) in temples and before home altars; and women greeting male relatives with a lamp and auspicious forehead mark (*nichāvar*), as well as seasonal and life-cycle rituals, such as the annual festivals of Holi and Divali and (especially) the rites of passage attendant on marriage and death—all are recurring motifs in popular films, which have developed certain audiovisual conventions for their representation. Their common uses include the alteration of mood (through an injection of solemnity, mourning, or festal gaiety), the development of character (for example, through the representation of piety), or the suggestion of the passage of time (as in the repeated ringing of temple bells in the 1975 hit *Deewaar* [*Dīvār*, The Wall], which signals the lapse of twenty years in the lives of the main characters). Even brief ritual episodes are often central to the development of a film's narrative—thus the shorthand representation of marriage rites near the beginning of the legendary *Mother India* (1957), accompanied by the first of the film's twelve songs, establishes the main character, Rādhā, as an auspicious bride and "Lakṣmī of the house" (embodying the goddess of prosperity and fecundity). This identification will be ironically referenced during a later moment of crisis when, abandoned by her crippled husband and facing likely rape by a village moneylender to whom she has gone to beg food for her starving sons, Rādhā angrily flings her marriage necklace at a silver statue of Lakṣmī enshrined in the moneylender's home. And in *Deewaar*, the early representation of a pious and long-suffering mother's *darśan* at a Śiva temple, participated in by her younger son but boycotted by his angry elder brother, prefigures the latter's climactic confrontation with the deity and offering of himself as a sacrifice (*balidān*) to save his mother's life.

Although the introduction of such portentous vignettes is commonplace, the most celebrated Hindi films of the past half century include two that are more centrally structured around ritual performances: *Jai Santoshi Maa* (*Jai Santoṣī Mā*, 1975; hereafter *JSM*) and *Hum Aapke Hain Koun . . . !* (*Ham āpke haiṃ kaun*, 1994; hereafter *HAHK*). Although classed in different cinematic genres ("mythological" and "social," respectively), these films show a number of intriguing similarities. Since each has enjoyed a success that may, without exaggeration, be termed phenomenal—exerting, in the opinion of both admirers and detractors, an impact on popular culture that has proven to be lasting—each has also become the subject of a modest body of critical literature.[3] In the remainder of this essay, I revisit these well-known films with a focus on their ritual dimension, which has been largely neglected in previous analyses. What I find particularly interesting about these films, apart from their remarkable success and sheer entertainment value, is that ritual performances function in each in both a narrative and prescriptive manner. That is, within the film the enactment of rituals is central to the unfolding of the plot and to its satisfactory resolution, and in the context of the film's reception, these practices have come to be widely emulated, in part through "ritualized" viewings of the films themselves.

Yet in focusing on one comparatively neglected dimension of these films, I do not intend to suggest reductively that their popularity depends primarily on this element of their structure. Feature films are multifaceted texts that are susceptible to a range of interpretations, and this is all the more so in the case of Hindi films, with their characteristic length and elaborate plotlines. I agree with John C. Lyden's assessment that the bulk of critical writing on popular cinema, at least from the standpoint of religious studies, has tended to privilege narrative content, examined from either a "theological" or "ideological" perspective—the former detecting religious "symbols" in plot and character, the latter critiquing both of these, often negatively, from such theoretical orientations as feminism, Marxism, and psychoanalysis (Lyden 2003, 17–35). Such approaches pay little attention to the specifically cinematic dimensions of film "texts" (cinematography and framing, mise-en-scène, sound and music, and so on) that may convey equally compelling (and sometimes internally contradictory, resistant, or even subversive) "messages" to audiences. In closely examining a few scenes from each film, I seek to supplement existing scholarly analyses by giving greater emphasis to these dimensions and by paying closer attention to the lyrics and staging of song sequences. These have been especially neglected in scholarship on Hindi cinema, although songs constitute one of its characteristic features, typically account for 20 to 30 percent of a film's running time, and enjoy wide post- and extrafilmic circulation.[4] Even scholars who concede the importance of song sequences tend to treat them as "interruptions" in the flow of the narrative, allowing for the eruption of "excess" in the form of emotion and spectacle (for example, Gopalan 2002; Thomas 1985). Yet in the case of both *JSM* and *HAHK*, it is precisely during song sequences that the most significant and imitated ritual activities occur. This is perhaps not surprising, since the repetitious and harmonious structure of music mirrors that of ritual and may also serve (as in the musical setting of the Catholic Mass or the lyrics of a Hindu *ārati*) to script and prescribe ritual practice. If filmmaking in general has been compared to ritual as a "world-making" activity that creates an alternative, self-contained universe structured according to orderly rules (Plate 2008, 1–13), then the Hindi filmsong, with its typical format of rhyming verses and echoing refrain, accompanied by complex and artfully choreographed "picturization," may be said to present a world-within-a-world that both encapsulates and mirrors the larger structure of the film and that accordingly warrants close analysis within the larger filmic "text."[5]

In the concluding section of this essay, I discuss an apparent shift that my focus on cinematic ritual suggests, from the turbulent 1970s to the decade of growing but uneven plenitude that characterized the 1990s: the fact that *JSM*'s subversive critique of dominant familial and religious structures appears largely undone in *HAHK*, which reaffirms those structures around a smiling but triumphalist brand of Hinduism. I also examine how the success of both films rested, in part, on their supplying scripts for individual and collective mimesis through ritual practice and ritualized viewing.

The Fast That Satisfies

The screenplay of *Jai Santoshi Maa* (Hail to the Mother of Satisfaction), attributed to one Pandit Priyadarśī of Hardwar, is unusual in that it is based on the genre of popular literature known as *vrat-kathā*. This refers to a story (*kathā*) intended for recitation during the performance of a votive "fast" (*vrat*) maintained in honor of a deity and intended to secure that deity's blessing or boon. Such observances

A tearful and singing Satyavatī (Kanan Kaushal) nears the end of her sixteen-week worship of the goddess Santoṣī Mā. From the film *Jai Santoshi Maa* (1975).

constitute one of the most widespread forms of Hindu practice and are especially prevalent among women. Although many *vrats* recur annually and are explicitly observed for the benefit of male kin, others are elective both in their timing and in their aims. *Vrat-kathās* are usually encountered as inexpensive and often crudely printed chapbooks sold in religious bookstalls. These texts detail the procedures for observing a *vrat* and then offer a story, the recitation of which will constitute one of its essential rites. The story may tell of the origin of the rite or, alternatively (and sometimes additionally), of its paradigmatic performance by an individual who must struggle against obstacles—often including an unsuccessful first attempt involving a ritual error that produces catastrophic consequences—before ultimately completing the *vrat* and obtaining its "fruit."

Historically speaking, Santoṣī Mā (Satisfaction Mother) seems to have originated in the 1960s in Rajasthan or western Madhya Pradesh, when a local goddess acquired this name. Whereas many such "mothers" are simply regarded as autochthonous protectors of a given locality (*bhū-devī*, or earth goddess), Santoṣī Mā acquired—when and where is uncertain—a non-Purāṇic origin story identifying her as the daughter of elephant-headed Gaṇeśa and his wives, Ṛddhi (Prosperity) and Siddhi (Success). This story links Santoṣī Mā with a pot-bellied deity known for his beneficence and also places her within an extended family that ultimately includes, as her paternal grandparents, the powerful Śiva and Pārvatī. This familial placement of Santoṣī Mā, which is in contrast to the relative autonomy of many other goddesses, seems important both for her general appeal to women and for the film narrative, and indeed may have contributed to the latter's most innovative plotline: a divine "family quarrel" that pits senior goddesses against the young "newcomer" Santoṣī Mā.

Like her father and grandfather, Santoṣī Mā is regarded as "easy to satisfy" (*āśutoṣ*, an epithet of Śiva). Her preferred offering is raw sugar and parched *gram* or chickpeas (*guṛ-canā*), among the most inexpensive foodstuffs, and her *vrat* simply requires an offering on Friday (the day sacred to her) of a small amount of these accompanied by abstention from sour foods (such as lime juice, tamarind, and curds) and the reading of her *kathā*. In its reputedly most efficacious performance, this is to be observed for a cycle of successive weeks (sixteen in the film but fourteen or twelve in some printed sources), followed by the celebratory feasting (with a menu from which sour foods are likewise banned) of a group of boys—a ceremony of thanksgiving and closure known as *udyāpan*. The completion of this extended ritual is said to grant any wish of the devotee. Limited evidence suggests that the popularity of this *vrat* was slowly spreading—by word of mouth and printed booklet and through a religious poster illustrating its key elements—among lower-class women for at least a decade prior to the film's production. Indeed Bombay filmmaker Vijay Sharma is said to have made, at his wife's suggestion, a pilgrimage to a Santoṣī Mā temple, where he received the inspiration to direct the film (Hawley and Wulff 1996, 4). It is equally clear, however, that large numbers of women had not heard of the goddess or her *vrat* prior to the release of the film, which repeatedly alludes to the "newness" of the cult.[6]

Incorporating both the birth story of Santoṣī Mā (with which it opens) and the tale of a heroic performance of her *vrat* by a sorely tried human devotee named Satyavatī (Kanan Kaushal), the film thus literally presents itself as the cinematic equivalent of a *vrat* pamphlet, complete with its obligatory *kathā* and with instructions for carrying out the sixteen-Fridays ritual graphically and dramatically illustrated. To these narrative elements is added another: the audacious story to which I alluded above, in which the goddesses Lakṣmī, Pārvatī, and Sarasvatī (the latter here called "Brahmāṇi," or "Mrs. Brahmā"), egged on by the mischievous and meddlesome sage Nārada (played by the comic actor Jeevan), attempt to stop the worship of their new "rival," Santoṣī Mā, by destroying the happiness of her exemplary devotee, Satyavatī. This narrative, enacted through witty and colloquial dialogue, exemplifies the kind of "domestication" of Hindu deities that is as common in the Sanskrit Purāṇas as it is in the regional folktales on which they may often have drawn and was reportedly greatly relished by theater audiences (Kurtz 1992, 14). But quite apart from its entertainment value, the story of the jealous goddesses, brief episodes of which alternate with longer ones devoted to the central tale of the long-suffering Satyavatī, allows the film to develop a remarkable parallelism that is absent from its written precursors (Das 1980, 49). By continually juxtaposing the assault on Santoṣī Mā by senior divine women with the persecution of Satyavatī by her jealous sisters-in-law and then ultimately thwarting both through Satyavatī's successful completion of the sixteen-Fridays *vrat,* the film makes what I term a "theo-visual" assertion of the oneness of deity and devotee—a unitary state that is both the premise and the desired outcome of much Hindu ritual, especially of the tantric variety. That such empowerment is potentially available not only to the film's heroine but also to any woman who undertakes the *vrat* is underscored by the changing manifestations of Santoṣī Mā in the course of the film: as a girl-child in the opening scene (wished for and welcomed by her adoring mothers but "created" only reluctantly by her frowning father); as a beautiful young woman (Anita Guha) who thrice appears to rescue Satyavatī and her husband, Birjū (Ashish Kumar), from the consequences of the goddesses' and sisters-in-law's wrath; and as a white-haired, gap-toothed crone who hobbles up on the sixteenth Friday of Satyavatī's fast and miraculously provides her with the handful of offerings that her in-laws and a greedy merchant had withheld, thus enabling her to complete her vow.

The film's four catchy devotional songs (*bhajans*) are all performed during acts of worship of Santoṣī Mā, thus establishing liturgical texts that may be used by worshipers—and indeed these songs have remained exceedingly popular and may still be heard on Fridays in temples and homes throughout India. The first, "Maiṃ to ārtī utārūṃ" (I perform [Santoṣī Mā's] *ārati*), immediately follows the scene of Santoṣī Mā's birth and similarly introduces Satyavatī, who sings it with an ensemble of female dancers in a large and apparently flourishing temple to this "new" goddess. The camerawork during this lively number provides a visual intimation of the unity of worshiper and deity that I have noted above, as well as a striking cinematic demonstration of the bodily and affective practice of *darśan* (literally, "seeing"). Many of the long shots offer near symmetrical views of the temple in which either the goddess or Satyavatī are framed by the moving dancers. Close-ups of Satyavatī's face alternate with comparable shots of an icon (complete with glittery, motorized halo) that closely resembles the young actress; in a third variant shot, the camera peers over the goddess's right shoulder to approximate the view of Satyavatī and the dancers whom (in the understood reciprocity of *darśan*) Santoṣī Mā sees. Indeed one full verse of the song revels in this theme of "visual communion."

Satyavatī (seen in long shot over the goddess's shoulder): There is great affection, great love in Mother's eyes.
Chorus (long shot of dancers): . . . In Mother's eyes!
Satyavatī (in close-up, followed by a reverse shot of the goddess's face): There is great mercy, power, and affection in Mother's eyes.
Chorus: . . . In Mother's eyes!
Satyavatī (in medium shot, followed by close-up): Why shouldn't I gaze, again and again, into Mother's eyes?
(in long shot over the goddess's shoulder): At every instant, a new miracle is seen in Mother's eyes!
Chorus (close-up of goddess): . . . In Mother's eyes!

Satyavatī's performance of this song, and her reported prayer to the goddess for a worthy husband, leads to a "chance" encounter with Birjū, the youngest of seven sons in a family of farmers. It is love at first *darśan* for the two young people, and (unexpectedly, given the usual protracted trials preceding cinematic "love marriages") their match is quickly sanctioned. This development is accompanied by several allusions to the auspicious union of Rāma and Sītā in the Rāmāyaṇa story. Thus Satyavatī's pious, widowed father (played by former star Bharat Bhushan in a cameo role) is reciting from the popular Hindi retelling of the epic Rāmcaritmānas of Tulsīdās when his daughter returns from her first encounter with Birjū, and he chants the well-known verse in which the goddess Pārvatī, to whom Sītā has prayed for a husband, assures her of the fulfillment of her request (1.236.7). But albeit made in heaven, this marriage, like that of Sītā, is soon to be sorely tried when Satyavatī runs afoul of the internal politics of her husband's extended family—her brothers- and sisters-in-law's jealousy of the pampered, artistic Birjū and resentment over the ease with which he has acquired a beautiful and self-chosen bride. When, through the machinations of the equally jealous celestial women (whom Nārada has informed of the growing popularity of Santoṣī Mā), Birjū learns that he is being fed the leavings of his brothers' meals, he storms off to seek his fortune, leaving his bride at her in-laws' mercy.

What ensues generally follows the *vrat-kathā,* though with repeated digressions to the innovative heavenly subplot. Although Birjū is believed to have drowned while crossing a river, he in fact prospers as the trusted assistant to a fabulously wealthy merchant. Meanwhile Satyavatī, branded an inauspicious widow, suffers as the slave of her in-laws, while the gloating goddesses regularly applaud from their perch above the clouds. When the family's abuse drives Satyavatī to attempt suicide, she is stopped by Nārada, who tells her about the sixteen-Fridays fast for Santoṣī Mā. The performance of this ritual—against the opposition of sisters-in-law and heavenly powers—is one of the climactic events of the film and is accompanied by a moving *bhajan,* "Kartī hūṃ tumhārā vrat maiṃ" (I perform your *vrat*). Satyavatī's pleading verses, accompanied by visuals that show the passage of time by the increasing number of oil lamps on her *pūjā* (devotional ritual) tray and the darkening circles around her eyes, alternate with musical passages dominated by a solo flute and accompanied by scenes of the Kṛṣṇa-like Birjū (whose name is an epithet for the amorous flute player), sporting in flower gardens with his employer's voluptuous daughter—a risqué episode facilitated by goddess-induced amnesia. His apparent total abandonment of his wife gives special poignancy to her cry (accompanied by visuals that again largely alternate between Satyavatī's now-anguished face and that of a more somber Santoṣī Mā icon) for the Mother's help:

> I perform your *vrat;* accept it, O Mother!
> I am caught in mid-current; carry me across, O Mother!
> O Mother Santoṣī, O Mother Santoṣī!
> I sit with high hopes in your court,
> Why do I weep while you look on, in this cruel world?
> Amend my fate, O amend my fate; make a miracle, O Mother!
> I am caught in mid-current; carry me across, O Mother!
> O Mother Santoṣī, O Mother Santoṣī!

When, after many trials, the *vrat* is successfully completed, Santoṣī Mā restores Birjū's memory, and he rushes home with the wealth earned in the merchant's service. Discovering his wife's plight, he builds a palatial new house for the two of them, complete with its own temple to their patron goddess. It is here that the film's earthly plot reaches its climax, during Satyavatī's *udyāpan* ceremony, which her sisters-in-law, inspired by the goddesses, attempt to thwart ritually by introducing sour food into the feast. This provokes Santoṣī Mā's wrath, which shakes both the earthly and celestial worlds. It leads, following another song in which Satyavatī entreats Santoṣī Mā (once again a series of close-up shot-reverse-shots alternate between the weeping wife and an icon that now appears sorrowful), to the goddess's miraculous epiphany in the courtyard, the in-laws' repentance, and, in a brief coda, the three celestial women's acceptance of Santoṣī Mā as an honored member of their divine family. The successful completion of the *vrat* thus signals both Satyavatī's triumph on earth and that of her chosen goddess in heaven.

Two Weddings, a Funeral, and a Dog

Whereas *Jai Santoshi Maa*, a "mythological" film about the tribulations and rewards of faith, draws on the folk literary genre of the *vrat-kathā*, *Hum Aapke Hain Koun . . . !* (Who Am I to You?), a largely comedic "social" film about the marital alliances of two uncommonly wealthy and harmonious families, intertextually cites a number of previous hits of Bombay cinema. Most notably it references director Sooraj Barjatya's first film, *Maine Pyar Kiya* (*Maiṃ ne pyār kiyā*, I Fell in Love, 1989), which was similarly set in a palatial home awash in consumer goods, cast six of the same actors in major roles, featured the same male star, Salman Khan, playing a romantic hero likewise named Prem (Love), and included the plot motif of a miraculous messenger-pet (a white pigeon in the 1989 film, a white dog in *HAHK*) who intervenes at a crucial moment in the narrative.[7] And whereas

Prem (Salman Khan) and Niśā (Madhuri Dixit) dance and tease one another during the exuberant ensemble number "Jūte do paise lo" (Give the shoes and take the money!). From the film *Hum Aapke Hain Koun . . . !* (1994).

JSM opens with a prologue set in Gaṇeśa's heavenly mansion, *HAHK*'s opening shot establishes an opulent earthly estate with verdant lawns big enough to allow family members to stage their own cricket matches. One is in progress as the film begins, played by gendered teams with caps that declare "boy" and "girl" respectively, announced by the comical servant Lallū Prasād (Laxmikant Berde) and umpired by the family pet, a straw-hatted Pomeranian named Tuffy. Astute viewers who guess, from the first moments of this 195-minute film, that its lighthearted plot will unfold in gamelike permutations, focus principally on romance, and involve Lallū and Tuffy as channels of higher authority will not be disappointed.[8]

As in *JSM* the Rāmāyaṇa is cited early on, in the context of a prospective marriage. Kailāśnāth (Alok Nath), a self-made industrialist who has foregone conjugal life in order to raise the two orphaned sons of his deceased brother and sister-in-law, now seeks a match for the elder boy, Rajeś (Mohnish Bahl), who is already a partner in the family business. A close relative, known simply by his title "Māmā-jī" (maternal uncle, played by Ajit Vachani), arranges a meeting at a pilgrimage place known as Rāmṭekrī (Rāma's hill)[9] with the family of Prof. Siddhārth Caudhurī (Anupam Kher), who has an eligible elder daughter named Pūjā (Renuka Shahane). Given that Professor Caudhurī and his wife (Reema Lagoo) turn out to have been old school chums of Kailāśnāth's, the meeting of the two families is especially warm; soon Rajeś and the lovely, domestically inclined Pūjā meet and shyly give their assent to an engagement.

The "Rāmṭekrī" shrine is an idealized soundstage set not unlike the temple in *JSM*, and it echoes with recitation of the Rāmcaritmānas and indeed with an excerpt from the episode of Rāma and Sītā's marriage cited in the earlier film (1.271.1).[10] These mythic allusions are emphasized by the first diegetic song, "Vāh vāh Rāmjī" (Bravo, Mr. Rām!),[11] in which members of both families celebrate the engagement (*sagāī*) of Rājeś and Pūjā while simultaneously participating in the *ārati* ceremony of Rāma and Sītā. This occasions—at the conclusion of a "secular" song that playfully "congratulates" the deity for having made such a good match—a *darśanic* shot-reverse-shot similar to those seen in the *ārati* sequence in *JSM*. Meanwhile Rājeś's younger brother, Prem, has already met and been charmed by Pūjā's spirited younger sister, Niśā (Madhuri Dixit), though their romantically tinged mutual teasing goes unnoticed by other family members in the excitement of the elder siblings' match. These initial rituals are soon followed by others that occupy much of the film's running time: a second, formal betrothal and gift-giving ceremony (*tilak, milnī*) held at Kailāśnāth's mansion; the wedding itself, incorporating a number of subsidiary rites (*bārāt, dāvat, vidāī,* etc.); the no less elaborate ceremony held to celebrate Pūjā's pregnancy (*god-bharā,* or full womb);[12] and then, unexpectedly, a heartrending funeral and wake, followed by a climactic second wedding.

By Hindi cinematic standards, *HAHK*'s plotline is sparse and linear, especially given the film's unusual length—a fact much remarked on in both popular and critical writings. During the course of Rājeś and Pūjā's engagement, marriage, and production of a son, Prem and Niśā gradually fall in love. Pūjā, happily learning of this (two hours and thirty-six minutes into the film), is about to "arrange" their engagement when she dies tragically in a fall, leaving both families devastated and her infant without a mother. When Professor Caudhurī proposes that his younger daughter take her sister's place as Rājeś's wife, Prem and Niśā realize the need to sacrifice their love for the greater good of the family.[13] Only the faithful servant Lallū knows their secret, and just as Rājeś's second wedding is about to be solemnized, he prays to the idol of Kṛṣṇa in the Caudhurī family's prayer room, asking for a "miracle" (*camatkār*). Kṛṣṇa provides this by causing the dog, Tuffy, to deliver Niśā's farewell love note, intended for Prem, to Rājeś instead. The latter, after a dramatic confrontation, magnanimously sanctions the lovers' union, declaring that Niśā can give no less love to his son as a *cācī* (paternal uncle's wife) than she could as a mother.

The relative simplicity of *HAHK*'s storyline is, however, compensated for by the baroque density of the film's mise-en-scène: the hyperbolic plenitude of the lifestyles of the two families, in homes overflowing with consumer goods, well-stocked with foodstuffs that are constantly being prepared, served, and consumed, and usually thronged with relatives, friends, and well-wishers observing joyous or solemn occasions—which unfold in a long series of comic and celebratory vignettes dense with jokes, songs and dances, and allusions to popular culture. For foreign viewers it may be challenging merely to keep the familial relationships straight, though Indians are guided by the nearly complete lexicon of Hindi kinship terms that pepper the dialogue (such as *māmī,* maternal uncle's wife; *būā,* father's sister; *jījī,* elder sister; *sasur,* wife's father-in-law; *bhābhī,* elder brother's wife; *samdhi-samdhan,* bride's parents; these terms are nearly always accompanied—in this world of ultrarich *noblesse*—by the respectful suffix *-jī*). This plethora of labels gives an ironic twist to the film's titular question, twice posed by Niśā to Prem—"Who/what am I to you?"—and then transformed, in a final animated title in which the word *kaun* (who) disappears, into "I am yours." Yet paradoxically it also highlights a key feature of *HAHK* that was remarked on by many viewers: its displacement of a central romantic couple by a diffused focus on what Patricia Uberoi terms "the emblematic family"—an idealization of the patrilineal joint family from which all systemic stressors have been carefully removed (Uberoi 2001, 311, 328, 338–40).

Indeed the darker side of affinal relations in North India, which is so prominent in *JSM*—the often agonistic relationship between bride-givers and bride-takers both during and after marriage—is, as Uberoi notes, smoothly elided in the familial world of *HAHK*. Greed for dowry is displayed only by a single character: a crassly materialistic and apparently sexually frustrated maternal aunt ("Māmī-jī," played by Bindu), who is as close to a villain as the film provides but whose attempted interventions pose no real danger and are usually played for laughs.[14] Other common manifestations of the traditionally perceived inequality between bride's and groom's families are either downplayed through hyperpolite dialogue and body language or permitted to manifest as vestigial but spectacular ritual practice, displayed in the ensemble numbers "Jūte do paise lo" and "Dīdī terā devar dīvānā" (both further discussed below). Interestingly these satirical allusions to real domestic tensions were—like the expressions of jealousy by the three senior goddesses in *JSM*—reportedly especially relished by audiences, and these two numbers remain among the most popular of the film's twelve songs (Uberoi 2001, 317, 328; cf. Kurtz 1992, 14).

That *HAHK*'s opening rituals at Rāmṭekrī are staged as celebratory fun rather than pious worship sets the tone for the depiction of most of the life-cycle rites that follow, and the songs accompanying these center on elaborately choreographed send-ups of folk customs (here termed *śakun*, or good omens) rather than Sanskritic rituals. Thus the actual "marriage" of Rājeś and Pūjā, solemnized by a Brahman priest's Vedic chants and the couple's circumambulation of the sacred fire, forms a mere background prelude to the spectacular ensemble number "Jūte do paise lo" (Give the shoes and take the money!), which depicts the attempts of the bride's junior female kin to steal the bridegroom's slippers and then "sell" them back to him for a substantial bounty—a teasing reversal, observed by some North Indian communities, of the dowry presentation. Prem and his coconspirators, Lallū and Tuffy, try to thwart the theft by hiding the slippers in a fancy sweetmeat box but are outsmarted by the ladies. The song's lyrics are presented as a verbal duel between male and female soloists and choruses, and the mise-en-scène takes full advantage of the Caudhurī house's vast two-storied atrium and grand staircase. The frenetic choreography features chases, as well as the dispensing (also celebrated in the lyrics) of abundant food—here intended to distract the "boys" from their attempt to regain the shoes.

Female singer: Have a cool drink. Male singer: Not in the mood!
Female: Take some *dahi baḍā*. Male: Not in the mood!
Female: Eat some *kulfī*. Male: I've had plenty!
Female: Take some *pān*. Male: I've had plenty!
Male chorus: We've had plenty, we've had plenty!

Although critics of the film condemned the materialist excess of such sequences (Bharucha 1995), the conspicuous display of both wealth and food has long been a central component in the non-Vedic rituals associated with Hindu marriage. Indeed Tulsīdās twice "interrupts" the first book of his epic to offer multipage descriptions of weddings (those of Śiva and Pārvatī and of Sītā and Rāma; Rāmcaritmānas 1.92–102; 1.286–342), which feature feasts served on golden platters as well as such non-Sanskritic rituals as women's song sessions in which the groom and his relatives are mocked. The poet's description is said to have influenced popular practice, even becoming, in some regions, a liturgical text to accompany weddings. In *HAHK* "Jūte do paise lo" similarly offers a model for wedding planners and an auspicious tableau of lavish consumption, even as its male-female duel serves the larger narrative by highlighting the developing romance between Prem and Niśā—who end up, after a final, frenzied chase, in an "accidental" embrace on a double bed.

An equally elaborate number is set after the film's intermission, when Pūjā's female relations and friends come to bless and celebrate her pregnancy, ritually placing a coconut in her lap and honoring her with oil lamps. In some families such rites include a women's singing program (*sangīt*) in which risqué songs that satirize male kin are performed. Here this custom—somewhat sanitized yet hyperbolically visualized—takes the form of the show-stopping "Dīdī terā devar dīvānā" (Big sister, your brother-in-law is crazy!), in which Niśā (as herself) dances with and mocks "Prem," impersonated by his female cousin Rītā, who is now cross-dressed and made up as Prem. The accusative refrain charging that he "flirts with girls" (*kuḍiyoṃ ko ḍāle dānā*) is graphically pantomimed, culminating in brisk activity under a sheet and Niśā's own feigned pregnancy. The song draws on the long and robust tradition of sexually tinged humor and slang regarding the "joking" relationship of sister- and brother-in-law within the extended family (the *bhābhī-devar* relationship), a "natural friendship" understood to include the frisson of possible sexual attraction and even intimacy. This is indeed a common subject of women's folk songs, as well as of both men's and women's pranks and skits during occasions of social license such as the Holi festival.[15] There is also a cultural tradition (dramatized in the film by Prem and his friends Lallū and Bholā) of men attempting to "crash" women's singing programs in order to enjoy the salacious lyrics as well as to find out what is being said about them. Here the friends' several attempts earn them abuse and mockery from the ladies but ultimately result in Prem's successful replacement of his drag double to complete the song in a saucy duet with Niśā (featuring the parodic opener "Bhābhī terī bahinā to mānā" [Oh Sister-in-law, please talk to your kid sister!]). In a further reversal, the song ends with Prem himself outfitted in a flimsy negligee and apparently pregnant.

Success, in Context

A shared feature of *JSM* and *HAHK* that I have not yet examined is that both were unexpected hits, whose success surprised and puzzled many observers. *JSM* was a low-budget B-movie by industry standards, with unknown actors and laughable special effects; it was intended for limited distribution mainly on provincial circuits, where it would presumably attract audiences of pious rustics and small-town women. Yet within weeks of its release, its fame, spread largely by word of mouth, caused it to be booked even in major urban areas, where it drew packed houses, eventually becoming one of the most lucrative films of 1975—a status it shared with the big-budget action dramas *Sholay* (Śole, Flames) and *Deewaar*, both featuring Amitabh Bachchan and other A-list stars. Although *HAHK* was an expensive film intended for wide release, the industry buzz about it, particularly after preview screenings, was that it would prove a disastrous flop: with no villains, no violence, almost no plot, and "too many songs," it was merely a "three-hour wedding video" that no one would pay to see (Ganti 2004, 168). However these predictions were quickly proven wrong; audiences flocked to *HAHK*, and it won most of the major industry awards and soon surpassed *Sholay*'s nineteen-year record as the highest-grossing Hindi film.

Interestingly both *JSM* and *HAHK*, which resolve their central crises through deus ex machina, were credited with "miraculous" success that benefited the wider film industry. Apart from being the cinematic incarnation of a *vrat-kathā*, *JSM*, as I have argued elsewhere, was also a kind of primer in the conventions of mainstream Hindi cinema, and its fame reportedly brought into theaters new audiences, especially lower-class women ("like those in the picture and others who never saw a cinema hall," as a film industry journal reported), some of whom would presumably develop a taste for cinema and come back for more (John 1975; for details on the cinematic "pedagogy" of the film, see Lutgendorf 2002, 26–35). *HAHK* was hailed as a "good, clean movie" suitable for family viewing, and its extraordinary success was said to have reversed a decade-long trend of the "classes" (an Indian journalistic label for the educated, urban middle and upper classes) abandoning cinema halls to the "masses" (uneducated, and mostly male, laborers). This trend, which reflected the availability of televisions and VCRs that permitted at-home viewing of films by the elite, as well as the numbingly violent *masālā* fare (often featuring episodes of rape) churned out by the industry during the 1980s, led to the growing dilapidation of many urban "picture palaces"—a fact noted with dismay by some who now returned to these halls to view *HAHK* (Uberoi 2001, 310, 341n9). As a result both theaters and films began to be "cleaned up"; *HAHK* is credited with launching a series of "feel-good" family-oriented spectacles that brought the "classes" back into cinema halls. This is especially notable since these films, too, quickly became available on videocassette (and soon thereafter on video compact discs and DVD), yet audiences continued to savor the experience of their collective viewing on the big screen.

Before I consider some of the practices that have developed around these two ritual-laden films, I would like briefly to place the initial success of each in its historical context. *JSM* appeared in the same year in which Prime Minister Indira Gandhi, faced with growing labor unrest, mass political agitation, and charges of electoral corruption, declared a state of national emergency and assumed draconian powers. In retrospect this move and the circumstances that provoked it revealed widespread disillusionment with the performance of the Indian government and economy since Independence—the failure of the state to deliver on its promises to its people—and presaged the end of the Congress Party's long mandate. In the decade that followed, India experienced the rise of regional and caste-oriented parties as well as the increasingly strident assertion of rights by traditionally disadvantaged groups. Scholars of Hindi cinema have similarly identified this period, in terms of its predominant narrative themes, as marking the end of the nationalism and optimism of the immediate post-Independence "Nehruvian" era. Tejaswini Ganti (2004, 30–33) thematically labels the next wave of films, beginning around 1973, the "crisis of the state," and M. Madhava Prasad (1998, 118, 138–59) speaks of a new "populist cinema of mobilization" centered on "angry" proletarian heroes, often played by Amitabh Bachchan. Although such a typology clearly fits the 1975 action hits *Sholay* and *Deewaar*, I apply it as well to that year's other, more unexpected cinematic success story.

Despite the demure piety and apparent nonassertiveness of *JSM*'s heroine, Satyavatī, she gradually achieves many of the pragmatic goals to which large numbers of Indian women aspired during this period: a companionate marriage to a man of her liking, an extended "honeymoon" with him (in the form of a pilgrimage to far-flung temples to Santoṣī Mā), and, ultimately, a prosperous household of her own, independent of her in-laws. The husband she chooses is a restless young man with similar aspirations, who tells his mother early in the film, "I don't want to spend my life like my brothers: same old plow, same old fields! Mom, my life will be something amazing, extraordinary!" With the blessings of the "upstart" goddess Santoṣī Mā, and through his wife's steadfastness and his own hard work, he achieves his goals, becoming, in effect, a "white-collar" businessman who has broken free of the rural subsistence economy. The catalyst for this couple's transformation is an extended ritual that is tenaciously performed by the young wife in the face of tremendous opposition: Satyavatī's *vrat* is pious worship, true, but also an "act of resistance" defying both heavenly and earthly powers. The "fruit" of her ritual is not merely confirmation of her near identity to the goddess she adores as well as the attainment of undreamed-of prosperity, but also independence from an "idealized" joint family that has gradually been revealed as dysfunctional and abusive. Through a female-oriented plot, and without recourse to themes of violence and revenge, *JSM*'s tale of a new goddess of "satisfaction" displays in its own way the unsatisfied aspirations that fueled the "crisis of the state" and offers its own model of "mobilization" to obtain desired fruits.

The period in which *HAHK* was released is likewise associated by film scholars with another major thematic shift, and Barjatya's *Maine Pyar Kiya,* with its "adoption of advertising imagery: rich, saturated color effects constantly emphasizing surface" (Rajadhyaksha and Willemen 1995, 451), has been identified as a key cinematic text presaging the "consumer revolution" of the 1990s. This reflected policies of "economic liberalization," and the growing political influence of the urban middle classes, with their links to a global diaspora of successful "NRI" (non-resident Indian) families (Ganti 2004, 33–43). Although these developments brought new prosperity to many Indians, they also sharpened the divide between haves and have-nots and contributed to the rise of reactionary religiopolitical movements seeking to impose a majoritarian ideology of Hindutva (Hinduness) on India's diverse population (Rajagopal 2001, 35–50). *HAHK*'s "feel-good" saga of a wealthy joint family epitomized many trends of this period: appearing to balance smoothly an opulent, consumer-oriented lifestyle (the family mansion boasts a large swimming pool, and Prem drives his own graffiti-covered Jeep) with reverence for "tradition," expressed through kinship terms and the cheery observance of gendered and age-ranked hierarchy—though this is tempered (as in the Rāmāyaṇa) by the voluntary mutual "sacrifice" of loving brothers. Rāma-related imagery indeed looms large (despite the intervention of the playful Kṛṣṇa through his canine agent), and the film has been declared symptomatic of "a deep internalization of the Hindu Right in popular and mass culture" (Bharucha 1995, 804). It is the spectacular performance of rituals—from the initial *ārati* at Rāmṭekrī through the choreographed rites of passage that occupy much of the film's running time—that seamlessly blends its diverse and even paradoxical themes. Rites generally associated with upper-caste North Indian Hindus are presented as normative expressions of a valorized "Indian" identity, based on patrilineal, extended-family "love" and reverence for (Hindu) tradition. These are trends that can be detected in many Hindi films of previous decades and indeed are connected with the rise of a more generic and mass-mediated "public culture" in India throughout the twentieth century, but they arguably acquired a particular force in the economic and political climate of its final decade.

Conclusion

It may appear that I am advancing—and, to an extent, I am—a reading of *JSM* as an unexpectedly "subversive" and progressive film and of *HAHK* as a far more conventional, even regressive one. Some of their contrasts may be summarized through a table:

	Jai Santoshi Maa **(1975)**	***Hum Aapke Hain Koun . . . !*** **(1994)**
Setting	rural economy of scarcity	urban economy of abundance
Highlighted ritual practice	innovative, individual	traditional, collective
Gender orientation	female	male
Presiding deity	unmarried Śaiva goddess	Viṣṇu (Sītā-Rāma, Kṛṣṇa)
Sociopolitical context	"crisis of the state," lower-class assertion	"economic liberalization," middle-class consumerism, Hindutva
Family depiction	oppressive joint family, ultimately abandoned	harmonious joint family, constantly reaffirmed
Plotlines	strong and multiple, with several villains	weak and singular, lacking villains
Principal textual reference	folk narrative genre (*vrat-kathā*)	Rāmāyaṇa, previous Hindi films

Yet, having identified these contrasts, I return to my earlier observation on the complexity of cinematic texts and the diversity of "messages" that individual viewers may draw from them. It appears, from Uberoi's limited interviews, that at least some who enjoyed the exuberant energy and inventive dialogue of *HAHK*'s conventionalized yet creative comedy of manners also maintained a critical distance, recognizing that the film's depiction of "good relations" within a joint family was a fantasy "not generally found in families" or identifying the film as a nostalgic evocation of a bygone era (Uberoi 2001, 312, 323, 328). To paraphrase a view that I once advanced in relation to the ideology and performance of the Hindi Rāmcaritmānas of Tulsīdās: a thorough consideration of what a popular text "says" also ought to consider what it "does"—or rather, what people do with it (Lutgendorf 1991, 439). This brings me back to the ritual content of these two films and to practices that have developed around their representation.

Although films are, in any single viewing, ephemeral performances, their experience is endlessly reproducible, especially with the advent of inexpensive technologies that allow for (legal and illegal) copying. In the Hindi film industry, it has long been understood that the most popular films generate substantial revenue through repeat viewings, and this is especially the case with the two being considered here. Indeed the American term *cult film*—used to designate a film with a coterie of dedicated fans who view it repeatedly, sometimes practicing participatory behavior such as dressing as film characters or reciting memorized dialogue and songs in unison with the screening (*The Rocky Horror Picture Show* and *The*

Sound of Music are two well-known examples)—assumes a different and rather more literal meaning in the case of these celebrated Hindi films.

The conventional assumption that film viewing belongs to a secular sphere of human activity that is categorically separated from the sacred or religious sphere has been challenged by a number of recent studies that call attention not simply to the mythic and theological content of films but also to the formalized practices that surround their reception by audiences (Lyden 2003, 108–36; Plate 2008, 1–17, 78–91). The experience of regular, congregationally shared viewing of massively projected, dreamlike images and stories suggests participation in mythic and ritual performances, and the assumed passivity of cinema audiences may merely reflect the relative lack of research devoted to film reception. In India "moving pictures" of deities, like other forms of divine representational embodiment, have readily elicited a devotional response from some viewers—for example, the reported prostrations that greeted the first on-screen appearance of Kṛṣṇa in one of the early films of D. G. Phalke, the "father of Indian cinema"—that has been scorned by critics who assume (as did early writers on cinema in the West) that credulous audiences believe that projected images are "real." Indeed that such behavior was repeated during screenings of *JSM* has been cited as evidence of a lack of "progress" in educating "the people" (Dharap 1983, 82–83). But such dismissive attitudes avoid the larger issue of how cinema viewers worldwide react to screen actors, idolizing them as stars and generating responses that often take the form of creative mimesis of the narratives in which they appear.

Jai Santoshi Maa, with its explicitly religious subject matter and its roots in the *vrat-kathā* tradition, offers, not surprisingly, the more obvious example of cultic behavior on the part of audiences, which began soon after the film's release. An article that appeared in the trade journal *Screen* in August 1975 noted the repeated garlanding by filmgoers of signboards advertising *JSM* in the lobbies of theaters and observed that "every Friday thousands of men, women, and children, particularly women, rush to the theatres showing the film like they were going to a temple to pay their oblations [*sic*] to the all-merciful Goddess" (John 1975). The reporter also noted the phenomenon of repeat viewings and its relationship to the *vrat* ritual depicted in the film, as well as other participatory behavior engaged in by audience members: "Inside cinema halls, men, women and children can be seen bowing their heads in reverence whenever a life-size frame of Santoshi Ma in all her splendour flashes across the screen and spontaneous cries of 'Jai Santoshi Ma!' rend the surroundings. . . . Then there are those people who go to see the film only to hear and sing the bhajans. As soon as a bhajan in the film begins a section of the crowd slowly starts chanting the same bhajan and sometimes the whole hall gradually gets into a mood and there is rhythmic clapping and singing in the hall."

Subsequent writings on the film describe periodic revivals in Friday matinee screenings that drew large female audiences; later the advent of videocassettes enabled women to view the film at home as part of their *vrat* ritual. The choice by viewers to engage so repeatedly with *JSM* did not, however, mean that they would favor the film industry's own attempts at repetition: several "mythological" spin-off films inspired by the success of *JSM* (including a 2006 remake that updated the storyline and boasted digital special effects) proved to be commercial flops.

Although it was not associated with a *vrat* or indeed with any explicitly religious activity, *HAHK* also famously prompted repeat viewings along with several kinds of participatory and mimetic behavior. Uberoi (2001, 310) observed that Delhi audiences included many who had memorized songs and passages of dialogue and would sing and recite along with screen characters and that viewers also responded loudly—with cheers, clapping, and retorts—to favorite moments in the story. As with *JSM* lore circulated regarding the number of repeat viewings indulged in by some fans; the most famous example was that of painter M. F. Hussain, who claimed to have seen the film sixty-seven times.[16] But like *JSM, HAHK* also inspired varieties of domestic performance, particularly in the execution of family life-cycle rituals. The popularity of grandiose weddings, of course, owes little to the film, yet the latter is credited with having helped popularize certain styles of nuptial celebration—including details of costuming and decor—as well as subsidiary rites (such as the theft of the groom's shoes), which would now often be accompanied by songs from the film. Notably *HAHK* is said to have provided a model for wedding planning among diasporic South Asians, who lacked regular exposure to the nuptial customs of their extended communities on the Subcontinent.

Indeed the critics' dismissal of *HAHK* as an interminable wedding video misses a key element of the film's ritual appeal. The opportunity to record and memorialize family life-cycle festivities on film, long enjoyed by the Western middle classes, became increasingly available to Indians following economic liberalization and began to trickle down from the elite—who could afford personal camcorders—to lower-middle-class families, who would engage local photographers to produce custom video compact discs that combined footage from family rituals with still photos, animation, special effects, and songs from Hindi films—including, of course, *HAHK*. This reflexive loop between popular practice and its mass-mediated simulacra is in fact twice celebrated within *HAHK* itself: when Prem watches a video of Niśā's performance, at Rājeś and Pūjā's wedding, of "Jūte do paise lo," at one point pausing the tape to gaze adoringly at her face (and thus revealing his love for her to the observing Lallū); and when Prem and his friends attempt to crash the ladies' performance of "Dīdī terā devar dīvānā" by barging in with a video camera and lights and insisting that they must record the event (they are, however, driven away, camera and all, with the threat of a ritual "shoe-beating").

To observe that *JSM* and *HAHK*, albeit inspiring similar forms of mimetic behavior among viewers, were fundamentally different in their class ethos and address may be accurate in the immediate historical context of each film, yet I feel that this assessment overlooks the aspirational dimension of film-inspired mimesis as well as the impact of India's material progress—however unequally delivered—over several decades. Viewers of *JSM* in 1975 lived in a country in which the majority of people lacked access to electricity, motorized transportation, television, and high-speed communication and in which the modest aspirations of many—for material prosperity, homes of their own, and greater independence in choosing careers and spouses—were appropriately shown as the kinds of satisfaction that could result from propitiating Santoṣī Mā. Two decades later massive if uneven infrastructural and market changes had considerably upped the ante on the kinds of possibilities to which lower- and middle-class people could aspire. The ostentatious life-cycle rites conducted in *HAHK* celebrate the satisfaction of sometimes conflicting wants and, indeed, suggest the possibility that one might "have it all": partake in a consumer cornucopia and yet espouse simple, traditional values; be a rich capitalist and yet a democratic humanist (Prem eventually heads his own automobile company yet continues to treat the family servant as a fictive "brother"); be materially successful yet artistically sensitive (Rājeś paints, and Prem plays the balalaika); be obedient to elders yet free to make key choices for oneself (when asked by Pūjā whether he wants an "arranged" or "love" marriage, Prem replies that he desires "a love-marriage, that you have arranged!"). Such goals may have remained impossible dreams for many of the film's enthusiastic fans—but then, cinema, like ritual, is about (among others things) the satisfaction of temporarily realizing the impossible.

Notes

An abridged version of this essay, with the title "Ritual Reverb," was published in *South Asian Popular Culture* 12, no. 1 (2012). The editors of the journal wish to thank the editors of this volume for permission to include it.

1. Further discussion of characteristic features of Bombay films may be found in Lutgendorf 2006.

2. The reference to cinematic narratives as typically "loose and fragmented" appears in Thomas 1995, 162; see also Thomas 1985 for a perceptive analysis of one successful *masālā* film.

3. On *Jai Santoshi Maa*, see Das 1980; Erndl 1993, 141–52; Kurtz 1992, esp. 111–31; Lutgendorf 2002. On *Hum Aapke Hain Koun . . . !*, see Bharucha 1995 and Uberoi 2001.

4. For example, one of the most influential monographs on popular Hindi cinema, M. Madhava Prasad's *The Ideology of the Hindi Film* (1998), ignores their musical component entirely. For an example of a recent study that offers insightful readings of song sequences in several films, see Mazumdar 2007, esp. 79–109.

5. Both *filmsong* and *picturization* are common terms in cinematic discourse in India; the latter refers to the choreography and mise-en-scène of song sequences, which are often eagerly anticipated by audiences, who have become familiar with the music through the prerelease of soundtracks.

6. For a detailed synopsis and fuller discussion of the film, see Lutgendorf 2002, 26–34.

7. An explicit reference to the earlier film occurs during the first wedding sequence in *HAHK*, when Prem receives a prank phone call from one of the bride's cousins, who identifies herself as "Suman" (the name of the heroine of *Maine Pyar Kiya*) and says she was his girlfriend "in a previous life." In addition to allusions to Barjatya's previous film, *HAHK* includes a "pass the pillow" game played during a family gathering, which features several well-known filmsongs as well as the performance, as the "penalty" exacted from "losers," of famous speeches from the films *Mughal-e-Azam* (1961) and *Sholay* (1975).

8. It is worth noting that the family's playing of cricket, like their staging of other "rituals," is elaborate, carefully coded, and parodic (thus Lallū pretends to be a sportscaster, "announcing" the game into a fake microphone) and helps to establish the film's surreal and comic tone. The initial match scene, which serves to introduce several principal characters, including the dog, is reprised later to introduce a song in which the daughter-in-law's pregnancy is joyously revealed.

9. Several pilgrimage sites (for example, in Ratanpur, Chhattisgarh; Dhandhuka, Gujarat; and Pune, Maharashtra) bear this name, but it is likely that the film intends no specific geographical reference. Other details of location appear intentionally vague—for example, the mansions of the two Hindi-speaking families seem to be situated in a southern "hill station," and a nearby "village" scene features a bricolage of assorted "rustic" styles. Vagueness with regard to geography (cf. the generic villages of "Mirpur" and "Sonpur" in *JSM*) is often intentional in Hindi cinema, reflecting filmmakers' desire to construct an "all-India" identity that will both project (desired) "national integration" and avoid targeting the film to a restricted regional audience.

10. The choice and use of epic quotations in each case deserves comment. In *JSM* Satyavatī's widowed father, who is worried over his daughter's marriage prospects, emotionally recites Pārvatī's blessing to Sītā for obtaining a worthy husband ("Listen Sītā, to my infallible boon: your heart's desire will be fulfilled"). In *HAHK* Pūjā's father, a mirthful professor and enthusiastic cook, has just broken a jar of spices in the kitchen; to forestall a scolding from his wife, he pretends to be absorbed in Rāmcaritmānas recitation, chanting a verse in which Rāma playfully confesses, to the enraged Brahman Paraśurāma, to having broken Śiva's bow in Sītā's *svayaṃvara* ("Lord, the breaker of Śiva's bow, must have been one of your servants"). Whereas both scenes assume an (ideal) audience with considerable familiarity with the Tulsīdās epic, the *HAHK* reference invokes it in the comedic mood characteristic of much of the film.

11. Earlier a title song accompanies the credit sequence.

12. This has been anglicized in the Eros Entertainment DVD's chapter menu as "baby shower"—not altogether inappropriately in light of the plethora of toys and gifts that flood the mansion.

13. Prem initiates this act of renunciation. Niśā at first misunderstands, thinking she is to be married to Prem, but when she learns the truth, she too accepts the propriety of the elders' choice. For some women viewers' critique of this sequence, see Uberoi 2001, 322.

14. Uberoi (2001, 330–33) astutely examines the manner in which this character is permitted to voice conventional and cynical attitudes that are otherwise repressed in the film's sanitized and sunny narrative.

15. The recent tendency for such songs to be co-opted by male singers and for the spectacle of female performance of them to be presented to a male gaze—both evident in this *HAHK* sequence—has been illuminatingly explored by Jassal (2007).

16. Hussain made no secret that the central focus of his obsession was the actress Madhuri Dixit, whom he declared to be the embodiment of "Indian womanhood" and later featured in a series of paintings as well as in a feature-length "art film," *Gaja Gamini* (*Gaja gāminī*, She with the Graceful Gait of an Elephant, 2000), which was a commercial failure. That Hussain is a secular Muslim indicates that at least some non-Hindu viewers did not find the film's allegedly Hindutva-friendly content culturally offensive. Yet Hussain's religious identity, and the fact that some of his painted goddesses were scantily clad, led to violent protests and even the destruction of some of his work by Hindu extremists.

References

Bharucha, Rustom. 1995. "Utopia in Bollywood: 'Hum Aapke Hain Koun . . . !'" *Economic and Political Weekly,* April 15, 801–4.

Das, Veena. 1980. "The Mythological Film and Its Framework of Meaning: An Analysis of *Jai Santoshi Ma.*" *India International Centre Quarterly* 8, no. 1: 43–56.

Dharap, B. V. 1983. "The Mythological or Taking Fatalism for Granted." In *Indian Cinema Superbazaar,* edited by Aruna Vasudev and Philippe Lenglet, 79–83. New Delhi: Vikas.

Dwyer, Rachel. 2006. *Filming the Gods: Religion and Indian Cinema.* London & New York: Routledge.

Erndl, Kathleen M. 1993. *Victory to the Mother: The Hindu Goddess of Northwest India in Myth, Ritual, and Symbol.* New York: Oxford University Press.

Ganti, Tejaswini. 2004. *Bollywood: A Guidebook to Popular Hindi Cinema.* London & New York: Routledge.

Geertz, Clifford. 1973. *The Interpretation of Cultures: Selected Essays.* New York: Basic Books.

Gopalan, Lalitha. 2002. *Cinema of Interruptions.* London: British Film Institute.

Hawley, John Stratton, and Donna Marie Wulff, eds. 1996. *Devi: Goddesses of India.* Berkeley: University of California Press.

Jassal, Smita Tewari. 2007. "Taking Liberties in Festive Song: Gender, New Technologies, and a 'Joking Relationship.'" *Contributions to Indian Sociology* 41, no. 1: 5–40.

John, Ali Peter. 1975. "The Miraculous Success of a Mythological." *Screen,* August 29, 10.

Kurtz, Stanley N. 1992. *All the Mothers Are One: Hindu India and the Cultural Reshaping of Psychoanalysis.* New York: Columbia University Press.

Lutgendorf, Philip. 1991. *The Life of a Text: Performing the* Rāmcaritmānas *of Tulsidas*. Berkeley: University of California Press.

——. 2002. "A Superhit Goddess/A Made-to-Satisfaction Goddess: *Jai Santoshi Ma* Revisited." *Manushi, a Journal about Women and Society* 131: 10–16, 24–37.

——. 2006. "Is There an Indian Way of Filmmaking?" *International Journal of Hindu Studies* 10, no. 3: 227–56.

Lyden, John C. 2003. *Film as Religion: Myths, Morals, and Rituals*. New York: New York University Press.

Mazumdar, Ranjani. 2007. *Bombay Cinema: An Archive of the City*. Minneapolis: University of Minnesota Press.

Plate, S. Brent. 2008. *Religion and Film: Cinema and the Re-creation of the World*. London: Wallflower.

Prasad, M. Madhava. 1998. *Ideology of the Hindi Film: A Historical Construction*. Delhi: Oxford University Press.

Rajadhyaksha, Ashish, and Paul Willemen. 1995. *The Encyclopaedia of Indian Cinema*. New Delhi: Oxford University Press.

Rajagopal, Arvind. 2001. *Politics after Television: Hindu Nationalism and the Reshaping of the Public in India*. Cambridge: Cambridge University Press.

Thomas, Rosie. 1985. "Indian Cinema: Pleasures and Popularity." *Screen* 26: 3–4, 116–31.

——. 1995. "Melodrama and the Negotiation of Morality in Mainstream Hindi Film." In *Consuming Modernity: Public Culture in a South Asian World*, edited by Carol A. Breckenridge, 157–82. Minneapolis: University of Minnesota Press.

Uberoi, Patricia. 2001. "Imagining the Family: An Ethnography of Viewing Hum Aapke Hain Koun . . . !" In *Pleasure and the Nation*, edited by Rachel Dwyer and Christopher Pinney, 309–51. Delhi: Oxford University Press.

PART 2

Innovations

Globalization and the Hindu Diaspora

The Politics of Ritual among Murukaṉ's Malaysian Devotees

ELIZABETH FULLER COLLINS AND K. RAMANATHAN

> The ways in which a people apprehend the divine is in large measure a statement about the way they see themselves and their context in a given moment. . . . At certain times in the Murukaṉ tradition, myth-makers and interpreters consciously adapt the god to changing cultural circumstances while, at the same time, seeking to link him to an authenticating past either of his own or of other gods from whom he inherits authority and power. At other times, the shift of imageries appears to be more nearly unconscious.
>
> *Fred W. Clothey (1978, 8–9)*

For Malaysian Hindus the Tai Pūcam (Thaipusam) festival, which honors Murukaṉ (Murugan), is the major religious event of the year.[1] Tai Pūcam is an occasion for ritual vow fulfillment. Ritual performances have both cognitive and emotional content (Ortner 1978, Wittgenstein 1979, Tambiah 1985, Bell 1992). In our analysis ritual is treated as a performative statement that gives symbolic expression to claims about a person's identity and his or her relationship to others. In this essay we examine the history of the Tai Pūcam festival to illustrate the politics of ritual: how ritual performances give expression to group identities and contested relations of power. We show how claims to ritual authority are expressed in the community of Tamil Hindus in Malaysia, which is deeply divided by caste and class differences. The caste-conscious Nattukottai Chettiyars worship Murukaṉ as Subrahmaṇia (Subrahmaṇya), who is associated with Brahmanic orthodoxy, while working-class devotees of Murukaṉ worship him as Taṇṭāyutapāṇi, the ascetic youth of the Palani Temple who rejects caste orthodoxy. We also show how the image of Murukaṉ has changed over the last thirty years during which a transnational Hindu reform movement has promoted a vision of Hinduism as an egalitarian, inclusive, and universal religion. At the same time, an Islamic resurgence and violent clashes between Hindus and Muslims in

India and Malaysia have made the minority Hindu community defensive. Increasingly Murukaṉ is represented as the warrior god who has been given his lance, the *vēl*, for the coming battle with the demon Sūrapadmaṉ.

The Tamil Hindus of Malaysia

Deep fault lines divide the community of Tamil Hindus in Malaysia into three groups: conservative, caste-conscious Nattukottai Chettiyars; middle-class professionals whose forebears came from Sri Lanka; and working-class Tamils, who are descendants of the low-caste and untouchable laborers brought to Malaysia to work on the docks, build the railways, and provide labor on plantations (Glick 1968).

The Chettiyars may have been established in Malaya as early as the Malacca Sultanate (1402–1511), but it was during the colonial period that they became an important presence (Ramanathan 1995, 90–102). Soon after the British opened up Penang for commerce in the late eighteenth century, the Chettiyars established themselves as moneylenders, providing capital to small-scale local entrepreneurs, tin miners, and planters. The Chettiyars maintained association with their ancestral temples in Chettinad in India and observed strict caste endogamy.[2] The Chettiyars in Penang took control of the Nagarathar Śivan Temple on Datu Kramat Road in Penang in 1871, renovating and expanding it in accord with Āgamic principles. They brought Brahman priests and other ritual specialists from India to serve in this temple, where four daily devotional rituals (*pūjās*) are performed (Ray Ramasamy 1996). Later they built the Nattukottai Chettiar Temple on Waterfall Road for Subrahmaṇia, whom they worshiped as their caste deity according to rules prescribed in Āgamic texts.[3] In the past worship in Chettiyar temples was restricted to the Chettiyar community.

English-educated Tamils from Ceylon, also known as Jaffna Tamils, served in Malaysia in clerical, technical, administrative, and managerial positions. They tended to identify with their British employers rather than the Tamil laborers whom they supervised. By the end of the colonial era, Ceylonese Tamils had begun to be prominent in the legal and medical professions and in the private sector. Some representatives of this well-educated group of upwardly mobile Tamils were secular in their orientation, but others were drawn into Hindu reform movements, such as the Malayan Śaiva Siddhānta Sangam, the Ramakrishna Mission, and the Divine Life Society.[4] Although they rejected the ideology of caste, they built Āgamic temples to Śiva and maintained their high status through restricting marriage within the community (Rajakrishnan Ramasamy 1988, 123).

The majority of Hindus (roughly 80 percent of Indians in Malaysia) were brought from Tamilnadu to Malaya to provide labor for the colonial enterprise. They brought with them the village goddesses they had worshiped at home along with clan and caste deities such as Muṉiāṇṭi, Maturai Vīraṉ, Karippacāmi, and

Aiyaṉār, as reflected in the large number of Hindu temples and shrines on estates and along railway lines (said to number eighteen thousand in 1999). Originally these deities were served by non-Brahman priests or shaman-diviners (*pucāri*) and were offered blood sacrifices. Some temples in urban areas have undergone a process of Sanskritization through renovation and the emulation of rituals practiced in Āgamic Hinduism, but in general Tamil laborers, who resent both Ceylonese Tamils and the Chettiyars for their attitude of superiority and lack of compassion, have insisted on the authenticity of their own traditions. These include ritual performances involving blood sacrifice, fire walking, and vow fulfillment by piercing the body with skewers and hooks or driving a spear through the cheeks and/or tongue (Collins 1997, 55–61).

Temples and Festivals as Sites of Ritual Contestation

Temples tend to be sites of contestation for social status in Tamil Hindu communities, and the major temple festival is generally the context in which conflict takes place.[5] At the conclusion of a temple festival, sponsors and notables are awarded recognition through the distribution of temple honors, which serve as an important symbol of status. As a result the right to sponsor or organize a temple festival and receive temple honors may be hotly contested. In colonial Malaya, from the nineteenth century until 1956, conflict in plantation temples frequently emerged between the Ceylonese Tamil clerical and managerial staff and the Tamil labor force over membership on temple management committees. In urban temples built collectively by different caste or occupational groups, disputes over the control of temple resources and the right to offer services, including special worship on the days preceding a festival day, frequently ended in court cases.[6] In temples founded by an individual or dominated by a particular caste group, conflict tended to emerge upon the death of the founder or when a rising caste group made claims to precedence (Collins 1997, 36, 89–105; Ramanathan 1995, 68–215). As the major festival of Malaysian Hindus, Tai Pūcam has been a locus for ritual politics and expression of the tensions and hostilities that divide Tamil Hindus in Malaysia.

The Tai Pūcam Festival: Caste, Conflict, and Convergence

The first shrine dedicated to Murukaṉ in Malaysia appears to have been a simple place of offering on Penang Island at the edge of George Town, located next to the waterfall that descends from Penang Hill. It was established in the late eighteenth century by Tamil laborers who marked the site with Murukaṉ's *vēl,* the lance with a leaf-shaped head. Subsequently when Sir Francis Light purchased the island from the Sultan of Kedah in 1786, he noted that Tamil laborers brought fresh water from this site to George Town using water carts. These water carriers appear to have initiated the celebration of Tai Pūcam, perhaps as early as 1800 (Ramanathan

2002). The first description we have comes from James Low, who witnessed the festival in the 1830s. His account expresses outrage and disgust at the forms of vow fulfillment by Tamil laborers that would later be echoed by Hindu reformers.

> The Hindus perform here all the absurd and often monstrous rites in their religion. . . . The usual swinging on tender hooks in public and disgusting exhibitions . . . in a civilized colony is a nuisance and an offense against public decency and feeling. When people forsake their own country and voluntarily settle in another, they should be satisfied with the permission to celebrate their religious rites only which do not outrage the proper feelings of the other portions of the community, and which are not injurious to public morals and the decencies of life and order. (Low [1836] 1972, 297–98)

Despite such views, in 1854 when British authorities decided to build a reservoir in the waterfall catchment area, they granted an eleven-acre site to relocate the Murukaṉ shrine (Ramanathan 2002). The Arulmigu Bala Taṇṭāyutapāṇi Temple (hereafter the Penang Hill Murukaṉ Temple) was built on this site in 1855.

In 1875 the Nattukottai Chettiyars built a hall on Waterfall Road at the foot of Penang Hill for the exclusive use of the Chettiyars. In the 1890s they expanded this hall, which became the Nattukottai Chettiyar Temple (hereafter the Waterfall Road Subrahmaṇia Temple), and ordered a silver chariot from India to carry an image of Murukaṉ on the annual Tai Pūcam procession. This initiated the celebration of Chetti Pusam on the day before Tai Pūcam, marking an important shift in the festival. Formerly the Tai Pūcam chariot procession started at the Maha Mariamman Temple on Queen Street in the heart of George Town. This temple, consecrated in 1833, was built by a consortium of different caste groups on land granted by British authorities to the *kapitan* of the Indian community in 1801. From the base of Penang Hill, the image of Murukaṉ was carried to the hilltop Murukaṉ Temple. With the establishment of the Chettiyar chariot procession, the route was changed so that it began at a shop-house owned by the Chettiyar community and ended at the Waterfall Road Subrahmaṇia Temple. In this way the Chettiyars asserted their position as the dominant caste in the Hindu community of Penang (Collins 1997, 46–47, 55). On Chetti Pusam, Chettiyars fulfilled vows to Murukaṉ by carrying a *kāvaṭi,* a wooden arch decorated with palm fronds or peacock feathers (symbolic of Murukaṉ's peacock vehicle) with two small pots of milk offerings attached, and performing a trancelike *kāvaṭi* dance.

The success of the Chettiyars in asserting their role as patrons of the Tai Pūcam procession appears to have been caused by conflicts over control of the Queen Street Maha Mariamman Temple. These conflicts led to court cases, which were resolved temporarily in 1904 when the colonial office appointed a British official as trustee of the temple. In 1906 the Hindu and Muslim Endowments Ordinance

Chettiyar vow fulfillment—performing the *kāvaṭi* dance.
Photograph by Patricia Seward.

was passed, establishing British authority over the administration of all temples and mosques in the Straits Settlement built on land granted by the colonial office (Ramanathan 1995, 160–86). In 1916 the temple management committee for the Queen Street Maha Mariamman Temple acquired a chariot and attempted to reestablish the original Tai Pūcam procession but was not successful in challenging the prestige of the Chettiyar community and the Chetti Pusam procession (Ramanathan 1995, 183n245).

In 1933 the Queen Street Maha Mariamman Temple was the first in Malaysia to open its doors to lower castes and untouchables. This challenge to caste hierarchy and orthodoxy grew out of the "temple entry movement," a campaign mounted by the Pan Malayan Dravidian Association that was inspired by the Adi-Dravida movement of low caste and untouchable groups in Tamilnadu (Arasaratnam 1979;

Collins 1997, 55, 101). The temple entry movement can be dated to 1929, when E. V. Ramasami Naicker (1879–1973) visited Malaya to promote the Tamil "self-respect" movement known as Dravida Kaḻakam, which called for the rejection of caste. Dockworkers in Penang formed the Hindu Mahajana Sangam, a social welfare association, which organized protests against the exclusion of untouchable worshipers from temples. In 1935 the Hindu Mahajana Sangam won control of the management committee that was responsible for the Maha Mariamman Temple and the Penang Hill Murukaṉ Temple (Collins 1997, 55; Ramanathan 1995, 181). This led to the conflation of two festivals on Tai Pūcam, the Chetti Pusam procession of the Nattukottai Chettiyars and the festival of vow fulfillment organized by the temple management committee of the Queen Street Maha Mariamman Temple and the Penang Hill Murukaṉ Temple.

Working-class devotees who fulfilled their vows on Tai Pūcam invented dramatic forms of vow fulfillment. Some constructed large metal arches, which were flamboyantly decorated with ornaments as well as milk offerings; in their *kāvaṭi* dance, they swirled and dipped in imitation of a male peacock courting his mate. Others chose to fulfill vows by hanging small pots with milk offerings from hooks in their chest or piercing their cheeks with the lance of Murukaṉ or piercing their body with long metal skewers attached to their *kāvaṭi.*

Working-class devotees of Murukaṉ with hook-piercing dance on Tai Pūsam. Photograph by Patricia Seward.

The Tai Pūcam celebration in Kuala Lumpur has a similar history of conflict over sponsorship of the festival. The Murukaṉ Shrine in the Batu Caves was established in 1891 during the tin boom in Selangor by K. Thambusamy (1850–1902). His father, Kayarohanam Pillai (d. 1884), had been influential in organizing renovation of the Mariamman Shrine, which became the Kuala Lumpur Mariamman Temple on Jalan Tun H.S. Lee. The Murukaṉ Shrine in the Batu Caves immediately attracted worshipers, and the decision of a British official to close the caves to public access led to strong protests. The district officer finally ordered that the shrine be left undisturbed. The first official Tai Pūcam celebration at the caves took place in 1892 (Nadaraja, no date). Following Thambusamy's death conflict broke out when the Writers Association (an organization of government clerks) and members of the Mukkolatar Association (composed of three caste groups) challenged the Vēḷāḷa (or Piḷḷai) caste group, which dominated the committee that managed the Mariamman Temple, the Batu Cave Shrine, and the Gaṇeśa Temple on Court Street. This dispute ended up in the courts in 1924, and in 1930 the chief judge of Malaya ordered that the temples and their property be handed over to representatives of fourteen groups that sponsored festivals at the temples. These groups were granted the right to elect representatives to a temple management committee.[7] This decision did not, however, end conflict over temple rituals. The new management committee terminated the sponsorship rights of Thambusamy's descendants and gave them to a group claiming to represent Sentul residents (Ramanathan 1995, 134–39).

In the 1940s a Dravida Reform Movement that called for the reform of ritual practices common among lower-caste Hindus spread from Tamilnadu to middle-class Hindus in Malaysia and Singapore. On the grounds that "spike *kāvaṭis*" and body piercing were exhibitionistic practices and not authentically Hindu, reformers attempted to ban these forms of vow fulfillment in the 1950s. Lower-caste and working-class devotees of Murukaṉ clung to their own forms of ritual vow fulfillment, choosing to fulfill vows at shrines and temples they controlled. The management committees of prominent temples soon realized that alienating worshipers from lower-caste groups led to loss of both income and prestige for a temple. They decided to content themselves with promoting reform through education and limited bans (Collins 1997, 51–53).

Despite these conflicts the celebration of Tai Pūcam grew in popularity in both Penang and Kuala Lumpur. Conflicts between groups were elided through the worship of different forms of Murukaṉ. The Chettiyars worshiped Murukaṉ as their caste deity, representing him as Subrahmaṇia, the teacher of Brahmā, who stands for orthodox Brahmanic Hinduism. Middle-class professionals who belonged to Hindu reform movements emphasized the path of spiritual insight or knowledge (Sanskrit: *jñāna*), which they said was symbolized by Murukaṉ's

The milk-offering form of vow fulfillment promoted by reformers.
Photograph by Patricia Seward.

lance. They sought to reform forms of vow fulfillment that they found primitive, including piercing the body and fire walking. Hindus from the Tamil labor force worshiped Murukaṉ as Taṇṭāyutapāṇi, the ascetic youth of the Palani Temple who rejected caste, and as the bringer of divine trance.

The Hindu Community in an Independent Malaysia

With the independence of Malaya in 1957, the social and economic circumstances of the Chettiyars, Ceylonese Tamils, and Tamil labor force changed significantly. The caste-structured world of Tamil Hindus in Malaysia had been destroyed by the Japanese occupation of Malaya. The Chettiyars lost an estimated three-fourths of their wealth as a result of the Japanese occupation and the nationalization of their assets in Burma following the independence of that country in 1948 (Chakravarti 1971, 68; Mahadevan 1978). When Malaysia became independent, many sold their properties and returned to India or migrated to western countries. Of those who stayed in Malaysia, most gave up moneylending and became lawyers, engineers, doctors, and businessmen. The race riots that broke out in Malaysia on May 13, 1969, when Chinese-based opposition parties celebrated major gains in national elections, led more Chettiyars to leave Malaysia, further reducing the size and importance of the community and ending their claim to the status of dominant caste.

In contrast Ceylonese Tamils tended to accept Malaysia as their home after Malaya was granted independence, especially as violence escalated between Tamil rebels and the government in Sri Lanka. The disappearance of their sinecure in the civil service as well as the racial politics of Malaysia, however, made Ceylonese Tamils more aware of their place in a vulnerable minority community. Some became leading figures in Malaysian branches of the secular Dravida Kal̲akam, the movement of Tamil "self-respect," social reform, and cultural revival led by E. V. Ramasami Naicker (also known as EVR). After EVR visited Malaya in 1954, the Dravida Kal̲akam began to build ties with Tamil estate workers and to work for reforms in the workers' practices and lifestyle, promoting a form of Hinduism based on universal values and stressing egalitarian ideals (Lee and Ackerman 1997, 93, 108–11).

As the poorest and most marginal group in Malaysia, plantation laborers were the most affected by Japanese efforts to extract labor from the population. Between 1937 and 1947, the Indian community suffered an absolute decline in population. The occupation led to growing political awareness among plantation laborers. Some joined the Indian National Army for the liberation of India, founded in 1943 by the militant nationalist Subhas Chandra Bose (1897–1945?) with support from Japan. Others became guerrilla fighters against the Japanese (Arasaratnam 1964). During the rubber boom of the 1950s, those who had been active in resistance to the Japanese began to establish labor unions for plantation workers. On many estates plantation workers attempted to wrest control of plantation temples from the clerical and managerial staff (Jain 1970, 324–27; Wiebe and Mariappen 1978, 142–60). In the 1970s some Tamil laborers began to leave plantations in search of jobs in cities, but many others found themselves trapped on plantations in ghettos of poverty.

The Malaysian Indian Congress (MIC), a largely middle-class organization established in 1946 to support the nationalist movement in India, attempted to unite Malaysian Indians as a political force. But the failure of most Tamil plantation laborers to claim citizenship when Malaysia became independent in 1957 reduced the political clout of the MIC. The MIC joined with the dominant political party, the United Malay National Organization (UMNO), in the National Front Coalition (Barisan Nasional). As a member of the ruling coalition, the MIC was granted cabinet positions only as long as its leaders did not challenge Malay dominance. The MIC was not able to resist or modify the New Economic Policy and affirmative action programs favoring Malays introduced after the anti-Chinese race riots of 1969. Under affirmative action programs, the number of Indians accepted into lower ranks of the civil service declined in favor of Malays. The introduction of Malay as the language of instruction for all schools further disadvantaged Tamils and reduced opportunities for educated Tamil speakers to obtain higher education

(Nagata 1984, 56). Although today Malaysian Indians constitute approximately 8 percent of the population, they make up 14 percent of its juvenile delinquents and 41 percent of its beggars. Malaysian Indians own less than 2 percent of the country's national wealth (C. S. Kuppuswamy 2003, 1). Working-class Tamils felt betrayed by the failure of the MIC to address their needs effectively.

Religion and Politics Intertwined

The tensions between working-class Tamils and MIC leaders have often been expressed through conflicts over control of temple committees. In the 1970s T. Subbiah, a lawyer and well-known member of the Chettiyar community, was the head of the Penang Branch of the MIC (Ramanathan 1995, 173–81). In 1973 he was appointed chairman of the Hindu Endowment Board (HEB), and he used this position to arrange for the renovation of the Penang Hill Murukaṉ Temple, thereby positioning himself as patron of the major temple associated with the Tai Pūcam festival. In 1982 Subbiah was elected to the Penang State Legislature as the MIC candidate. He then proposed to build a temple to his personal deity Ayyappaṉ on Penang Hill above the Murukaṉ Temple. This action was taken as an affront to the prestige of the Murukaṉ Temple by the Hindu Mahajana Sangam (HMS), the militant working-class organization that had led the temple entry movement earlier in the century, and the Malaysia Mukkolatar Association, an organization representing three low-caste groups. These organizations accused Subbiah of using religion to advance his political career and announced that they would organize the celebration of Cittrāpaurṇimai (Citraparvam) as an alternative to the Tai Pūcam festival. While this strategy was not successful as only about three hundred fifty worshipers participated in the celebration of Citraparvam, the protest against construction of the Ayyappaṉ Temple received support from two middle-class organizations, the United Hindu Religious Council and the Penang Branch of the Malaysian Hindu Sangam (MHS), a reform organization established in 1965. The MHS was led by N. Shanmugam from the opposition political party, the Democratic Action Party (DAP). He succeeded in obtaining an injunction against construction of the Ayyappaṉ Temple and defeated Subbiah in the election for the Penang Legislative Assembly in 1986 (Ramanathan 1995, 174–77).

The conflict over construction of an Ayyappaṉ Temple on Penang Hill led the Chief Minister of Penang to form an ad hoc committee to review the activities of the Hindu Endowment Board (HEB). The committee recommended various changes designed to depoliticize administration of the Queen Street Maha Mariamman Temple and the Penang Hill Murukaṉ Temple, including the exclusion of all persons actively involved in politics from the HEB. The proposed reforms were supported by DAP leader N. Shanmugam, but MIC president Samy Vellu objected. The conflict over control of the HEB and management of temples in Penang simmered on into the 1990s. When MIC politicians regained a dominant role on the HEB, leaders of the MHS and the opposition party DAP called for the dissolution of the HEB. This led the Penang state government to set up a new committee to recommend further changes in the HEB.

As the Islamic revival strengthened in the late 1980s, efforts were made to bridge the gap between the Hindu Endowment Board, which was dominated by middle-class Tamils with MIC connections, and the working-class Hindu Malaysian Sangam. In 1989 the two organizations joined together to raise money for a new chariot for the Queen Street Maha Mariamman Temple. When the chariot arrived from India, however, conflict broke out anew over who owned it (Ramanathan 1995, 183–86).

Islamization and Malaysian Hindus

In 1974 Anwar Ibrahim, leader of the Muslim student organization Angkatan Belia Islam Malaysia, organized a campaign attacking UMNO, the ruling party, for failing to deal with Malay poverty. The "Baling Demonstrations" led the government to adopt policies designed to co-opt and contain opposition framed in the language of Islam. The government established its own Islamic missionary organization, Yayasan Dakwah Islamiah, and in 1978 the National Fatwa Council was set up to coordinate state religious council activities and to issue rulings on religious matters.

Even before the Iranian Revolution in 1979, small groups of Islamic extremists were active in Malaysia. Between December 1977 and August 1978, twenty-eight Hindu temples along the main road from Malacca to Perak state were attacked (Das 1978; *Asia Week* 1979; *New Straits Times* 1978a). When leaders of the MIC appealed to the government for protection of Hindu temples, informants say they were told that Hindu leaders should take responsibility for protecting temples (Dr. Sankaran Ramanathan, personal communication). Consequently MIC leaders working with temple management committees arranged for the formation and training of "security forces" for temples. On the morning of August 19, 1978, the security force of the Kerling Subramaniar Temple confronted a group of attackers. Before the police arrived, four Muslim extremists were beaten to death (*Asia Week* 1978). The temple guards were arrested and charged with murder.

The government attempted to suppress news of this inflammatory incident and launched a campaign promoting religious tolerance, but stories of the "Kerling Incident" spread. The Hindu community rallied in defense of the temple guards. In January 1980 six guards were sentenced to jail terms ranging from two and a half to four years. In explanation of the sentences, the judge said:

> If I impose a sentence that is too deterrent against these eight people, it can be viewed as an encouragement to would-be temple desecrators. It would make the guards [of] places of worship so timid that they would not be able to perform their guard duties. If I impose too light a sentence . . . it can be viewed as an encouragement to people who would like or feel inclined to take the law into their hands. . . . I would admit freely that on the night of August 18, 1978 . . . the accused persons were good citizens who were caught in a situation not of their own choosing. That they acted as they did was because of the background of temple desecrations perpetrated by unknown persons before August 19, 1978. (Das 1980)

Many influential Hindu leaders felt betrayed by this verdict, which crystallized a sense that the Hindu community in Malaysia was under attack. Four more Hindu temples were desecrated before an attack on a police post in Batu Pahat, Johore, on October 16, 1980, ended with the capture of the extremists. By that time many middle-class Hindus, who had formerly been more secular in their orientation, were committed to the reform of Hinduism and to raising the prestige of Hinduism in Malaysia.

To counter the growing appeal of the opposition Islamist Parti Islam Semalaysia (PAS) after the Iranian Revolution of 1979, the government adopted "Islamic" policies. In 1983 an Islamic Bank and the International Islamic University were established and the study of Islamic civilization at universities mandated. In 1980 the Tamil-language daily *Tamil Malar* had its license to publish withdrawn for slandering Islam. In 1981 and 1983, amendments to the Societies Act of 1967 threatened unregistered (Hindu and Chinese) temples with relocation, demolition, or the confiscation of assets.[8] These actions exacerbated fears in the Hindu community. Prime Minister Mahathir sought to quiet these fears, announcing that the implementation of Islamic values in government "would not . . . threaten other cultures" or "impose regulations on non-Muslims" (*New Straits Times* 1983). Nevertheless Chinese and Indian community leaders formed the Malaysian Consultative Council for Buddhism, Christianity, Hinduism, and Sikhism to resist policies that threatened minority religions.

Reform and Resistance

The Malaysian economy grew rapidly beginning in the late 1980s and through the 1990s, and middle-class Malaysian Indians began to visit famous temples in India, where they absorbed ideas about the proper Āgamic ritual forms. They began to introduce reforms in the temples they controlled in Malaysia, accepting the Brahman-based Sri Śaṅkarācārya Maṭha in India as the authority on Āgamic Hinduism. The influence of the reform movement is apparent in temples across

Malaysia. Almost all Māriyammaṉ temples in urban areas have undergone renovation and have been reconsecrated to reflect Āgamic practices. Concrete images of the goddess have been replaced by granite ones said to be more suitable. Formerly non-Brahman priests served in most temples. The reformers successfully lobbied the Malaysian government for permission to bring Brahman priests trained in India to serve in their temples on a contract basis.[9] These priests are paid a salary, but they also earn income by performing special rituals (*ārccaṉai*) for individuals, which have become a popular sign of high status. There are now shops that sell ritual items imported from India. Commercial production of jasmine and other flowers for making garlands for worship has begun.[10] Many new temples have images from both Śaivite and Vaiṣṇava traditions, a reflection of efforts to unite Malaysian Hindus and promote the idea of a universal Hinduism.

Leaders of the reform movement include Sri Muthu Kumara Gurukal, who gives popular talks on the Vedas and is described in newspapers as the "Hindu high priest," and Dr. S. Jayabarathi, a self-taught expert on Tamil history and culture and author of scholarly and popular writings on Tamil Hindu traditions, who was formerly director of a hospital in Sungai Petani. An all-Tamil government radio station, RTMB Radio 6, has been established. Radio broadcasts and the pay-per-view satellite television network Astro Vanavil (in Tamil) provide new venues for spreading the reformers' message. Every day Hindu devotional songs are played in the morning, and there are talks on Hinduism addressed to younger Malaysian Hindus by the businessman S. Parameswaran.

Central organizations of the reform movement include the Ramakrishna Mission, the Divine Life Society, and the International Sri Satya Sai Baba Organization, which all produce literature and have booths with their publications at the Tai Pūcam festivals. Significantly the most important venue of reform appears to be the English-language magazine *Hinduism Today* (published in Hawaii), which is sold outside of major temples controlled by reformers. *Hinduism Today* features articles about leading Hindu figures known in the West, such as Sri Ramakrishna (1836–86), a major figure of the Bengali Renaissance and Hindu Revival of the late nineteenth century; Vivekananda (1863–1902), known for introducing Vedanta and yoga to the West and founder of the Ramakrishna Mission; Swami Śivananda Saraswati (1887–1963), author of works on Vedanta and yoga directed to a Western audience and founder of the Divine Life Society in 1936 (who lived for a time in Malaysia as a young man); Satya Sai Baba (b. 1926), head of the International Sri Satya Sai Baba Organization with branches throughout the world; and Haridas Giri, a follower of Gnanananda Giri (d. 1974), an almost legendary figure in Tamilnadu associated with a tradition of musical worship. In 1997 Haridas Giri with Namananda Giri founded the Sri Gnanananda Nama Sankirtana Mandali Malaysia.

The aim of these and other reformers is to teach an ecumenical and egalitarian form of Hinduism that would unite Malaysian Hindus. In a 1989 interview in *Hinduism Today*, then-president of the MIC Samy Vellu issued this plea:

> We must talk with the government with one voice. Islam has one voice. And to this effect I have proposed for years the establishment of a Hindu religious council for Malaysia to strengthen ourselves vis-à-vis the government, but this has not been accepted. We still have too much conflict in our views. But I still feel this is the answer, one Hindu council to get us organized and all pulling in the same direction. We can do it, we have the means. I feel that the temples, our temples of which we have so many, should be the center for educational programs, for social programs, for so many other things that we could do. (*Hinduism Today* 1989b)[11]

But conflicts over ritual practices between middle- and working-class Tamils persist. In 1998 Sri Muthu Kumara Gurukal urged devotees to carry a simple milk offering (*pāl kāvaṭi*), insisting, "There is no point really to carry big *kāvaṭi* or to pulling chariots with hooks attached to the back; at the end of the day, it all just becomes a side show." He argued that religious texts rather than oral traditions are the basis of authentic Hinduism and protested that "unlike practicing Muslims and Christians who read and study the Quran and the Bible, most Hindus do not study their religious scriptures in detail. Everything is accepted at face value and what is practiced are hand-me-downs from generation to generation here in Malaysia. What right do these people have to actually claim and show off that God is in them? Not only does it give Hinduism a bad name but it is also a serious case of blasphemy" (handout distributed in Penang in 1998). To this appeal a self-taught priest helping devotees to prepare for vow fulfillment responded to a newspaper reporter, "I never knew that there were religious scriptures in Hinduism. People have been doing things this way for decades and nobody said anything. So, why are they banning this and that all of a sudden?" (Muthiah 1998).

In 2006 the management committee for the Queen Street Maha Mariamman Temple and the Penang Hill Murukaṉ Temple made another attempt to ban forms of vow fulfillment to which they objected. The chairman of the committee explained, "Last year, we had a few devotees who carried *parangs* [machetes] as part of their *kāvaṭi* vows. And we still have some devotees who pierce themselves with long skewers. . . . What has the *parang* got to do with Lord Muruga [*sic*]? I am not aware of Hindu scriptures, sages, or custom saying one must pierce oneself with very long skewers" (*Star* 2006a). But most working-class devotees of Murukaṉ resisted the reforms. They joined in groups to pull a chariot with an elaborate altar by means of ropes attached to hooks pierced through the skin on their backs. Others attached the small pots of milk that they brought in offering to their chests with hooks impaled in the skin. As reformers banned one or another form of vow fulfillment, working-class devotees invented new ones. In 2005 some took up face painting.

Working-class resistance to middle-class control of temples and the Tai Pūcam festival is most clearly seen in the burgeoning cult of Muṉiśwaraṉ. In many places shrines to Muṉiāṇṭi, a deity traditionally worshiped by Tamils of low-caste origin, have been upgraded or transformed into Muṉiśwaraṉ temples, where the formerly semidemonic temple guardian is identified as a form of Śiva. In Tampoi outside of Johor Baru, a newly expanded and renovated Sri Muṉiśwaraṉ Temple has become an important site for vow fulfillment on Tai Pūcam. Renovation of the temple was funded in part by a grant from the Johor state government arranged by a local MIC politician to counter criticism that the party had failed to represent the interests of working-class Indians (Dr. Sankaran Ramanathan, personal communication).

Globalization and the Spread of Religious Militancy

Shortly after the destruction of the Babri Mosque by Hindu extremists in India in December 1992, the Perak state government launched a new program of temple

A devotee with piercing and small pots with milk offerings suspended from hooks in his chest. Photograph by Patricia Seward.

demolitions, igniting new fears among Malaysian Hindus (Ramanathan 1995, 42–62). The working-class MHS took the lead in demanding that the demolitions stop, but leaders in Hindu reform organizations argued for compromise. In their view there were "too many" temples, and they lamented that temples on estates and roadside shrines were not well maintained (Dr. Sankaran Ramanathan, personal communication). MIC president Samy Vellu sought to avoid a confrontation with the government while at the same time maintaining a position as spokesman for Malaysian Hindus. He asked that leaders of the Hindu community be allowed "to continue with the ongoing exercise of compiling information on the status of all temples in the state" so that they could advise the Perak government about which temples should be removed, relocated, or retained and "urged certain religious bodies not to make matters worse by making irresponsible statements lest the Hindus end up losers" (*Star* 1993). Ignoring the protests of the MHS, the Perak government sent out demolition notices to fifty temples. In the end Prime Minister Mahathir appears to have intervened and put an end to the demolitions (Ramanathan 1995, 255n100).

Throughout the 1990s there were sporadic outbreaks of violence between extremist groups of Muslims and Tamil Hindus, the most dramatic of which took place in 1998. As working-class Tamils in Penang mounted resistance to relocation of a shrine, seventeen shrines and temples of deities associated with lower-caste groups were attacked over a seven-day period.[12] Videos showing attacks on mosques in Coimbatore, India, in 1997 and 1998 were used to incite this violence, and Tamil Muslims were said to have taken a prominent role in organizing the attacks (Ramanathan 1998). This deepened divisions in the Hindu community as working-class Tamils protested that MIC leaders did not take a strong enough stand in protecting their temples.

In 2001 the state of Selangor mounted another campaign to demolish Hindu temples, igniting another round of protests (Perumal 2001). The state of Perak also set about demolishing Hindu temples that were said to interfere with development projects. At the same time, low-level outbreaks of violence between working-class Hindus and Malays erupted. Five Malays in Kampar were killed by Indian cattle herders, who maintained that they had complained to the police for years about poaching but that no action had been taken, so they took the law into their own hands (Spaeth 2000). In another incident the same year, Indians attending a Hindu funeral clashed with Malays celebrating a Muslim wedding, leading to the death of five Indians and an Indonesian migrant and injuries to thirty more people (C. S. Kuppuswamy 2001, 1).

As the MIC appeared to be ineffective in representing the interests of working-class Hindus, a coalition of Hindu groups formed the Hindu Rights Action

Force (HINDRAF), determined to mount a political protest against Barisan, the ruling coalition, and the MIC (Kuppusamy 2005; 2006). Taking the slogan "People Power" from nonviolent protest movements in the Philippines and Indonesia, they demanded the right of minorities to religious freedom. They organized protests against temple demolition and drew up a petition demanding restitution from the United Kingdom for bringing Indians to Malaya as indentured laborers. The Barisan government refused to grant HINDRAF a permit for a rally at the British High Commission in November 2007. Nevertheless thousands of protestors appeared for the rally, carrying signs demanding the right to express their opinion. They were attacked by police with tear gas and chemicals sprayed through fire hoses. HINDRAF leaders were arrested under the Internal Security Act on charges of sedition (B. Kuppusamy 2007). During the February 2008 Tai Pūcam festival, HINDRAF responded to the arrest of their leaders with a candlelight *kāvaṭi* procession.

The brutality of the police response to the HINDRAF demonstration shocked many Malaysians, especially those from religious minorities, and undermined support for the UMNO-led Barisan coalition. In the general elections of March 2008, there were large defections from the MIC to the opposition DAP, and the Barisan lost its two-thirds majority in Parliament. In October 2008 the government banned HINDRAF (Balasubramaniam 2008).

After the election of a new prime minister, HINDRAF resurfaced and continued to protest against temple demolitions by state governments. In 2009 HINDRAF demanded that the government take action when a group of Muslims brought a severed cow's head to a protest against relocating a Hindu temple in their neighborhood. This incident was resolved by UMNO leaders, who arranged for an official apology to the Hindu community. In 2011 HINDRAF launched further protests against *Interlok*, a novel by Abdullah Hussain included in the Malaysian school curriculum that it claimed promoted a negative stereotype of Malaysian Indians as pariah untouchables. On Tai Pūcam the temple committee refused to allow the HINDRAF protestors onto the temple grounds at the Batu Caves in Kuala Lumpur. While working-class Hindus tended to support HINDRAF, middle-class Hindus expressed embarrassment and concern that the protests antagonized Muslim leaders in Malaysia.

Conclusion: Religious Militancy and Ritual Politics

Over the past twenty-five years, the practice of Hinduism in Malaysia has been undergoing a transformation in response to political events in India and the Islamic resurgence in the Middle East and Malaysia. The rise of extremist Islamist groups in Malaysia in the late 1970s, the growing appeal of the Islamist political party PAS and the response of the UMNO-dominated government to these challenges have made the minority community of Malaysian Hindus fearful. The emergence of violent Hindu-Muslim conflict in India in the 1990s exacerbated these fears just as Hindu shrines in Malaysia became the target of state-organized demolitions and violent attacks by Islamists (*New Straits Times* 1978b). In this context middle-class Hindu professionals have strengthened their identification as Hindus and promoted reform of non-Āgamic ritual practices.

At the same time, the Tai Pūcam festival has grown in popularity as an assertion of Hindu pride and militancy. Vow fulfillment is recognized as a dramatic enactment of power. Each year Tai Pūcam attracts more worshipers. In 2008 newspaper reports estimated that 1.3 million people went to the Batu Caves in Kuala Lumpur, whereas the crowd addressed by MIC president Vellu in 1980 numbered only five hundred thousand. Large crowds were reported for Penang as well: in 2006 five hundred thousand worshipers went to the Penang Hill Murukaṉ Temple (*New Sunday Times* 2006; *Star* 2006b; 2006c). There is also a new emphasis on Murukaṉ, not as Subrahmaṇia, who represents Brahmanic orthodoxy, nor as Taṇṭāyutapāṇi, the ascetic youth of the Palani Temple who rejects caste orthodoxy, but as the victorious warrior who has been given his lance for the coming battle with the demon Sūrapadmaṉ. Among working-class devotees this militancy is echoed in the celebration of Skanda Śasti commemorating Murukaṉ's victory over Sūrapadmaṉ (Ramanathan 1996, 51).

Hindu pride and militancy are also evident in the installation of the world's largest statue of Murukaṉ in front of the Batu Caves in 2006. Similarly in Penang the management committee of the Queen Street Maha Mariamman Temple and the Penang Hill Murukaṉ Temple is undertaking to rebuild the Murukaṉ Temple at a cost of RM 5 million (approximately US$1.6 million). The new temple, which will look out over Penang Harbor, is modeled on Tirupati in Andhra Pradesh and will be the largest Āgamic temple in Southeast Asia (Dewi 2003).[13]

At the same time, schisms in the community are reflected in the number of temples (not controlled by reformers) that have organized local Tai Pūcam celebrations: in Johor Baru one hundred thousand people fulfilled vows or worshiped at seven different temples; in Ipoh one thousand devotees fulfilled vows at the Gunung Cheroh Sri Subramaniar Temple; Tai Pūcam festivals also took place in Sungai Petani at the Subramaṇia Swamy Temple and in Batu Berendam, Malacca, at the Sri Subramaṇia Temple; and a new celebration was initiated at the Sri Taṇṭāyutapāṇi Temple in Seremban (*New Straits Times* 2006).

Hinduism is a religion with enormous diversity in the ritual practices of its adherents. Some differences in ritual are an expression of identity, the distinguishing traditions of a particular group. But differences in ritual practice can also be a form of politics, a contestation over the power relations between different castes

Murukaṉ in front of the Batu Caves in Kuala Lumpur. Photograph by Patricia Seward.

and classes. In the minority community of Hindus in Malaysia, this ritual politics is particularly evident as leaders strive to present a united front in what they experience as a hostile environment.

Notes

1. The most common spelling used in Malaysia for names of deities, rituals, and festivals is placed in parenthesis after the transcription of the Tamil name.

2. The ancestral temple in Chettinad represents the final authority in all religious and social matters for the nine clans of Chettiyars (Mahadevan 1978).

3. While Murukaṉ is the most popular name for the son of Śiva in Malaysia, he is also known as Subrahmaṇia, Taṇṭāyutapāṇi, Skanda or Kārttikeya, and Kumāra.

4. The Malayan Śaiva Siddhānta Sangam is a religious educational organization that promotes a theology emphasizing ritual fused with intense devotion, which developed in Tamilnadu beginning in the seventh century. The Ramakrishna Mission, founded in 1897 by Swami Vivekananda (1863–1902), the disciple of Sri Ramakrishna, is an educational and welfare organization based on Vedanta, the theology of Shankara (788–820) as developed by Vivekananda. The Divine Life Society, founded in 1936 by Swami Sivananda Saraswati, is also based on Vedanta and the practice of yoga.

5. Arjun Appadurai (1981, 18–19) has provided a multidimensional definition of a South Indian temple that illustrates why it is a site for contestation over social status: "(a) as a place, or a *sacred space,* the temple is an architectural entity that provides a royal abode for the deity enshrined in it, who is conceived as a paradigmatic sovereign; (b) as a *process,* the temple has a redistributive role, which . . . consists of a continuous flow of transactions between the worshippers and deity, in which resources and services are given *to* the deity and are returned *by* the deity to the worshippers in the form of 'shares,' demarcated by certain kinds of honors; (c) as a *symbol* or, more accurately, as a system of symbols, the temple . . . serves to dramatize and define certain key South Indian ideas concerning authority, exchange, and worship at the same time that it provides an arena in which social relations in the broader societal context can be tested, contested, and refined."

6. For example the Queen Street Maha Mariamman Temple in Penang was built by the following groups: police, barbers, Nadars, Madurai scrap metal dealers (known as "Bottle Chettiyars"), and dockworkers. These groups later organized themselves as the Hindu Mahajana Sangam.

7. Today twenty groups or associations each have three representatives on the Kuala Lumpur Maha Mariamman Temple management committee, constituting a committee of sixty representatives.

8. The Societies Act originally aimed at containing the influence and activities of the Malayan Communist Party. After the May 13, 1969, riots, the act was applied to other groups the state wished to monitor. The Societies Act required all temples to maintain a register of members, conduct periodic elections of officials, and submit an annual financial report to the Registrar of Societies. Application of the act to Hindu temples led in some places to renewed conflict over control of temples focusing on the right to vote in the temple management committee election. It also forced temple management committees to improve the administration of resources (Ramanathan 1996, 53–54).

9. Some Malaysian Tamil priests have gone to Veda Agama Pada Salai, a traditional Hindu religious school in Tamilnadu, to study the Vedas and Āgamic rituals. There have also been initiatives to set up training schools for priests in Malaysia (*Hinduism Today,* 1989a).

10. Information on changes in the Tai Pūcam festival and ritual practices in Hindu temples in Malaysia was collected during field research in 1974–1977, 1980, and 2006.

11. Ritual politics played a role in the rise of Vellu to power in the MIC. In 1973 he was a member of the Kuala Lumpur Maha Mariamman Temple Management Committee (Ramanathan 1995, 139).

12. Shrines and temples that were attacked include the Raja Raja Madurai Veeran Temple on Jalan Sungai, a Muṉiśwaraṉ temple in Tanjung Bunga, a Muṉiśwaraṉ temple in Tanjung Tokong, the Veerama Kaliamman Temple in Gelugor, and nine (mostly Muṉiśwaraṉ) shrines on the mainland across from Penang (Ramanathan 1998).

13. The present shrine can accommodate approximately three hundred people at one time; the new temple will accommodate four thousand people (personal communication from a member of the temple committee).

References

Appadurai, Arjun. 1981. *Worship and Conflict under Colonial Rule: A South Indian Case.* Cambridge: Cambridge University Press.

Arasaratnam, Sinnappah. 1964. "Social and Political Ferment in the Malayan Indian Community, 1945–1955." Paper presented at the International Conference Seminar of Tamil Studies, Kuala Lumpur, Malaysia. www.tamilnation.co/diaspora/malaysia/arasaratnam.htm.

——. 1979. *Indians in Malaysia and Singapore.* London: Oxford University Press.

Asia Week. 1978. "Incident at Kerling." September 1: 15.

——. 1979. "The Ugly Spectre of Kerling Revived." June 8: 16–17.

Balasubramaniam, Jaishree. 2008. "Malaysia Bans HINDRAF; Indians Cry Foul." *Rediff India Abroad,* October 16. www.rediff.com/news/2008/oct/16hindraf.htm.

Bell, Catherine. 1992. *Ritual Theory, Ritual Practice.* Oxford: Oxford University Press.

Chakravarti, N. R. 1971. *The Indian Minority in Burma: The Rise and Decline of an Immigrant Community.* London: Oxford University Press.

Clothey, Fred W. 1978. *The Many Faces of Murukan̲: The History and Meaning of a South Indian God.* The Hague: Mouton.

Collins, Elizabeth Fuller. 1997. *Pierced by Murugan's Lance: Ritual, Power, and Moral Redemption among Malaysian Hindus.* DeKalb: Northern Illinois University Press.

Das, K. 1978. "Extremism rears its head: A series of temple desecrations has provoked fears of strife between fanatical religious groups." *Far Eastern Economic Review,* September 1: 12.

——. 1980. "Issues of blood and religion: Sensitive questions are raised by the case of eight temple guards found guilty of killing desecrators." *Far Eastern Economic Review,* January 25: 22.

Dewi, K. Kasturi. 2003. "RM 5m to Rebuild Temple." *New Straits Times,* January 17.

Glick, Clarence. 1968. "The Changing Positions of Two Tamil Groups in Malaysia: 'Indian' Tamils and 'Ceylon' Tamils." Paper presented at the Second International Conference Seminar of Tamil Studies, Chennai, Tamilnadu. www.tamilnation.co/diaspora/malaysia/glick.htm.

Hinduism Today. 1989a. "'We'll Train Our Own Priests,' Says Malaysia's Largest Temple." February. www.hinduismtoday.com/modules/smartsection/item.php?itemid=593.

——. 1989b. "Malaysia's Samy Vellu." May. www.hinduismtoday.com/modules/smartsection/item.php?itemid=624.

Jain, Ravindra K. 1970. *South Indians on the Plantation Frontier.* New Haven: Yale University Press.

Kuppusamy, Baradan. 2005. "Ethnic Indians Demand Fair Share of Prosperity." *Inter Press Service Agency,* October 17. www.ipsnews.net/2005/10/rights-malaysia-ethnic-indians-demand-fair-share-of-prosperity/.

——. 2006. "Malaysia's Minorities United against Sharia." *Asian Times,* January 14. www.atimes.com/atimes/Southeast_Asia/HA14Ae04.html.

——. 2007. "Facing Malaysia's Racial Issues." *Time,* November 26. www.time.com/time/world/article/0,8599,1687973,00.html.

Kuppuswamy, C. S. 2001. "Ethnic Tensions in Malaysia: A Wake-Up Call for the Malaysian Indian Congress." South Asian Analysis Group, Paper no. 213, March 20. www.southasiaanalysis.org/%5Cpapers3%5Cpaper213.htm.

——. 2003. "Malaysian Indians: The Third Class Race." South Asia Analysis Group, Paper no. 618, February 28. www.southasiaanalysis.org/papers7/paper618.html.

Lee, Raymond L. M., and Susan E. Ackerman. 1997. *Sacred Tensions: Modernity and Religious Transformation in Malaysia.* Columbia: University of South Carolina Press.

Low, James. [1836] 1972. *The British Settlement of Penang.* Singapore: Oxford University Press.

Mahadevan, Raman. 1978. "Pattern of Enterprise of Immigrant Entrepreneurs: A Study of Chettiyars in Malaya, 1880–1930." *Economic and Political Weekly,* January 28–February 4, 146–52.

Muthiah, Wani. 1998. "The Real Meaning of Thaipsuam." *Star,* February 9.

Nadaraja, R. (n.d.). "Batu Caves Sri Subramaniar Swamy Devasthanam." murugan.org/temples/batumalai.htm (accessed February 14, 2005).

Nagata, Judith. 1984. *The Reflowering of Malaysian Islam.* Vancouver: University of British Columbia Press.

New Straits Times. 1978a. "Hindu Temples Desecrated." August 20.

——. 1978b. "Temple killings: 8 to stand trial." November 3.

——. 1983. "PM on Islamic Values and Non-Muslims." October 17.

——. 2006. "Temples Prepare for Thaipusam." February 9.

New Sunday Times. 2006. "Paying Homage to Lord Murugan." February 12.

Ortner, Sherry. 1978. *Sherpas through Their Rituals.* Cambridge: Cambridge University Press.

Perumal, Elan. 2001. "MB Tells Why Temples Have to Go." *Star,* October 27.

Ramanathan, K. 1995. "Hindu Religion in an Islamic State: The Case of Malaysia." Ph.D. diss. University of Amsterdam.

——. 1996. "Hinduism in a Muslim State: The Case of Malaysia." *Asian Journal of Political Science* 4, no. 2: 42–62.

——. 1998. "Hindu-Muslim Religious Clash in Pulau Pinang April 1998." Prepared for the Malaysian Indian Congress (MIC). Unpublished.

——. 2002. "Bala Thandayuthapani Murugan Temple, Hilltop, Waterfall Road, Penang" and "Timeline of History of the Bala Thandayuthapani Temple." Prepared for the Temple Committee as part of a proposal for a new temple building. Unpublished.

Ramasamy, Rajakrishnan. 1988. *Sojourners to Citizens: Sri Lankan Tamils in Malaysia, 1885–1965.* Kuala Lumpur: Rajakrishnan.

Ramasamy, Ray. 1996. "A Short History of the Śivan Temple." In *Penang Nattukkottai Nagarathar Arulmigu Mangalambikai Markkandeswarar Śivan Temple Consecration Souvenir Magazine.* Penang: Ganesh.

Spaeth, Anthony. 2000. "A Heritage Denied: Decades of Official Discrimination Have Turned Malaysia's Ethnic Indians into a Disgruntled Underclass." *Timeasia,* August 21. www.indianmalaysian.com/heritage_denied.htm.

Star. 1993. "Samy Vellu: Temple issue must be settled politically." April 26.

——. 2006a. "Temple sets rules on kavadi." February 4.

——. 2006b. "50, 000 join chariot procession to Batu Caves for Thaipusam." February 10.

Tambiah, Stanley J. 1985. *Culture, Thought, and Social Action.* Cambridge, Mass.: Harvard University Press.

Wiebe, Paul, and S. Mariappen. 1978. *Indian Malaysians: A View from the Plantation.* New Delhi: Manohar.

Wittgenstein, Ludwig. 1979. *Remarks on Frazer's Golden Bough.* Edited by Rush Rhees. Doncaster: Brynmill.

Women, Ritual, and the Ironies of Power at a North American Goddess Temple

CORINNE DEMPSEY

This essay focuses on ritual ironies that take place at the Śrī Rājarājeśwarī Pīṭham in the town of Rush in upstate New York. These ironies, in turn, invite contemplation about the complexities of gendered humanity and divinity and the relationship between the two within the ritual setting. Put most simply, it is ironic that, while ritual performances at Rush gleefully disregard traditional gender distinctions and exclusivity, the powerful *effects* of ritual performance are understood to highlight gender distinction such that, in some cases, it curtails women's—and not men's—participation. The latter portion of this equation involving the potentially negative effects of ritual on women furthermore has to do with the quality of sacred powers ascribed to male—and not female—divinity.

Viewed from a slightly different angle, ironies at Rush emerge from the temple's dedication to increased ritual opportunities for women and, at the same time, to an adherence to strict ritual orthopraxy. While these two themes are typical of diaspora temples in the United States, the Rush temple amplifies and synchronizes them such that female devotees brazenly break into what is normally an elite male ritual domain by performing central, elaborate priestly roles.

The detail that renders many women vulnerable to some of the very powers to which they have specialized ritual access—and the crux of Rush ritual ironies—is menstruation. The following is an attempt to fill out, unpack, and, to the best of my ability, untangle this theme of ritual irony as interpreted by Rush temple theology. I follow the twists and turns of a ritual irony that essentially hinges on the problems of menstruation and aspects of male divine power amid a celebration of exceptional female privilege and authority.

Rush Temple Ritual in Context

First, to expand upon the ways that the Śrī Rājarājeśwarī Pīṭham ritually situates itself within the context of diaspora Hinduism in the United States, it would be fair to say that in a variety of ways, the Rush temple, established in its current location in 1998, is an oddity.[1] Although founded and guru-led by a charismatic Sri Lankan gentleman whom devotees refer to as Aiya, the temple departs from typical guru ashrams that tend to downplay ritual practices (Coward 2000, 161–63; Coward and Goa 1987, 79). To the contrary the Śrīvidyā Tantric tradition upon which the Rush temple is based revels, by nature, in ritual performance. The aim of Śrīvidyā and the resulting reputation of the temple is the successful production of divine power, made possible through elaborate offerings of mantras, movement, and matter.

This flourishing of ritual performance, orchestrated by Aiya with contagious aplomb, is in many ways consistent with a diaspora trend noted by Fred Clothey in which rituals represent a conscious "return to orthopraxy," effectively linking participants to ancestral roots, conferring status upon the event, and enhancing "the power of ritual to achieve its intended aims" (Clothey 1992, 130; see also Vertovec 2000, 152). The Rush temple likewise gives considerable attention to detail, accuracy, and abundance in ritual performance as a means for garnering divine power and religious authenticity. Yet a crucial difference remains. At other ritually oriented diaspora temples, "Brahmanic priests, tutored in the performative traditions of their forefathers to preside over the ritual life of the temple," provide the center of gravity (Clothey 1992, 129). At the Śrī Rājarājeśwarī temple, male Brahman ritual specialists, trained in India or Sri Lanka and traditionally an important link to orthopraxy and its benefits, are—by deliberate design—nonexistent.

The Rush temple's most visibly dramatic deviation from other South Indian–style Hindu temples—in the North American diaspora and elsewhere—has to do not only with the absence of traditional Brahman priests, but also with the presence and range of women's participation within ritual contexts. This partly reflects a feature common to diaspora Hinduism in which women have inched their way onto new terrain because of necessity and changing cultural circumstances. In some cases, for example, women compensate for the lack of English skills of Brahman priests (Leonard 1997, 111–13); in others they insist that their religious roles expand while on new turf (Waghorne 1999, 123–24). As noted by Karen Leonard (1993), women as traditional bearers and preservers of culture can often be, somewhat inversely, in the forefront of cultural adaptation and change. Diaspora Hindu women's increased religious participation typically spans from serving on temple boards, carrying processional palanquins, and cooking temple food to conducting temple tours (see Waghorne 1999; Leonard 1993, 1997). Yet the Rush temple extends women's participation to the point of completely leveling traditional divides between roles for men and women. At Rush women of all backgrounds are encouraged—and on occasion gently coerced—to perform the priestly functions of ritual leadership during public *pūjā* worship and Vedic *homam* (*homa*) fire rituals.[2] Aiya's conviction that it is as much a woman's right as a man's to lead temple rituals is such that he often strategically brings seasoned female practitioners into the limelight during major festivals as a means, in part, to broadcast his agenda.

The flexibility Aiya's diaspora position offers him is not something he takes for granted. He believes he could never get away with his unconventional agenda for women and non-Brahmans were his temple not in North America. Although he sometimes faces the ire of conservative members of the local South Asian community, Aiya dramatically claims that if the Rush temple were operating in South India or Sri Lanka, he likely would have been killed by now or, at least, have had a few choice bones broken.

The Rush temple thus inhabits an interesting—and, for some, threatening—juncture of conformity and nonconformity within the diaspora context. Consistent with larger temple trends, it opens ritual opportunities for women and emphasizes the authenticity and power of orthopraxy. Yet it defies such trends when it mixes the two—when, in a context of ritual orthopraxy and purported authenticity, it insists upon central leadership roles for women. This is the temple juncture that, as described at this essay's outset, produces interesting ritual ironies. The temple's

Temple devotee performs *pūjā* to Rājarājeśwarī, July 2008.
Photograph by the author.

broad approach to religious authority and its emphasis on ritual power furthermore create a set of concerns for its participants that are slightly different from the concerns of other diaspora temples. Moreover, because of the predetermined devotional focus of the temple (which does not result from committee vote or community clout) and the eclectic makeup of its more dedicated members (many but certainly not all of whom are Sri Lankan Tamil), the usual diasporic preoccupations with ethnic, communal, and national identity formation widely reflected in North American temple practices do not coalesce as definitively at Rush (Williams 1992). The central concerns of Rush practitioners, honed through their focus on worship and training, are less entrenched in relationships with national, regional, or ethnic bodies than with—and no less consequently so—the bodies of temple deities and their powers. While the ritual ironies that affect women may be rooted in part in the community's explicit support for women's ritual participation, their flip side hinges on cosmic and theological conundrums that can be far more difficult to unravel.

Blazing Trails

I draw the following reflections upon women's access to ritual performance and power at the Śrī Rājarājeśwarī Pīṭham based on exposure to the temple over the past dozen or so years. Yet many of the finer points and quotes from Aiya on this topic are gleaned from conversations that took place between the two of us in early January 2006.[3] My anecdotal point of departure, however, is a ritual event that occurred back in 1999 on a Sunday during Memorial Day weekend. This three-day holiday weekend in 1999 celebrated the first *pratiṣṭhā,* or anniversary celebration, of the temple's consecration and installation of Rājarājeśwarī and her entourage in a renovated barn in Rush, just south of Rochester, New York. (Prior to the Rush barn, Aiya and his wife Amma's one-and-a-half car garage hosted Rājarājeśwarī, a number of other deities, and regular devotional activities.) At nine in the evening of the second day of the festival, wrapping up a day of elaborate *pūjās*, *homam* fire rituals, *bhajan* hymns, and *abhiṣekam* (*abhiṣeka)* milk baths for the deities, Aiya announced in Tamil and English to the crowd of roughly four hundred that it was time for Devī's procession in her newly constructed *capparam* chariot. This procession, he insisted, was to be conducted by women only. No men allowed. A murmur swept through the crowd while a group of women clamored to the gold-plated processional image of the goddess stationed on a small palanquin. To the cheers of "Aro Hara!" they hoisted the goddess's palanquin onto their shoulders and carried her to the waiting chariot. After the goddess was situated inside the *capparam,* Aiya climbed in next to her and performed *ārati* to her with a camphor flame. Women of all ages, meanwhile, toppled over one another to grab a length of chariot rope before the procession began, bound first around the parking lot and then around the temple itself. Designated to lead the way were women carrying two blazing fire lamps and two large red and yellow decorations in the form of a sun and moon perched on top of poles. Bringing up the rear to keep the *capparam* lights shining was a whining generator.

As is the case for most temple activities at Rush, this event was designed with cultural authenticity in mind. Members duplicated as best they could a processional atmosphere on Sri Lankan streets: families set up and decorated card tables that doubled as makeshift house fronts and stopping stations along the procession route; the parking lot itself became a village. At each family's station, traditional sweets such as rock sugar, raisins, and nuts were ready for distribution along with not-so-traditional gummy bears and Hershey's kisses. The most visibly nontraditional aspect of the procession, not only straying from Sri Lankan cultural norms but consciously so, was the exclusively female crew of chariot pullers, pushing and elbowing (the elderly women were the most aggressive) to claim a portion of the *capparam* ropes.

Temple participant performs *abhiṣekam* during Śivarātri while others wait their turn, 2007. Photograph by the author.

For many women in the crowd, this was a first-time honor; the thrill of the moment was such that the initial enthusiastic pull of the chariot nearly toppled the entire structure, complete with guru and exquisitely decorated deity, onto the asphalt. The men, unable to assist physically, were helpless to do anything but anxiously shout directions—most commonly commands such as "Slowly! Slowly!"—as the chariot finally lurched along, negotiating obstacles such as speed bumps, tree limbs, and telephone wires along the way. As the women maneuvered the chariot's course, a number of men continued to yell commands that were, for the most part, drowned out by raucous female laughter and cheers of "Aro Hara!" Amid their laughter and frivolity, women discussed among themselves the best way to chart their course (the elderly women were the most insistent). Occasionally the women looked up to Aiya, seated next to Devī in the chariot behind them, who motioned with his hands to stop to refuel with sweets whenever they had arrived at a new station. An observer to the event might have concluded that the men, although certainly seen and heard, were—with the exception of Aiya—rather expendable to the procession process.

The Śrī Rājarājeśwarī Pīṭham's practice of allowing only women to carry palanquins and pull chariots, still rare in North America but not unique (Waghorne 1999, 124), seemingly leaves the men, ritually speaking, in the proverbial dust. The feature of the temple that distinguishes it from others—the extent to which women are encouraged to assume traditional ritual leadership roles—moreover appears to render even traditionally trained male Brahman priests expendable. Some temple priests have in fact expressed concerns to Aiya that the Rush temple threatens their livelihood, to which Aiya responds that priestly roles should have more to do with devotion and vocation than livelihood. Furthermore when Aiya, a non-Brahman, openly teaches the conventionally male Brahmanic Śrīvidyā path to women (as well as non-Brahman men), he challenges gender and caste privilege and entitlement—not to mention secrecy—carefully guarded by many in the Śrīvidyā tradition. For this he also receives occasional critique and rebuke. Closer to home, some traditionally oriented South Indian and Sri Lankan laypeople, while not necessarily feeling their livelihood or privilege threatened by Aiya's approach (although it is hard to tell for sure), simply believe that the Rush temple goes too far in its agenda of gender equity.

Within the range of women's involvement at the Rush temple, from less threatening chariot pullers to more threatening leaders of Vedic *homam* fire rituals, an isolated ritual event that managed to test the boundaries of tolerance of even some regular temple members and supporters was a sacred thread ceremony, traditionally an exclusively male rite of initiation, that Aiya performed several years ago. The event was prompted by a thirtysomething New Jersey Brahman woman who approached Aiya and asked if he would perform the rite for her. As he blithely described it, people, including family members of the young woman, were disturbed by the conferring of the thread to a woman, "and [were] even more disturbed that there was a nutcase who would give it to her." In part Aiya validates this unusual event by noting historical (but long-ignored) precedent, particularly as documented through scripture and through ancient temple sculptures of women wearing the sacred thread.[4] Regardless of precedent, Aiya's concession to perform the ceremony reflects his straightforward belief in the entitlement of women to full ritual participation. As he described it, "What can I do? If I say something and I believe in it, I have to practice it. It's not only theory. And so she came and asked me, 'Could you give me the thread?' and I said, 'Of course.' We had a full thread ceremony for her."

Although a woman's thread ceremony breaks with conventional gender restrictions, it nonetheless marks caste privilege, something against which Aiya also rebels. For this reason he does not, as a high-caste non-Brahman, wear a thread himself in spite of his guru's offer long ago to perform the ceremony for him. Noting this discrepancy that Aiya willingly performed the ceremony on a Brahman woman but not, in accordance with tradition, on Brahman boys, I jokingly asked if he would perform a thread ceremony for a clearly noncaste woman such as me. Again, in sync with his principles, he responded, "Yes, of course," adding, "but you can't selectively wear it when you go to the temple and then take it out and hang it on a nail when you go to a party. You have to wear it all the time."

Religious Rationales for Religious Transgressions

The above comment raises another foundational theme within the Rush temple ethos: rituals are not merely aesthetically rich play or meaningful metaphor. They are to be taken seriously, performed with orthoprax precision, and understood as essential for the temple's emanation of and reputation for divine energy in abundance. Instances in which women at the Rush temple perform *homams* and *pūjās* and, on rare occasions, receive the sacred thread are not simply for show or display of a feminist agenda. Conversely women's ritual leadership does not, for participants at Rush, minimize the value and power of the rituals they lead. Temple rituals function not only to confer divine blessings upon those within their purview; they also give religious credibility and authority to those who have mastered them.

The logic behind Aiya's insistence on the right of women to perform temple rituals—sometimes seemingly relegating men into the background—is multilayered. Fundamentally he considers the notion of menstrual pollution, a concept that traditionally diminishes a woman's ritual status even when she is not menstruating, to be an erroneous cultural imposition. He insists that there is nothing intrinsically polluting about menstruation and therefore nothing potentially damaging or harmful about interactions with women while they are menstruating. Reflecting this view is the fact that Aiya's daily interactions with menstruating women are no different than those with other women: he eats food they have cooked, sits in close proximity, and offers them blessings when approached. Nonetheless he does insist that women stay clear of the temple while menstruating. His rationale for this seemingly paradoxical, if not contradictory, stance is taken up later in this chapter. For now suffice it to say that it is based on a set of concerns that have nothing to do with pollution.

Aiya also thumbs his nose at traditional notions of widow inauspiciousness that can limit widows' activities. As a result he gives widowed *upāsikās* (initiates) the same rights to perform temple *pūjās* and *homam* fire rituals as he allows to married and single women. When a woman's husband dies, Aiya asks that she does not follow funerary tradition and remove the signs of her auspicious married status, such as the gold wedding *tāli* around her neck or her red spot of *kuṅkum* on her forehead. He does not necessarily encourage the removal of these auspicious indicators outside the funeral context, either. Rather, as he described it, "I tell them, 'It's up to you. It's up to you if you want to conform to what society expects you to do. Because if society expects you to remove the *pottu,* the *tilaka* [forehead mark of an auspicious married woman], the flowers, and the earrings—all those things—you have to make up your mind. Do I want to do this after being widowed? I was married to a husband and I was married to him for life. Just because he has left halfway does not mean I am no longer able to wear the signs of married auspiciousness. And if you choose to keep them that is your choice.'" Statements such as this, in addition to being part of Aiya's crusade against widow inauspiciousness in general, accord with his theological belief that women are embodiments of the eternally auspicious goddess, unmanifest source of all divine feminine entities and energies. Nevertheless once widowed, women do often choose to remove their signs of married auspiciousness. In many cases they seem to do so in conformity with societal expectation, yet thrown into the mix is a personal need to mourn a husband's death.

Aiya garners support for his unconventional approach from ancient art, legend, and scripture, as well as from the encouragement of his own maverick guru, who he calls "Guruji" and who lives in Andhra Pradesh. One of the narratives he relates to demonstrate the historical access of women to the temple sanctum—something he suggests religious authorities have subsequently and conveniently ignored—is from a ninth-century legend featuring one of the sixty-three Tamil Nāyanār saints, Kungiliya Kalāya Nāyanār, found in the Periya Purāṇam. This legend, featuring Kungiliya Kalāya's extreme selfless devotion to Śiva and his consequent spiritual powers, includes a cameo appearance of a woman in a temple. Although the story traditionally focuses on the saint's powers and position, Aiya, in an exegetical move familiar to his storytelling style, adjusts the lens such that the nameless woman in the supporting role becomes the focus of the tale.

The story begins with the exploits of Kungiliya Kalāya, whose single-minded devotion to Lord Śiva is such that he, against common sense, spends all his money honoring Śiva in his village temple by burning incense. When he burns his last bit of worth, exchanging his wife's final piece of gold jewelry for yet more bags of incense, Śiva miraculously blesses Kungiliya Kalāya with material abundance. Thus begins Kungiliya Kalāya's reputation as a powerful Śiva *bhakta* (devotee). The nameless woman enters the story in the following scene, as described by Aiya:

> Two towns away, there's a big Śiva temple. A lady goes to the temple and exactly as it is enjoined in the scripture, she bathes in the tank and, with wet clothes, she goes into the temple, carrying a garland, with a cloth tied around her. [*Aiya mimes tying a cloth around his upper chest, under his armpits.*] And she goes and she tries to garland the Śiva *lingam* [*liṅga*].[5] And the cloth slips. So out of modesty she holds the cloth with her arms. [*Aiya flaps his elbows down to his side.*] And she's struggling to put the garland on the *lingam.* [*Elbows at his sides, Aiya shows how her reach becomes limited.*] And Śiva, the all-knowing, takes the *lingam* like this [*Aiya uses his arm to demonstrate the* lingam *leaning at an angle*] and accepts the garland. And the Śiva *lingam* stays that way.

At this point, thinking that Aiya was finished, I laughed with delight and thanked him for the great story. Not quite done spinning out his point, he patiently responded, "Now. I'll complete the story and come back to the point." So he continued:

> So, the story gets around, the king's soldiers come, and they try to straighten the thing. Nothing doing. They go to the king and the king comes and says, "Oh my God, this has happened!" and he ties his royal elephant to it and they try to straighten the thing up. Kungiliya Kalāya Nāyanār hears about this. And he goes there and with the garland that he's wearing, he puts it on the Śiva *lingam* and says, "Om nama Śivaya," and the thing comes up. [*Aiya demonstrates with his arm the* lingam *returning to an upright position.*] Then he's become even more powerful.
>
> Now the sideline to this story is this lady, the very fact that she went to the Śiva *lingam*—the Śiva *lingam* always, in a Śiva temple, is in the sanctum. Okay? And she was allowed to garland it. To garland you have to go really close. That means women had access.

Suspecting that Aiya's elaboration on the narrative was not a common one, I interjected that surely this was not a point most people took away from this story. "That is not the point. But I always make sure that I tell people this. She had access there and somewhere along the line these fellows changed it. Now, they might give the explanation, 'Oh, that Śiva *lingam* was not inside the sanctum. It was outside.' Bull."

Amid his use of historical precedent and his disdain for traditional notions of female impurity and inauspiciousness, Aiya's most commonly expressed rationale not only for encouraging women to assume ritual leadership roles but also for their privileged position in this regard has to do with Śrī Rājarājeśwarī Pīṭham's nature as a goddess temple. Aiya argues that no one could more appropriately honor the Mother than a human mother, actual or potential: "I will not shy away from doing rituals in Sanskrit just because they're being done by women. In my mind, they have equal rights. In the worship of the divine Mother, they have even a greater right to worship her, because they are the ones who are the mothers. So I think that they are more primed for it than the men who are doing the *pūjā*, who are doing the rituals."

Female Presence, Power, and Balance

Not surprisingly a high percentage of participants at Śrī Rājarājeśwarī Pīṭham—from casual visitors to serious initiates—are women. Men from the Sri Lankan Tamil community, it seems, often get dragged along to the temple behind their much more enthusiastic wives. Aiya described the typical scenario: upon arriving at the temple, the woman, excited to participate in temple activities, goes immediately inside, while "the husband is left standing outside enjoying his cigarette. Eventually he will hear the commotion inside with the bells and the chanting and the [conch] shells. He'll hear this and then [*Aiya mimes the man throwing down his cigarette and smashing it with his foot*] he'll come inside to see what's going on." This way, as Aiya sees it, men get reeled, often unwittingly, into the temple atmosphere. He recently estimated that a large proportion of his *upāsaka* students who have reached the highest stage of spiritual advancement, around 75 percent, are women (*upāsikās*). He believes this imbalance is due in part to contemporary cultural expectations—both in North America and in South Asia—in which men are hesitant to involve themselves fully in religious practices. "It's a macho thing—because they think that they will be laughed at by their peers. Women don't have such a hesitation to go into these things; they are not afraid to express this. So most of them tend to be women."

The crowning layer to this seemingly ubiquitous female presence and spirit at the Rush temple is its focus on female divinity, most visibly in the form of the Śrī Rājarājeśwarī *mūrti,* stationed front and center, exquisitely carved from black granite.[6] Yet in accordance with temple and Śrīvidyā convention, the goddess resides in other forms, as well. The *śricākra yantra,* composed of forty-four interlocking triangles and stationed beneath the Śrī Rājarājeśwarī *mūrti,* is understood to represent and emanate the goddess's power when charged with the fifteen- or sixteen-syllable Śrīvidyā mantra (see Khanna 1979, 44, 70). The mantra itself is considered to be the goddess's body in subtle form. The goddess's power, fueled by the mantra, emanates from the *yantra* into the *mūrti* and into the temple atmosphere. As a result, as Aiya likes to say of the main Rājarājeśwarī *mūrti* who receives *pūjā* offerings three times a day, "she is pulsating with life." Another subtle form of the goddess, present at the temple at least once a week, is the *homam* fire into which devotees regularly offer fine saris and female accoutrements.

True to the temple's Tantric tradition, however, Aiya insists that the goddess does not and cannot stand alone. Male and female properties are vitally and inextricably linked. Douglas Brooks, in his account of Śrīvidyā in South India, likewise notes that the great goddess central to the tradition emerges as independent yet never completely severed from her male consort, Śiva. The female Absolute thus becomes a dyadic divinity composed of masculine and feminine complements (Brooks 1992, 60–61). One tangible representation of this dyadic female structure is the *śricākra yantra,* which contains five downward-pointing triangles at its center representing female divinity and four upward-pointing triangles representing male divinity. Likewise the *homam* fire is a blend of male and female principles. As Aiya described it to me, "You can't separate the fire from the heat. The fire is Śiva; the heat is Devī [Śiva's consort]. It's one cohesive unit." Reflecting on the vital nature of male and female complementary energies, Aiya continued, "And history is replete with figures, great historical figures, who have tried the single approach and have failed. And gotten into real trouble—spiritual trouble." To illustrate his point, he recounted the Adiyātma Rāmāyaṇa, popular in Kerala, in which Rāmā represents Devī and Sita represents Śiva. This version depicts Rāvana, a great Śiva *bhakta,* as making the lethal mistake of trying to separate Sita from Rāmā, Śiva from Devī. As Aiya described it, "He wanted Śiva to accept him completely. And Śiva was not about to do that without the Devī. If he had worshiped Śakti [the goddess] as well, then the story would have been changed. Nobody would have been able to defeat him."

During our conversation Aiya also compared the crucial balance of feminine and masculine properties in female divinity to the necessary balance of estrogen and testosterone found in human women: "Just like in a woman, the feminine energies are greater because of the hormonal structure. It does not mean that the woman's body does not contain testosterone. It is reduced. If it dominates, then she will become masculine." Likewise, although feminine energy dominates in the Rush temple, male energy is essential to its ritual efficacy. The same would be true in reverse for temples dedicated to male deities. The one exception of which Aiya is aware is the Śiva temple in Honolulu, exclusively dedicated to Śiva. Aiya chalks up its neglect of the goddess's power to diaspora unawareness. As he put it, "What

I do, the Hawaiians don't do. They're not really Hindu, and I don't think they're Śaivite because Śaivism, in the land of its birth, not in America, not in the Hawaiian islands, in the land of its birth, it has always accepted Devī as the power of Śiva."

The Quandary of Male Presence and Power

The most tangibly apparent way in which the Rush temple accounts for its requisite portion of male divinity is through its installation of numerous male Śaiva deities, such as Ganeśa, Murukaṉ, Bhairava, and, most important and prominent, Śiva. Visible male energy, in other words, is not in short supply at Śrī Rājarājeśwarī Pīṭham. Furthermore, unlike the din of men's instructions during the female-driven *pratiṣṭhā* procession described above, this energy cannot so easily be ignored. A context in which women in particular are advised not to underestimate the presence and consequences of divine male energy, particularly Śiva's energy, has to do with the menstrual cycle.

In spite of the unconventional and overwhelmingly privileged place women enjoy at the Śrī Rājarājeśwarī Pīṭham, a traditional restriction that Aiya stands by is one in which women, as a rule, are requested not to enter the temple during the first three days of their period. This traditional mandate might seem to present not simply an inconvenience for many female practitioners but also, in a setting where women regularly assume ritual entitlement and authority, a frustrating irony or worse. As mentioned above, mitigating the contradiction—although not its consequence—is that Aiya does not adhere to notions of female impurity typically associated with menstrual taboos.[7] His reasoning for retaining the restriction has nothing to do with the potential of women's menstrual pollution harming temple rituals; rather he turns convention on its head and insists that temple rituals have the potential to harm menstruating women.

This distinction is sometimes lost on the women of the Rush temple. In 1998 I was present with my tape recorder when the subject of menstrual taboos was broached by a female temple devotee on break from graduate school at UCLA. At the time the barn temple was less than a year old. Yet Aiya's response made clear that hers was already a ubiquitous question, asked by women devotees who felt the pinch of what seemed to them a fundamental contradiction between temple teachings and practices. Aiya began his explanation with the statement "That is a very good question, and I have answered it lately only about fifty times." He obligingly went on to explain again the risks of ritual power on menstruating women, using scientific and medical terminology to fill out his argument:[8]

> At that time [of the month], Amma, the uterus will expel blood. Right? Okay? And all the blood vessels that have formed during that twenty-eight-day period get expelled along with the blood and everything. For those three or four days,

> the top layer of the uterus is raw. It's in a very tender state. Especially if you have Śiva *mūrtis* inside the temple like a Śiva *lingam*, like a Bhairava, right? The mantras that are absorbed by those are in the alpha to gamma range. So when you walk into the temple, even without doing the *pūjā*, these things are continuously being emitted from them. They are harmful to you. . . . They can go down to the cellular structure and can cause problems around the mitochondria, in the cells in that region. And then scar tissue in that area will start. Later on you might have endometriosis, prolapse, all these problems will be there. It'll also affect the mesenteries that suspend the uterus.

When Aiya finished his explanation, I asked, just to make sure, "So what you're saying is that it's not about pollution." He continued by offering his assessment of how tradition gets derailed in the first place: "No, not at all. But that is exactly how you can convince the peasants: 'Now, don't go in there, you'll pollute the temple.' So they'll be careful. You see how these things have come about? And then some fellow will take it into his head and write it down and say, in Sanskrit couplets, 'Okay, if you go at this time, this will be polluting.' And then all the other pandits will now keep chanting that and say, 'Oh, see, it is written.'"

During our more recent discussion of temple powers and their potentially harmful effects, I asked if Aiya knew of any instances in which divine female emanations were particularly detrimental to men. He could think of none. Female energy, in his experience, was harmful only when in highly concentrated form and therefore produced levels of power beyond the limits of human tolerance, male or female—particularly during this degenerate era, often referred to within the Hindu context as the Kali *yuga*. Furthermore, unlike male divine power, female divine power, in his experience, is never intrinsically harmful to devotees. Even potentially ferocious Kālī, as far as he is concerned, is like a gentle mother in the company of those who take refuge in her. Reflecting on this point, Aiya noted an analogous phenomenon in human nature: "If you look at a man and a woman faced with a situation, before the woman will respond, the man will pick up a sword and cut someone. Look at the world situation. [This was in 2006.] We've chosen one person to lead us. If there had been a woman at the helm at this time—Condoleezza Rice excepted—they [*sic*] wouldn't have walked into. . . . They wouldn't have thought of violence straightaway. They'd try other options." After reflecting in silence for a few moments, Aiya admitted that his distinction between the nature of male and female power—straying slightly from the Śrīvidyā understanding of a benign great goddess who nonetheless harbors potential for harm—has likely been formed by his own life experiences.

> But you know, maybe it's just the way I've been conditioned. At age twelve my dad was removed. From age one to twelve, I watched how the masculine figure

> behaved in the house. With his drinking and putting pressure on my mother, things like that. When he died, I was actually relieved—as a twelve year old. I think that I really was relieved and thought, "Here was this guy, and now he is not going to give any more problems to my mother, any more pressure." And the way that she brought me up: silent, yet fully supportive. . . . When I think of it, that is what is at the back of my mind when I approach the Devī as the Mother. Because I think she cannot be any different. So maybe in some kind of situations or in some other forms of the Devī—emanations—she can be harmful. But up to now she has not been for me.

Aiya confirms that the ambivalent nature of Śiva's power is not unique in and of itself. What, however, can we make of the double standard it seems to keep? Should devotees infer that Śiva—who as a male energy source cannot be dispensed with or ignored at the woman-centered Rush temple—is somehow anti-woman? Joining Aiya and me in our discussion of these matters was Saru, Aiya's daughter in her late twenties. Understandably bothered by the implied course of our conversation, she came to Śiva's defense, noting that the energy from the Śiva *lingam* is not harmful to menstruating women who have kept their practice up to a certain level. She suggested that potential harm is therefore not Śiva's fault; it is the woman's fault for falling short in her devotion. While this is important to consider, a problem nonetheless remains: while Śiva's energy is understood to harm women who lack proper devotion, he appears to leave impious men alone.

Vindicating Śiva

This seemingly negative impact of Śiva's powers on women becomes mitigated if not reconciled when we step away from the view cast by temple energy dynamics and consider him instead from his narrative and devotional perspectives. As legend and temple tradition often have it, Śiva preserves a special place in his heart not only for women but also, more concisely, for the particular needs and concerns of women. According to temple traditions found across India, the same Śiva *lingam* that causes trouble for some women's reproductive systems under certain circumstances contains the capacity to confer fertility. Driving home his point that Śiva not only accommodates women's concerns but also disregards traditional notions of purity and pollution, Aiya related to me a story from Madurai. Briefly put, this locally circulated tale describes a woman who goes into labor with no one to help her, as her mother at that moment is stranded on the other side of a monsoon-swollen river. Śiva, in his compassion, appears in the form of the laboring woman's mother and performs for her the duties of a midwife—duties that are traditionally considered highly polluting because of their inevitable involvement with blood and other bodily fluids. When the real mother eventually returns home and finds a baby in her daughter's arms, her divine double has disappeared without a trace.

Another instance that, for Aiya, demonstrates Śiva's accommodation to womanly concerns is found in the tale already related above, in which the woman in the temple struggles to garland the Śiva *lingam.* In his telling of the Tamil Nāyanār story, Aiya adjusts the narrative to demonstrate the historical access of women to the temple sanctum. One could also emphasize the *lingam*'s sideways lean as Śiva's miraculous invitation to a woman he deems worthy of worshiping him—a gesture that, at the same time, graciously allows her to uphold her feminine modesty and dignity.

Saru's concern that we not represent Śiva as antiwoman is thus somewhat mitigated through narrative and tradition, yet the problem of the sometimes-harmful effects of Śiva's temple energies on women remains. It seems as though Aiya's answer to the conundrum was not to dismantle it for the sake of gender equity but to view it from the perspective of the complexities of power. "Even the male power that comes out of the *lingam* in carefully controlled measured conditions—it can be used to energize healing. You can shrink alpha waves into it and then shrink tumors. But if it is just into tissue, it can cause trouble." When I suggested that Śiva—who seemingly advocates for women's particular concerns as well as posing potential harm to the same—could therefore be your friend or your adversary, Aiya responded, laughingly, "Of course. Electricity can be your friend or fry you. You can do anything you want with it or you can put it in water and electrocute a whole lot of people!"

Conclusion: Untangling Ritual Ironies?

During our string of discussions on this topic, it seemed that Saru and I kept hoping to stumble upon resolutions to the two ritual ironies facing us, a hopefulness in which Aiya seemed much less invested. The first irony, having to do with the temple's nonconventional policy that encourages women to enjoy full ritual participation while, more true to convention, their participation is curtailed once a month, was not something Aiya felt a need to deconstruct or "correct." Since he bases his views about woman's nonparticipation on "scientific" understandings of divine power generated during ritual performances—rather than, as he sees it, erroneous cultural (and textual) superimpositions about menstrual pollution—he makes no apologies for his position and, in the end, sees no contradiction in need of unraveling. That his policy of women's limited ritual participation amid full priestly leadership comes at some cost, drawing women who revel in ritual responsibilities and angering and alienating some of the same along the way, does not appear to weaken his resolve or incite his need to "fix" the apparent irony.

The second troubling irony, encased in the first, has to do with the nature of divine power, in particular Śiva's power, that can in certain ritual contexts harm women for whom, as narrative tradition attests, he displays a particular fondness. While Aiya is interested in considering Śiva from a variety of angles and in deepening the complexities of the deity's image and powers, he makes little effort to resolve the deity's mixed messages. Unlike Saru and me, Aiya seems more comfortable, in general, with gendered ritual conundrums and possible incriminations against beloved male divinities. He makes no attempt to assuage or explain away, for the sake of the two women sitting with him, the sting of contradictions or the problem of Śiva's questionable behavior. Thankfully—as far as I am concerned—he does not try to rationalize all things in an attempt to appeal to audience expectation.

Rather than following Aiya's lead, however, I close by offering partial resolutions to the quandaries embedded in the performance and power of Rush temple rituals. I respond first to the twists and turns of interlocking ironies by superimposing a theological framework, and I finish by reflecting on the practicalities—if not inevitabilities—of ritual selectivity. My aim is modestly to suggest ways to make sense of these gendered conundrums from the inside out and, as such, partially explain how they manage to live on, relatively unchallenged, in an environment full of outspoken and religiously critical women.

A theological framework that could be used to address Rush's enduring ritual ironies emerges from the Śrīvidyā Tantric tradition upon which the temple is founded. In spite of Aiya's indebtedness to Śrīvidyā, he never offered this Tantric logic as a means for thinking our way out of seemingly entrenched conundrums. This is likely because it did not occur to him—perhaps because he was not straining, like Saru and I were, to solve the issues at hand.

Basically speaking, Śrīvidyā theology understands the divine foundation for the tradition, the great triple goddess Lalitā Tripurasundarī, as containing inextricable dualities of power in much the same way that Śiva does. In his analysis of Lalitā, Brooks notes how the goddess's power not only contains complementary opposites on a variety of levels but also does so necessarily. Her traces of violence, eroticism, and inauspiciousness are not realms that devotees normally emphasize or encounter (exemplified by Aiya's description of the all-loving, all-patient mother goddess), since she is for them primarily, if not entirely, benign, independent, and auspicious. But in principle devotees must assent to the existence of these negative complements in order for her positive power to be meaningful and complete in a world of dualities.

> Lalitā's violence, like her asceticism and eroticism, is calculated and necessary to sustain order in the universe. Were Lalitā utterly benign, the forces of evil would prevail; were she not erotic, Śiva would create an imbalance through his ascetic *tapas;* and were she not married and [made to] appear submissive to

> Śiva, she would not be able to project her full potential as the source of power; were she not the source of auspiciousness and inauspiciousness, the world of complementary opposites would cease to be of interest. Lalitā not only balances and counters Śiva, but demonstrates how Śiva is ultimately dependent on her. (Brooks 1992, 67)

Following this Śrīvidyā line of reasoning in which complementary opposites confer positive power and meaning on female divinity, the conundrum of women's ritual vulnerability and authority seems to unravel—or, more accurately, emerges with its own parallel logic. One could argue that, like the Śrīvidyā goddess's power for her devotees, Śiva's capacity for benevolent power sustains its fullest depth and meaning when it is part of a polarity that includes potential ritual danger—a polarity that, as we have seen, is operative more for women at the Rush temple than for men. Thus when reconsidering the 1999 *pratiṣṭhā* procession that began this essay, it is perhaps significant that the men thought they were running the show, yelling commands to a raucous, half-listening band of women. Within the context of insistent male ritual leadership, women's lighthearted initiative seems all the more meaningful. Likewise when women at the Rush temple more directly assume priestly leadership roles during rituals, against the grain of domestic and diasporic Hindu trends, the fact that they occasionally ruffle the feathers of orthodox privilege and entitlement deepens the impact of their position.

In a temple setting that promotes and celebrates women's ritual authority and spiritual advancement, the fact that women—not men—are potentially vulnerable to harmful ritual energies, particularly male energies, is indeed ironic. Yet when framed by Śrīvidyā, one side of the equation is impossible without the other: positive ritual power—whether in the form of human priestly authority or divine efficacy—cannot be realized fully without acknowledging at least the possibility of its (albeit unbalanced in this case) opposite.

Since I have never heard this theological perspective consciously promoted or even raised at the Rush temple, I suspect it might be helpful to select devotees only as an undercurrent at best. Viewed from a more direct and practical angle, a nontheological solution to temple ironies seems to arise from Aiya's charismatic, largely feminist-inspired leadership. Whether or not women buy into his scientifically worded theories about harmful male energies, periodic exclusion from the temple is a trade-off that many are willing to make in order to reap its benefits. Contributing to this willingness to comply with temple restrictions is the fact that Aiya's rationale for menstrual exclusion is not informed by ideologies of purity and pollution that are intrinsically demeaning to women. This rejection of negative associations likely helps women overlook the compromises they must make in order to uphold ritual involvement and authority.

This phenomenon of women's ritual selectivity recalls observations made by Madhu Kishwar about inconsistencies inherent in women's devotion to their favorite male deity. Kishwar notes that in domestic ritual settings, women portray Śiva in ways that seem to disregard Purāṇic depictions of him as "the least domesticated and the most rebellious of all the gods, one whose appearance and adventures border on the weird" (2000, 247). As she puts it, "Hindu women have selectively domesticated him for their purpose, emphasizing his devotion to Sati/Parvati, as well as the fact that he allowed his spouse an important role in influencing his decisions. At the same time, these women conveniently overlook the many very prominent and contradictory aspects of his life and deeds" (ibid.).

This propensity to overlook Śiva's undesirable behavior allows women to honor and invoke a beloved male deity as well as a divine marital relationship that is unequivocally joyful, passionate, and equitable—qualities that, given ritual efficacy, flow into the human realm as well. Ritual selectivity, also perhaps at play for female leadership at Rush, is certainly not unique to women or to Hindu traditions. As Aiya argues throughout this essay, selective recollections of women's religious capacities are what enable patriarchal traditions to flourish. Reversing this pattern, Aiya endeavors to restore memory at Rush in order that women regain their rightful place. Whether participants believe that women's rightful place is fully or partially regained at the Rush temple and whether compromises are recognized and considered worth the cost will, of course, depend on individual interpretations of and faith in divine efficacy and guru leadership.

Granted that all religious performance is interpretative and therefore selective, the question that remains is the extent to which ritual selectivity and its emergent ironies weigh heavily, lightly, or not at all on practitioners. It is a question, in turn, about whom—divine and/or human, male and/or female—is calling the shots and why.

Notes

1. For instance the Rush temple is not, like most U.S. diaspora temples, a community organization established by a temple trust and run by a temple board (Waghorne 1999, 119); the deities that reside there are not a result of committee vote or heated debate (Narayanan 1992, 175); and it does not boast what Joanne Waghorne has referred to as the "new American Hindu pantheon" (1999, 118) that celebrates a range of sectarian and regional traditions aimed at supporting—and garnering support from—the largest swatch of the local South Asian diaspora possible. See also Leonard 1997, 112, and Eck 2001, 84–85. The Rush temple unabashedly and exclusively represents the Śaiva-Śakta tradition, worships in Sri Lankan Tamil style, and is established and run by a charismatic guru figure, Sri Chaitanyananda, known as Aiya by his students. Although a trust fund and active temple board exists, Aiya is at the helm, taking advice yet unquestionably steering the course of the temple.

2. This essay uses the transliteration of the South Indian/Sri Lankan Tamil lexicon for ritual activities and ritual paraphernalia favored at Rush. The North Indian/Sanskrit forms, used elsewhere in this volume, are placed in parentheses on first occurrence. Aiya's proper name (see note 1 above) appears without diacritical marks as is his preference.

3. During my visit in January 2006 I geared many of my questions to Aiya with this essay in mind. Beginning in the summer of 1998 until 2002, I conducted numerous formal taped interviews at Rush. See Dempsey 2006 for the product of that earlier research.

4. The Ṛg Veda (10.109.4), Yama Smṛti, Hārita Smṛti, and Paraskar Grihya Sūtra include references to women wearing the sacred thread dating from ancient times up through the first several centuries in the Common Era (Manjul 2002).

5. This is the aniconic, often pillar-shaped, stone form in which Śiva is most typically worshiped in a temple.

6. The story behind the Rush temple's main *mūrti,* chiseled from granite by a temple artist in Andhra Pradesh and initially installed in an ashram in the Pocono Mountains, is recounted in Dempsey 2006, 50–56.

7. See Marglin 1985 for a discussion of the origins of menstrual taboos within the Hindu traditions. For more on cross-cultural constructions of menstruation and menstrual taboos, see Buckley and Gottlieb 1988 and Van de Walle and Renne 2001.

8. Aiya's argument is also documented in Dempsey 2006, 138–39. His use of scientific terminology to explain temple power is in some ways a trademark approach of his. See Dempsey 2008 and 2006 for more reflections on the use and meaning of science in the temple context.

References

Brooks, Douglas Renfrew. 1992. *Auspicious Wisdom: The Texts and Traditions of Śrīvidyā Śākta Tantrism in South India.* Albany: State University of New York Press.

Buckley, Thomas, and Alma Gottlieb. 1988. *Blood Magic: The Anthropology of Menstruation.* Berkeley: University of California Press.

Clothey, Fred W. 1992. "Ritual and Reinterpretation: South Indians in Southeast Asia." In *A Sacred Thread: Modern Transmission of Hindu Traditions in India and Abroad,* edited by Raymond Williams, 127–46. Chambersburg, Penn.: Anima.

Coward, Harold. 2000. "Hinduism in Canada." In *The South Asian Religious Diaspora in Britain, Canada, and the United States,* edited by Harold Coward, John Hinnells, and Raymond Brady Williams, 151–72. Albany: State University of New York Press.

Coward, Harold, and David Goa. 1987. "Religious Experiences of the South Asian Diaspora in Canada." In *South Asian Diaspora in Canada: Six Essays,* edited by Milton Israel, 75–90. Ontario: Multicultural Historical Society.

Dempsey, Corinne. 2006. *The Goddess Lives in Upstate New York: Breaking Convention and Making Home at a North American Hindu Temple.* New York: Oxford University Press.

——. 2008. "The Science of the Miraculous at an Upstate New York Temple." In *Miracle as Modern Conundrum in South Asian Religious Traditions,* edited by Corinne Dempsey and Selva Raj, 119–38. Albany: State University of New York Press.

Eck, Diana. 2001. *A New Religious America: How a "Christian Country" Has Now Become the World's Most Religiously Diverse Nation.* San Francisco: HarperCollins.

Khanna, Madhu. 1979. *Yantra: The Tantric Symbol of Cosmic Unity.* London: Thames & Hudson.

Kishwar, Madhu. 2000. "Yes to Sita, No to Ram! The Continuing Popularity of Sita in India." In *Off the Beaten Track: Rethinking Gender Justice for Indian Women,* edited by Madhu Kishwar, 234–49. New York: Oxford University Press.

Leonard, Karen Isakson. 1993. "Ethnic Identity and Gender: South Asians in the United States." In *Ethnicity, Identity, Migration: The South Asian Context,* edited by Milton Israel and N. K. Wagle, 165–80. Toronto: University of Toronto Centre for South Asian Studies.

——. 1997. *The South Asian Americans.* Westport, Conn.: Greenwood.

Manjul, V. L. 2002. "Backed by Scripture, Girls Get Their Sacred Thread." *Hinduism Today,* December 31.

Marglin, Frederique Apffel. 1985. "Female Sexuality in the Hindu World." In *Immaculate and Powerful: The Female in Sacred Image and Social Reality,* edited by Clarissa Atkinson and Constance Buchanan, 9–60. Boston: Beacon.

Narayanan, Vasudha. 1992. "Creating the South Indian 'Hindu' Experience in the United States." In *A Sacred Thread: Modern Transmission of Hindu Traditions in India and Abroad,* edited by Raymond Williams, 147–76. Chambersburg, Penn.: Anima.

Van de Walle, Etienne, and Elisha Renne. 2001. *Regulating Menstruation: Beliefs, Practices, Interpretations.* Chicago: University of Chicago Press.

Vertovec, Steven. 2000. *The Hindu Diaspora: Comparative Patterns.* London: Routledge.

Waghorne, Joanne Punzo. 1999. "The Hindu Gods in a Split-Level World: The Sri Shiva-Vishnu Temple in Suburban Washington, D.C." In *Gods of the City: Religion and the American Urban Landscape,* edited by Robert A. Orsi, 103–30. Bloomington: Indiana University Press.

Williams, Raymond. 1992. "Sacred Threads of Several Textures." In *A Sacred Thread: Modern Transmission of Hindu Traditions in India and Abroad,* edited by Raymond Williams, 228–57. Chambersburg, Penn.: Anima.

Hindu Ritual in a Canadian Context

PAUL YOUNGER

During the last 150 years, new Hindu communities have come into being in many different parts of the world. This development started in 1838 when the British began sending Indian laborers to other parts of their empire, and significant Hindu communities were established in Mauritius, Guyana, Trinidad, South Africa, Fiji, and East Africa (Brown 2006; Younger 2010). After the colonial era ended, a second wave of emigrants began to leave India and settle voluntarily in Europe and North America. Those emigrants are now forming Hindu communities as well (Vertovec 2000; Brown 2006). In Canada there are now more than a half million Hindus and hundreds of temple communities.

Scholars have not found it easy to figure out how to study these new Hindu communities. One line of inquiry followed by a variety of social scientists has concentrated on the pattern of community formation and has asked only tangentially how Hindu religious practice affects the formation of the community (Israel 1994; Vertovec 2000; Kurien 2007). Starting from a very different perspective, scholars who have studied Hindu ritual in India shift their research to one or more of these new locations and describe the temples that are being built, the religious specialists who have emerged, and the Hindu rituals that are found in these new settings (Williams 1988; Narayanan 1992; Pechilis 2004; Waghorne 2004; Dempsey 2006). In this essay I bring these two lines of inquiry together. I ask whether there are ways in which the social characteristics of a diaspora community help explain the ritual decisions a certain segment of that community makes. Or, looked at from the opposite side, whether the type of ritual choices temple communities make reveals anything about the role that a worshiping community will develop for itself in the new social setting.

In the context of this inquiry, "ritual" is taken to refer to the religious practices of a legally constituted body of worshipers or a temple community. Because in Canada religious communities are so clearly defined, freelancing gurus are not as prominent as they are in India, and the individual styles of "spirituality" for which India is known are hidden from view by the commitment people make to their temple community of choice. That commitment itself is in some ways a new form of Hindu religiosity, but for the sake of this inquiry we will take that as a given framework of Hindu practice in Canada and ask what ritual styles local communities have chosen to establish within that framework.

The Social Setting

Canada evolved into nationhood gradually, over a fairly long period of time. The early French adventurers developed a working relationship with many different groups of native people, and they moved far and wide across the continent before settling primarily in Quebec. Somewhat later, English-speaking communities settled on the land, first in the geographically limited areas of the east coast and later further inland in what they called Upper Canada or what is known today as Ontario. By 1867 the French and English had the good sense to form a confederation, and the new political entity was in a position to push a railway to the west coast and invite other immigrant groups to help populate this vast territory. Because of this history, the "imagined community"[1] of Canada emphasizes its ethnic plurality and the "openness" of the land, and immigrants from the beginning have been encouraged to develop their own style of life.

In the political context of the early twentieth century, the open invitation to immigrants was destined to suffer a temporary setback. In order to finish the railway, Chinese laborers were brought in in large numbers, but when that task was finished there was great confusion as to whether or not the Chinese would be allowed to stay. Soon after the railway was completed, Queen Victoria's Sikh honor guard was brought back from her golden jubilee of 1887 along the newly opened railway, and the members of the guard fell in love with the prospects of the still largely uninhabited west coast. Within a few years, thousands of Sikhs immigrated and were soon an important part of the forest industry and the early agricultural endeavors of British Columbia.[2] By 1914, however, the colonial authorities in Great Britain were panicking about what appeared to be a growing possibility of war with Germany, and they insisted that the Canadians look for German influence in the political activity of the Sikhs on the west coast.[3] In actions that now seem regrettable to Canadians, the authorities of the day responded by cutting off the immigration of both Chinese and Sikhs. It would be a half century before that anomaly was corrected and immigrants from those two communities once again became major parts of west coast society.

Correction of the immigration policy occurred in 1967 when the Pierre Trudeau government pushed through legislation removing all country-of-origin considerations from the policy. Because Canada was undoing decisions made earlier in the century, and because Chinese and Sikhs were poised and ready to renew the development of their earlier settlements, the changes that occurred in Canadian society after 1967 were far-reaching. Within a generation of those changes, Canadians had come to imagine themselves as a nation in which new immigrants constituted the most energetic segment of the population and essentially the fourth part (along with Aboriginals and French- and English-speakers) of the multicultural confederation.

People from every area of the globe flooded into Canada under the new immigration policies, and there was no "Hindu immigration" as such (Bramadat and Seljak 2005; Coward 2000; Younger 2012). Hindus came from many different parts of the world, and it was only after they discovered Hindus from other locations among their neighbors that they began to be curious about the idea of forming a Hindu community. Many founders of temple communities proudly describe how indifferent to religion they had been during their youth and how they discovered their need for religion in this new setting. In this setting Hinduism in its traditional ritual forms was not so much brought into Canada; rather Hindu immigrants somehow formed themselves into communities and then set about establishing new ritual forms.

Among the first immigrants to arrive were an exceptionally large number from Guyana. The Canadian immigration law changed just as the oppressive Forbes Burnham government took over monopoly power in Guyana and a large percentage of the better educated among the population found it easy to get work in Canada. A bit later a similar flood arrived from East Africa after Idi Amin expelled Indians from Uganda in 1972 and Indians all over East Africa became nervous about their future. By the 1980s Tamils fleeing the civil war in Sri Lanka began to arrive and eventually became the largest single block of Hindus in the country. Because of the refugee-like nature of the migrations from Guyana, East Africa, and Sri Lanka, these three communities have tended to remain semiseparate segments of Hindu society. This kind of self-separation has, in turn, influenced the decentralized pattern that characterizes the whole Hindu community of Canada.

Another important factor influencing the way Hindu communities were formed after the enactment of the new immigration laws of 1967 was the aggressive style of the Sikh leadership. The Khalsa Diwan Society, established in Vancouver in 1908, continued to provide leadership for Sikh immigrants, who once again began arriving in large numbers.[4] Partly because of the disappointment associated with the fact that immigration had been denied to Sikhs between 1914 and 1967, Khalsa Diwan Society leaders not only managed the *gurudwāras* or temples but also encouraged new Sikh immigrants to become active in politics and to insist that wearing turbans and carrying *kirpins* (daggers) was their religious right. Hindus were puzzled by the new Sikh insistence on putting a distance between themselves and their Hindu neighbors, and after an Air India plane was apparently bombed by Sikh advocates of a separate homeland in 1985, Hindus became more certain than ever that they did not want the type of bold and controversial leadership the Sikhs had.

Some Hindu immigrants, of course, began informal ritual practice as soon as they arrived, and there are many stories of home altars (Gunn 2007; Pearson 1999), local *bhajan* (devotional singing) groups, and semipublic celebrations of festivals in schools and churches during the early years. Temples as such only began to be discussed when people realized that marriages could not be held without provincial permission. Provincial authorities, however, quickly made clear that marriages could be conducted by anyone provided they were designated as "clergy," and that designation could be made by any legally constituted board representing a group that considered itself a religious community. Because this process for licensing someone to perform weddings involved no prior theological considerations and involved no national religious body, Hindus in different localities began to form into groups and define themselves as a temple community. While the democratic nature of this procedure was totally new to the immigrants at first—and led to some awkward moments as people learned how to discuss issues of a religious nature and how to compromise—it was the legal basis for establishing a temple community in Canada and soon became the way in which Hindus decided their ritual forms.

Ritual Choices

Hindu Samaj: Community Temple Ritual

A fairly typical example of the discussions about ritual that took place in the early community temples of Canada can be seen in the Hindu Samaj of Hamilton, which opened for worship in 1976.[5] Hamilton is a major industrial city on the western end of Lake Ontario. The first notable Hindu presence in the city came with the arrival of the family of Om Prakash Bhargava in 1963 when he took up work as an engineer in a steel company. He was a religiously well-educated North Indian Brahman, and his mother, while unable to speak English, was revered by the community of Indians. For years she held the picture of Lakṣmī while others performed *ārati* (the waving of lights) to the image or reverentially held a tray of camphor lights in front of it. The following year, a husband-and-wife team of Indian physicians moved to the city, Hindu professors were hired in metallurgy, electrical engineering, and applied mathematics, and two professors began teaching Hinduism at McMaster University. During the mid-1960s, the Indo-Canadian Society served as the institutional base of this community, which included Sikhs, Muslims, and Syrian Christians from Kerala as well as Hindus, and arranged the worship experiences and dramas for a host of Indian festivals. After the changes in immigration law in 1967, the two steel companies in the city hired large numbers of Guyanese and Punjabis, and the community suddenly expanded. By the end of the decade, Sikhs and Muslims were busy forming a local *gurudwāra* and mosque, respectively, and the Hindus set about hesitantly talking about a temple.

The formation of a Hindu community was not easy. The great majority of laborers initially expected the Brahmans and professors who had been leading the Indo-Canadian Society to continue in that role. That group was suddenly divided, however, between those of South Indian background, who had specific ritual requirements in mind, and those from North India, who spoke for the majority who wanted a Hindi-speaking priest and a minimal amount of ritual. A compromise was eventually reached when the board designated S. V. Subramanian, a Brahman metallurgy professor from the South, as the worship leader and then hired a Hindi-speaking priest. Today there are South Indian ritual specialists brought in for the installation of images, and the priest is required to follow a daily routine in the feeding, bathing, and worshiping of the deity images. On the other hand, a casual weekend visitor to the temple would come away remembering the robust Hindi-language *bhajan* singing that takes place on Sunday afternoon and the shared meal that follows the worship. During this congregational-style service, the elected lay leaders make numerous announcements and try to cultivate the informal sense of community or *samāj* of which the temple is proud.

Once the South Indian/North Indian differences in the community were recognized and satisfactorily sorted out, the community began to resolve its other differences over ritual in a consciously generous and inclusive way. Smaller segments of the community, such as those from Guyana and Gujarat, were given prominent roles on the board, and a lay leader from Guyana now conducts an English-speaking worship service on Sunday morning before the longer afternoon service in Hindi. Discussions about which deities were to be worshiped were long and careful. The building in which the temple was first housed had once served as a church, and the sanctuary was a long rectangular hall. Initially the community hung pictures of various deities along a long side wall. After some time it decided that there should be five separate shrines of roughly equal size but slightly different architectural style constructed along that wall. The final result is that a large, black granite Gaṇeśa from South India is on the worshiper's left, followed by white marble images from North India of Rām/Sītā, Kṛṣṇa/Rādhā, and Durgā, with a granite *liṅga* (a kind of icon) of Śiva, once again from South India, is on the far right. For the major Sunday afternoon worship, only a brief *pūjā* (worship service) is conducted by the priest at each of the deity shrines as he presents the worshipers' offerings, and at the end of the service the congregation lines up in five separate lines to perform *ārati* at each of the shrines, with many worshipers performing it for a number of different deities and a few for all five.

The Hindu Samaj is still the only Hindu temple in Hamilton, and the compromises the community made about ritual when it was first established seem to have proved satisfactory to a large and diverse worshiping community. Most medium-sized cities across Canada have similarly established "community" temples, and the ritual decisions made in those cases were much the same as those made at the Hamilton temple. While one hears about hard-fought elections and some disputes within the temple boards, in all cases of which I am aware, the democratically elected board has remained in charge and a regular process of renewal within the leadership has taken place. There is a distinct ritual conservatism in these community temples, and when after 9/11 the Hindu Samaj was burned to the ground in an act of arson, new images of exactly the same five deities were installed in the new building.

This community-style temple ritual entails a very marginal role for the priest, who is usually brought from India and seldom stays more than five years (Sekhar 1999). In some smaller cities, hiring a priest at all proved too cumbersome, and a variety of laypersons have taken over the priestly role. In this setting ritual is defined as "the religious practice that the board determines," and no claim of "authenticity" or direct link with Indian practice is made. The prevailing attitude seems to be that ritual provides a sacred center to the life of the community, and, while it is recognized that the ritual was determined by the founding membership, it is now treated as authoritative.

Vishnu Mandir: Guyana Temple Ritual

When laborers were first taken to Guyana in 1838, the freed West African slaves were just moving from their plantation slave quarters to settlements they established at the edge of each of the many plantations. Many of these newly freed slaves were already Christian, but in the settlements they were able to establish locally built churches. After five or ten years on indenture contracts, the Indians were also free to move into the settlements, and they quickly established *mandirs* (Hindu temples) very similar to the nearby churches. The pandits who led the worship in the *mandirs* were from traditionally educated Brahman families and could recite and sing from the Tulsīdās Rāmcaritmānas, so the Sunday morning services they conducted were similar to those in the churches nearby in that they centered on story recitation (*kathā*) or a sermon based on a verse from their scripture. The congregation gathered at the feet of the pandit, who sat on an elevated *āsanam* (throne), and, after a time of singing *bhajans*, he would deliver his *kathā*. On his right a collection of donated images were grouped together, and, at the end of the *kathā*, prayers were addressed to the group as a whole. During the rest of the week, there was seldom worship in the *mandir* (Younger 2004, 2010).

The worship system of the Vishnu Mandir in the Richmond Hill suburb north of Toronto is an interesting example of a number of Guyana-style temple rituals introduced into Ontario. In this case an experienced pandit from a prominent family of pandits in Guyana was hired as a heart surgeon in 1975, and he immediately set out to be a leader who could represent Hinduism in the Canadian context. Dr. Bhupendranath Doobay started by establishing a television program called *The Voice of the Vedas* in 1976 and quickly joined the Canadian branch of the Hindu Temple Society of North America, which had from 1972 on been formulating plans for a temple in Richmond Hill. When Doobay realized that all the plans of that group involved building authentic South Indian Brahman temples with priests from South India, he decided to move forward on his own. By 1981 he had bought a prominent piece of land on the edge of Toronto and built the Vishnu Mandir on Yonge Street in Richmond Hill. In 1987 he continued his controversial leadership by leading a *yātra,* or public protest march, from his temple to a school board meeting in nearby Scarborough, where he demanded that they name a school after Mahātma Gandhi and erect a statue there. The school board denied the demand, but, more important, most Hindus criticized Doobay for trying to "represent" them in that public way.[6] From then on his leadership efforts were focused primarily on the community from Guyana.

In spite of his controversial style, Guyana Hindus found the leadership Doobay offered as a pandit to be familiar, and they quickly helped him make his temple one of the most prominent in the city of Toronto. Although he adamantly insisted that the worship was "Vedic Hinduism" and hired assistant priests from Banaras, the style of worship one finds in Vishnu Mandir is a reproduction of that which one would find in Guyana, along with some added touches from the "megachurch" traditions of North America. The six- or seven-hundred-strong congregation gathers on Sunday morning at the feet of Doobay for an extended time of music, homily, and worship in English. He sits on a huge *āsanam* throne fitted with microphones and light dimmers. An orchestra is in the front rows, and a computer operator sitting beside the *āsanam* projects a constant stream of scripture verses, musical lyrics, and announcements onto the overhead screen. Doobay leads the music, quotes extensively from the Rāmcaritmānas and sometimes other scriptures, makes all the announcements, and generally conducts an extended homily for more than two hours. At the end of that time, he announces plans for the worship of the images. The pattern of image worship seems to vary from week to week. I once saw a full *abhiṣeka* (form of ritual bathing) of the Viṣṇu image, with the priest from Banaras reciting all the chants and Doobay pouring the water. More commonly worshipers are invited to take their offerings from the offering table where they sit during the homily and place them before one or another of the seven or eight images (of differing sizes) placed around the altar area.

(The South Indian images of Viṣṇu and Ayyappa<u>n</u> are treated differently in that only priests go to the corner of the altar where they have recently been installed.) Finally, usually after an interlude of music, everyone is invited to participate in *ārati*, and people go to the front of the altar and then to Doobay, who stands beside the *āsanam*, with their tray of camphor flame.

In a Guyana temple, there is a strong sense of community, but it is a sense established some generations past in the Caribbean (Trinidadians also worship in these Guyanese-led *mandirs*) and not one developed with new partners in Canada. It is the pandit who defines the ritual, and he is free to make changes in the ritual even as the worship is taking place.

Ganesha Temple: From Brahmanic Ritual to Sri Lankan Community Ritual

The Ganesha Temple was started in 1984 by a small group of South Indian Brahmans. As we have already noted, they began their discussions in 1972 as part of the Hindu Temple Society of North America, and in many ways they were influenced by the vision of that group, which wanted to provide temples that would "show" North American society what the most "authentic" Brahmanic Hindu rituals were like. While in the United States that vision had a major influence on the development of Hinduism and major temples were established by the group in Flushing (Queens, New York), Pittsburgh, Houston, and other places (Hanson 1999; Eck 2001), in the Ganesha Temple in Richmond Hill, that vision disappeared soon after the doors of the temple were opened. What happened in Toronto was that by the mid-1980s a flood of Sri Lankan refugees had begun to pour into the country, and they quickly became the majority on the board of the Ganesha Temple. After major quarrels most of the original founding members of the temple board eventually left the temple management to the Sri Lankans.

The original plan of the temple was to establish a close replica of the South Indian temple style with a high surrounding wall enclosing a network of open walkways or *prakāras* and a large number of separate shrines housing individual deities. The arrangement of the deities for the Ganesha Temple was determined by the *ācārya* (leader) of the Kāñcīpuram monastery in India. There are two full *vimānas* (sacred towers) that project out through the roof to the outside, one on the left as one enters for Kārttikēya or Muruka<u>n</u> and one on the right for Viṣṇu in the form of Veṅkatēsvara. In the center, and in line with the main *gōpura* (gateway tower), is the shrine of Gaṇeśa or Vināyaka<u>n</u>. To the left of Kārttikēya is the rest of the Śiva family, with separate shrines for the *liṅga* form of Śiva, for Pārvatī, and for Natarāja. Across the major walkway, there is a larger shrine for Durgā that faces north in the auspicious direction. On the Viṣṇu side, in addition to the main shrine, there are separate shrines for the consorts Devayanai and Valli. The *naivēdya* (feeding), *abhiṣeka* (bathing), and *dīpa* (showing of the camphor lights)

Ganesha Temple central shrine. Photograph by the author.

are done four times each day for each of these deities, with the evening rituals accompanied by live temple music. The original Brahman temple priests were brought from Madurai, with two specifically assigned to the Viṣṇu deities and six or so to the Śaiva deities.

The ritual practices of the temple remind one very much of the worship practices of Brahman temples in South India and Sri Lanka. Families arrive during auspicious hours (normally 8 A.M.–1 P.M. and 4–9 P.M. daily), buy *archana* (prayer) tickets of various kinds at the front window, and take them along with their other offerings to a priest at the deity shrine or shrines of their choice, where special prayers or other rituals are performed specifically for them. Having adorned themselves with sacred ash and *kuṅkum* (red powder) and having received the blessing of the deity's camphor flame, holy water, and *prasāda* (sacred food), they prepare to go home.

In addition to the daily ritual, the temple takes great pride in providing ritual for a couple dozen festivals each year. On a half dozen occasions, these are ten-day celebrations, and on two of these they pull the deities around the outside of the temple on great wooden chariots. On these occasions crowds fill the temple corridors, and the festivities often go way into the night. In the festival the deity is transformed into the *utsava*, or movable form, usually in a small image, and is carried into the life of the worshiping community. Because of the cold of Canada, the temple is enclosed in this case, but the openness of the *prakāras* (walkways) makes it possible to imagine the deities on extended trips that enable them to share in the life of the worshipers.

Because the vast majority of the worshipers are Sri Lankan and a majority of the priests are still from India, there are sometimes disagreements on how a festival should be conducted. In 1994 I witnessed a sharp disagreement during the major Ārdrā Darśana festival. Part of that festival involves the fifth-century saint Māṇikkāvacakar singing his hymns for Śiva.[7] In Cidambaram and other places in South India, an *ōtuvār* or traditional singer is dressed up as Māṇikkavācakar and, after considerable ceremony, sings each of his twenty hymns interspersed with other ceremonies. In the Ganesha Temple in 1994, an elderly *ōtuvār*, who no longer sings regularly, was dressed by the priests and ceremonially made into Māṇikkavācakar. In Sri Lanka women usually sing these songs because they express the lovelorn longing of women for the deity, so after the first hymn, the *ōtuvār* handed the songbook to a Sri Lankan woman standing beside him. The priests were appalled and stopped the ceremony for a considerable amount of time while negotiations took place among members of the board. Because the vast majority of the worshipers are now Sri Lankan and they control the board, the festival resumed after some time, and the classically trained woman sang the hymns with great beauty (Younger 2002).

While the ritual details of the Brahmanic practice of the temple might appear to be unchanged after the Sri Lankans took over the board in the 1980s, the overall tone of the ritual has been altered in a number of important ways. There is a fundamental difference between the ritual intentions of the original board that wanted to "show" the Canadian public what Hindu ritual was like and the present board that wants to provide a ritual center for the far-flung Sri Lankan Tamil community. The bitterness between these two perspectives is great, and the Sri Lankans regularly express the view that if the original board had not been so concerned with having a grand entrance facing busy Bayview Avenue, the temple and deities would face east in the religiously appropriate direction rather than west. The new board is now hiring Sri Lankan priests, and the festival activities are modified each year with the interests of Sri Lankans in mind. Even in the daily ritual, a Sri Lankan woman now sings a hymn after the evening *abhiṣeka* is finished at each shrine, and the worshipers touch her feet and honor her as a member of their community. Although the ritual of this temple is still elegantly Brahmanic in some important ways, the ritual system of the temple is gradually being transformed so that it can serve as a community temple of the Sri Lankans at the same time.

Vaisno Devi Temple, Sanatana Mandir, and Hindu Sabha: New Ethnic Community Temples

After the first excited wave of immigrants had settled into Canada under the new legislation of 1967, a somewhat different style of immigration began as family and ethnic groups sponsored their friends, and a second wave of immigrants came to join those who were already settled down. To some extent this second wave of immigration allowed subgroups an opportunity to cluster together in the different suburban regions that surround Toronto. In this new setting, some groups organized themselves around their culture of origin and began to think of new temple communities designed with their subculture in mind. We will discuss the ritual patterns in three temples of this type that were built between 1991 and 2001.

The first example is the Vaisno Devi Temple, which was opened in 1991 on the outer edge of Oakville, the suburban city to the west of Toronto that has the highest per capita income of any city in Canada. This temple is sometimes spoken of as a Punjabi temple because a Punjabi donor put up much of the money for the original construction and insisted that the central deity be the powerful pilgrimage goddess popular in the Punjab. Even though the temple had a major donor, an elected and legally constituted board in the style of Canadian temples officially manages it. What is different about the management is that the priest from the Punjab, who was chosen by the original donor and has been there now for almost twenty years, is responsible for financial management and is expected to make the final ritual choices after hearing from the board.

Given the differences at the management level, it is a bit surprising to see how indebted the ritual choices made in this location are to those made a decade earlier by temples such as the Hindu Samaj and the Vishnu Mandir. The main worship takes place on Sunday afternoon and culminates in a community meal much as it does in the Hindu Samaj. On the other hand, in a way reminiscent of the Vishnu Mandir, the priest makes all the announcements and even plays a major role in leading the music, and it is his assistant who does the *pūjās* for the various deities as the singing takes place. Although the priest is now quite comfortable in English and uses English for most of the announcements, he goads his upper-class westernized congregation regularly about the need to learn Hindi and always presents his *kathā* or sermon in Hindi.

As the issues already discussed show, the ritual choices of this temple are similar to those of early community temples in that the interests of the lay members of the congregation determine the overall ritual direction. On the other hand, the priest enjoys the support of a homogeneous congregation and operates more like the Guyana priests in making ritual decisions that give the temple a distinct and singular ritual focus. Even though the major donor had wanted the focus of worship to be on the goddess Vaiṣṇo Devī and the board had agreed to give the temple that name, the congregation wanted to worship a number of different deities. The ritual arrangements finally made were that all the deities are grouped together and elevated on a stage two steps above the rectangular congregational area, an image of Vaiṣṇo Devī—twice the size of the others—is placed in the center directly in front of the steps, and the other deities are arranged in a semicircle around her in accord with the natural or clockwise pattern of worship. As one moves around the semicircle, Gaṇeśa and the Śiva *liṅga* come first, then Viṣṇu/Lakṣmī, Kṛṣṇa/Rādhā, at the far back a Nātha or ascetic sage revered by the major donor, then Hanumān, and finally Rāma, Sītā, and Lakṣmaṇa on the congregation's right. All the images are made of marble, and the adornment of the images at a given time is much the same so that they appear as one community of divine representatives. In the performance of *ārati,* worshipers go only to the base of the stage, and the reverence of the camphor lights is directed toward the divine company as a unit.

Because the decision was made from the beginning to worship all the images together and not use a separate worship tradition for the Vaiṣṇo Devī image, the temple came to be known for its contemporary style of worship, and no mention is made about "authentic" worship of the Devī. The socializing among the well-off congregation both in the congregational hall and the dining area in the basement is notable and clearly one of the major motivations for attending this congregationally centered place of worship. Even the priestly leadership is clearly focused on meeting the needs of the current congregation, and the priests are now known primarily for the large number of weddings they perform.

The second example of the new ethnic community temple is the Sanatana Mandir of the Gujaratis opened in 1995. The Gujarati percentage in the Hindu population of Canada is smaller than it is in the United States, and during the first wave of immigration, most Gujaratis fit into the local temple communities in a helpful minority role. As time went on and the number of immigrants from both East Africa and India increased, the wealthier Gujarati business families tended to congregate in Markham, a suburb to the north of Toronto, so that they could assist one another in their far-flung business enterprises. In 1995 they built their major community center there with a relatively modest temple attached. The community center has a vast parking lot and half a dozen halls where weddings, conventions, and other community activities can be held.

The priest on duty in the temple acknowledges that the community center management largely leaves him to perform the rituals as he learned them as a child in Gujarat. The management does expect him to include in his ritual routine worship of the donated statues of Mahāvīra, Swāminarayan, Gandhi, and Hanumān, and he has placed them on the outer edges of the row that originally had only Gaṇeśa, Viṣṇu, and a goddess. During the week a folding wall closes this area off so that only a single row of worshipers can sit briefly for worship, but on the weekend and during festivals the wall is folded back, and the deity images become part of one of the large meeting rooms.

The most dramatic ritual innovation in the temple is the celebration of the Raas Garbha dances during Navarātri in early October each year. Based on an old Gujarati custom, in which girls go to their neighbors' gardens with a pot symbolizing the goddess and do a circular dance, the Sanatana Mandir dances involve thousands of males and females banging on sticks and dancing for hours to live folk music supplied by professional bands. The community hall is designed so that these dances can go on in a number of halls at the same time, and on the last of the nine nights, the whole exercise is moved to the arena at the Canadian National Exhibition grounds so that ten thousand elegantly dressed dancers can take part. For Gujaratis in Canada, that celebration at the exhibition grounds provides a powerful sense of community. The brief ritual to the goddess that precedes the dance gives it a thread of ritual legitimacy and a sense that this ritual dance keeps the community grounded in religion and its ethnic heritage.

The third example of a temple of this type is the Hindu Sabha, which is now the most prominent temple for Hindi speakers or North Indians in Canada. The worshiping community with that name goes back to 1975, but the community met in rented locations for years. The land it had purchased west of Toronto for its temple increased dramatically in value over the years, and just as the temple was opened in 2001, malls and elegant houses went up on every side of it. The temple building itself is modernistic and does not immediately remind one of a traditional Indian temple. Inside is a huge hall with the deities arranged in a tableau of three tiers with Viṣṇu/Lakṣmī high above, Rām/Sītā/Lakṣmaṇa and Kṛṣṇa/Rādhā in the middle tier, and the Śiva *liṅga,* Durgā, and Hanumān in the front at a lower level. Worshipers are able to approach only the three at the lower level for individual worship and normally sit back toward the middle of the hall and view the whole divine assembly. In contrast to the sense of awe that one has in the large hall, a cavelike walkway has been provided behind the divine tableau, and along this popular walkway, there are a half dozen opportunities to worship (a *liṅga,* some sages, epic murals, and so forth) at close range.

The temple has large entrance corridors and places for shoes and coats, and it was clearly designed to be able to handle a large number of worshipers coming and going. There is a steady flow of worshipers throughout the day, many of whom are commuters. When the expensive housing went up around the temple, many Sikhs moved in, and it is now common to see Sikhs walking to the temple for a brief prayer. Few worshipers seem to know one another, and the expectation

Hindu Sabha. Photograph by the author.

is simply that in the hurried context of an urban world, an up-to-date style of Hindu worship is available. The cluster of priests who are brought from India on a rotating basis provide the prayers worshipers request, and the efficient board manages the temple through its office staff. On Sundays at noon, the board itself can be seen sitting in a circle in the main hall counting the money for the week before it holds its regular meeting.

This temple more than any other in Canada has accepted the Canadian government's assurance that any community is free to worship in any way it chooses as long as it has a board to determine how that worship will be arranged. This board thinks of itself as part of the "new India" and wants the urban commuters who worship there to feel that the heritage of the deities displayed in the dramatic tableau at the front of the hall can be appropriated without the anachronistic rituals of village India. The sense of reverence worshipers feel as they make their quick trips to this temple is a general one that is not focused on a specific image or deity, but it does give grounding to their busy lives, and they appear to be thankful that they can have that grounding in an aesthetically pleasing atmosphere.

The Ayyappan Temple and the Ati Para Sakti Temple: The Storefront Ritual Style

By the beginning of the present century, the majority within the Indian community was feeling comfortable in the Canadian environment. Partly because others were doing so well, those within the Tamil community from Sri Lanka were socially uncomfortable and concerned about the problems within their community. A whole generation within the Tamil community of Sri Lanka had grown up in the middle of the civil war between the Liberation Tigers of Tamil Eelam (LTTE), or Tamil Tigers, led by Velupillai Prabhakaran and the Sinhala-led government. For this generation the Tamil school system hardly functioned, and most youths served for years in the Tiger military. Once these refugee families arrived in Canada, mothers were usually successful in winning their daughters' loyalty back from the LTTE and sending them off to school, but the poorly educated men found it hard to get work, and many formed gangs of friends with whom they could pass the time. For those from Vēḷāḷa or landlord caste backgrounds, the rituals of a Brahman temple such as the Ganesha Temple were appealing; but for the majority with other caste backgrounds, the grandeur of that temple actually made them realize how much they missed the other worship traditions of Sri Lanka. These restless members of the community stopped going to temple altogether for a time before some among them realized how easy it was to form temple communities of their own in Canada. It was not long before dozens of small storefront temples sprang up in the Scarborough area of Toronto, where Sri Lankans are concentrated. The two that I describe below are among the more successful of this new style of temple worship.

The first example is the Ayyappan Temple opened in 1999. A Nair caste gentleman from Kerala had been in Canada for some years when he observed that there were temples going up on every side, but there was no place to worship Ayyappaṉ, the mountain deity of central Kerala. He bought an abandoned farm on the eastern edge of Toronto and turned the cattle shed into a temple for Ayyappaṉ. The Tamil priest he hired to care for the deity had been on the arduous pilgrimage to the forest shrine of Ayyappaṉ, to which about ten million South Indian males go during a forty-day period in January–February each year. Within a few blocks of this farm temple is the area of Toronto where the refugee immigrants from Sri Lanka are concentrated and where, by 1999, many of the young Sri Lankans who had served with the LTTE in Sri Lanka were getting involved in crime. The youth began visiting this unusual temple setting, and it was not long before a bond developed between the priest of this traditionally male-centered cult and the restless youth with military backgrounds. The priest of the temple recognized the social problems of the Sri Lankan youth, and he challenged them to try the arduous yearly pilgrimage to the home shrine of Ayyappaṉ high in the Kerala mountains. Soon a vigorous, youthful male clientele was crowding into his small temple, and seventy to a hundred of them were preparing yearly for the pilgrimage, a pilgrimage that entails strict vows, severe ascetic behavior practiced by a group, and a final, male-only trek to the mountain shrine (Younger 2002).

Once the Sri Lankan pilgrims became the center of the Ayyappaṉ community, the ritual of the community was changed in a number of important ways. The Nair gentleman who had started the temple allowed the new board time to find a new Ayyappaṉ image and then moved the original one to the Vishnu Mandir Temple, where, as noted earlier, it is now in a side altar. The arrangement of the deity images in the temple is unusual but is described by the priests and worshipers as the only possible arrangement consistent with the special power of each deity. The Ayyappaṉ image is in a fully enclosed and elevated shrine that faces west but is near the middle of the temple area, except that it is offset to the south. The powerful goddess is outside the door of that shrine facing south, and Ayyappaṉ faces Bhairava, the dangerous form of Śiva, who is in a niche at a distance on the far wall. Worship begins with the worshiper approaching three images on a table at the rear or eastern end of the hall. These deities are Aiyanār, a deity somewhat similar to Ayyappaṉ that is found in villages of Tamilnadu and Sri Lanka; a goddess; and the snake deity revered by the Karaiyar or fisherman caste that leads the Tiger military. With the blessing of these deities, the worshipers move on to Ayyappaṉ and the main goddess, and then they carefully ward off the anger of Bhairava by stopping at his shrine as they leave. The temple atmosphere buzzes throughout the week with priests loudly explaining to worshipers how to keep from offending the deities and bare-chested pilgrims performing service for the deities and energetically preparing themselves for the challenges of the pilgrimage.

The temple board has now had a medium-sized temple built on the lot beside the cattle shed. There was some hesitation about moving the deity; some worshipers feared that on the second story of the new building the deity would be less powerful because he would not have the power of the earth, and especially of the area long inhabited by cows, directly underneath him. The priests eventually altered the design to meet those concerns and, with Namboodri Brahman priests recently recruited from Kerala, the ritual of the temple is moving in a more Brahmanic direction.

The second example of a storefront-style temple is the Ati Para Sakti Temple opened for worship in 2002. For most Sri Lankan immigrant women, the absence of local goddess shrines for intimate daily worship was a difficulty when they arrived in Canada. Aware of this problem, a majority of the storefront temples in the part of the city where Tamils have concentrated are goddess temples of some sort. One of the Tamil women living in this area and longing for a suitable place to worship during the 1990s was Vasanthi. She had grown up in a rural area of Sri Lanka and had assisted her grandfather when in retirement he had built a Durgā temple on the family property. When the civil war started, the family had arranged for her youngest sister to go to Chennai in South India to study medicine, and Vasanthi went along to keep her company. During this time she spent much of her time in Melmaruvathūr, where the local priest had developed a major cult around the worship of the supreme goddess, Āti Para Śaktī. Most of the ritual in this cult is led by women, and Vasanthi participated in the leadership and memorized hours of ritual detail. When the whole family later immigrated to Canada, they found it difficult to get suitable work and were often unemployed. Vasanthi began to spend much of the night performing severe rituals for the goddess, or "Amma," and was soon known among family and friends as someone with exceptional spiritual power. In 2002 she and her friends received permission from the priest in Melmaruvathūr to open a congregational branch of the Āti Para Śaktī movement in a storefront.

This storefront temple now functions seven days a week, with all-day services and meals on Saturday and Sunday and evening services the rest of the week. Vasanthi is clearly the worship leader (addressed as *talaivī,* "leader" or "actress" in colloquial Tamil) when she is there (every day except Friday, when she serves another location), but there are twelve other women designated to lead the ritual, and at least half of them are busily engaged in assisting people in their worship at any moment during the service. These women are not exactly priests in that worshipers perform their own acts of worship, but the leader recites the prayers and demonstrates the motion of the hand that is required as the worshiper repeats the prayer. Men and children make up about a third of the worshipers and help with the food, but they do not lead in the ritual, except for the closing exercise that involves expelling the evil spirits from the building.

The object of worship in this temple is the goddess Āti Para Śaktī, sometimes referred to as Om Śaktī, who is considered by the worshipers to be the supreme divinity. For some years now, she has been embodied in Arulthiru Bangaru Adigalar, the priest of Melmaruvathūr, whom the worshipers address as "Amma" as well. The altar of the temple is a table six feet from the back wall, and in the center of this heavily adorned table is a small metal image of the goddess. As one approaches her moving in a clockwise direction, one first meets a small Gaṇeśa on the end of the table and then a picture of Bangaru Adigalar possessed by her. Having worshiped from that side, the worshiper backs away, rather than crossing in front of the goddess, and goes to a nine-foot-high cutout of Bangaru Adigalar in the back left corner and then across the back to a similar cutout in the back right corner. Finally the worshiper approaches the other end of the worship table, where there is a replica of the sacred feet of Bangaru Adigalar and a second opportunity to worship the image of the goddess.

The common congregational part of this worship experience takes place every day when for about forty-five minutes the congregation, seated to the side, recites from a prayer book the antiphonal prayers and hymns that are led by one or more of the leaders. For hours before and after that common prayer, most worshipers come anxious to do their own prayers, make garlands, create rice powder *kolams* (designs in front of the altar), or recite 108 names of the deity or 108 petitions to the deity. Throughout this bustle of ritual activity, a dozen or more congregants are busily engaged with the preparation of the meal in the kitchen, and extended conversations on life's problems go on between one of the leaders and every worshiper. Ledger books are constantly passed from hand to hand as peoples' memberships are noted, prayer requests are made, and the financial contributions on the altar are counted. Before leaving, a few men, women, and/or children take camphor lights in coconuts and, after asking permission from the goddess, go to every corner of the hall, the kitchen, and even the washrooms to gather up the evil spirits lurking in those corners. They then go to the front door and, looking at the goddess, smash the coconuts on a grinding stone.

There is no public speaking of any kind during this extended ritual, and everyone's attention is directed to ritual action at all times. Nevertheless the sense of community is strong, and everyone greets everyone else as they move about the room. Most people act as if they know everyone else, and they quickly tell others seated near them about their personal problems and why they brought those problems to the goddess. Because everyone eventually adopts the style of the leaders and assists others in their worship in some small way, the line that normally marks off community activity from ritual activity almost totally disappears. The goddess is described as the supreme deity, but people reassure one another that she is forgiving and tolerant of human error and will comfort them both here in the hall and as they go back to their difficult lives. Late in the temple day, topics shift from how to perform this or that ritual to how to sweep up and wash the floor and how to find a ride home. It is as if the goddess now possesses the whole community much as she does Bangaru Adigalar and now goes with them as they destroy the evil spirits and move out into the world for another day.

The many storefront temples now available in the urban and suburban malls of Canada represent a distinct new style of Hindu ritual. Because the financial investment need not be a major issue and it does not take a long period of time to build the community, the primary focus is on the theological promises the ritual for the chosen deity offers. In the two cases described above, the name of the deity and the ritual style associated with it were from India and were not initially familiar to the Sri Lankan community. On the other hand, because the deities had established reputations, the ritual style was similar to familiar Tamil ritual styles, and gifted Tamil-speaking leaders were involved in each case, the newness of the ritual turned out to be one of the attractions in this new social setting.

Conclusion

Based on the evidence presented here, what are the factors affecting the ritual development of Hindu temples within the Canadian context?

One factor that might easily be overlooked is the sense of cultural openness provided by the Canadian tradition of social pluralism. A legislative expression of this tradition was proposed in 1971 in the Multiculturalism Act that was finally passed in 1988, but the tradition is deeply rooted in Canadian history. The immigrants' first experience of this tradition sometimes seems like a form of indifference as neighbors offer new immigrants the assurance that they are free to worship in any way they choose. A few self-appointed leaders within the Indian immigrant community arrived in Canada with a very different view of the cultural encounter that was about to take place, and they offered to "represent" Hinduism in a way that challenged the Canadian public and put the community in a good light. Most of the early immigrants were unsure what to expect in this regard, but as they saw no evidence of a difficult encounter, they chose to ignore the appeals of those who wanted to "represent" them in this confrontational way. Gradually they turned their attention toward other Hindus in the vicinity and began a period of introspection.

Having turned inward and having begun to examine themselves, groups of immigrants soon heard a second surprising thing about their new situation, namely, that if a number of them agreed, they could call themselves a temple community and have one of their number licensed to perform Hindu weddings. This seemed odd at first because Sikhs, Christians, and Jews had national organizations that handled these matters, but it was a big break for Hindus because they came from many different places and were finding that they had little in common with one another and no national organization. Although they had started their discussions about a Hindu community primarily to satisfy government officials, those discussions soon blossomed, and barriers of language, caste, and gender were soon left behind as people voted on the images that they were planning to worship and on the duties laypersons and priests would have for those deities. As we saw in detail in the case of the Hindu Samaj of Hamilton, the ritual system set in place by these democratic discussions was put together piece by piece and carefully tested in the worship practice of the temple over an extended period of time.

A third factor in the development of ritual systems in the Canadian setting was that, as temple communities became established over longer periods of time, the ritual system came to be taught to the second generation as an authoritative form of Hindu practice. Although the management of the temple continued to be in the hands of a democratically elected board, the ritual system established by the founders came to be understood as part of the revered tradition of the temple.

When by the end of the last century the pace of immigration continued to expand and more and more immigrants came to join family and friends who had been in Canada for some time, a fourth factor began to influence the development of the ritual practices of temples. Superficially one might describe this as the development of ethnic or regional temples, because some of these newer temples served suburbs of Toronto where immigrants from certain regions of India had started to congregate. It would be a mistake, however, to think that the ritual of these temples involved an effort to produce "authentic" examples of ritual systems of India. These newer temples continue in the now-established Canadian tradition of inviting worshipers to design a ritual tradition that meets their needs as a community. What is new about these temples is that instead of focusing on the number of deities to be worshiped, as the early temple communities did, they create a worship atmosphere that is comfortable for the ethnic subcommunities that use them. One feature of this comfort is the use of the traditional language. In general, however, there is no effort to reestablish traditional forms of worship, and the temples have been daring in establishing worship styles that are aesthetically comfortable in terms of whom these worshipers are today.

Finally the storefront temples allow the many different temple traditions, which have been developing in Canada from the beginning of Hindu immigration, potentially to expand into infinite varieties. The two that we examined in detail follow ritual patterns that are borrowed from India, but even they, in the Canadian context, are understood to be under the direction of a board chosen by the membership. Each board is autonomous and, while responsible to the government on tax matters, is responsible only to its membership on matters of theology and ritual. In practice the founders' wishes in relation to ritual are treated with reverence, and in the case of these two storefront temples, that reverence brings them in line with established Indian traditions.

Although there are now hundreds of temple traditions established in Canada, no two are affiliated together. There was an attempt to form a Canadian Council of Hindus in the 1980s, but it was abandoned when the founder died because, like the other leadership efforts of the Hindu Temple Society and Dr. Doobay, it seemed to be addressing a perceived need to fight for one's rights that few in the temple communities felt. The government encouragement of the temple communities was certainly a factor in their widespread development, but it also seems to be the case that the opportunity to define their own ritual practices made it possible for Hindus in Canada to determine for themselves a faith appropriate to their new identities. Instead of trying to convince their children to adhere to religious practices designed for a very different cultural environment, Canadian Hindus seem to have found a way to practice rituals with which they are comfortable and which they feel comfortable passing on to their children.

Notes

1. I use the concept of "imagined community" developed by Benedict Anderson (1983) in referring to the Canadian polity because I think it brings out well the unwritten consensus that has long governed Canadian behavior. Part of my argument about Hindu immigrants is that they picked up this sense of unwritten consensus and, instead of following those who wanted to articulate Hindu rights and develop a "represented community" for them, allowed ritual behavior to define their role in Canadian life.

2. Sikh history in Canada has been thoroughly studied both by outside scholars and scholars of the community. N. Singh's 1994 study is the best from inside the community.

3. The political movement they feared was the Ghadr movement based in Berkeley, California, but influential among Sikhs in Canada as well. See Juergensmeyer 1989.

4. Sikhs are as numerous in Canada as are Hindus, and they are better known by the Canadian public because of their confrontational style and the role they now play in politics (Mahmood 2005).

5. I use the local spellings for the names of all temples.

6. I follow the work of Kaplan and Kelly (2001) in using the term "represented community" to create a sharp contrast with "imagined community."

7. There are widely different dates suggested by the scholarly community for the life of Māṇikkavācakar. I have dealt with that matter at length in Younger 1995.

References

Anderson, Benedict. 1983. *Imagined Communities: Reflections on the Origin and Spread of Nationalism.* London: Verso.

Bramadat, Paul, and David Seljak, eds. 2005. *Religion and Ethnicity in Canada.* Toronto: Pearson Longman.

Brown, Judith. 2006. *Global South Asians: Introducing the Modern Diaspora.* Cambridge: Cambridge University Press.

Coward, Harold. 2000. "Hinduism in Canada." In *The South Asian Religious Diaspora in Britain, Canada, and the United States,* edited by Harold Coward, John R. Hinnels, and Raymond Brady Williams, 151–72. Albany: State University of New York Press.

Dempsey, Corinne G. 2006. *The Goddess Lives in Upstate New York: Breaking Convention and Making Home at a North American Hindu Temple.* New York: Oxford University Press.

Eck, Diana. 2001. *A New Religious America: How a "Christian Country" Has Now Become the World's Most Religiously Diverse Nation.* San Francisco: HarperCollins.

Gunn, Janet. 2007. "Poiesis/Praxis/Puja: Constructions of Self and Culture in Diasporic Hindu Household Ritual." Paper delivered at the American Academy of Religion Annual Meeting, San Diego.

Hanson, Richard Scott. 1999. "Sri MahaVallabha Ganapati Devasthanam of Flushing, New York." In *Hindu Diaspora: Global Perspectives,* edited by T. S. Rukmani, 349–66. Montreal: Chair in Hindu Studies, Department of Religion, Concordia University.

Israel, Milton. 1994. *In Further Soil: A Social History of Indo-Canadians in Ontario.* Toronto: Toronto Organization for the Promotion of Indian Culture.

Juergensmeyer, Mark. 1989. "The Gadr Syndrome: Immigrant Sikhs and National Pride." In *Sikh Studies: Immigration and the Experience beyond Punjab,* edited by Gerald Barrier and Verne Dusenberry, 302–21. Delhi: Chanakya.

Kaplan, Martha, and John D. Kelly. 2001. *Represented Communities: Fiji and World Decolonization.* Chicago: University of Chicago Press.

Kurien, Prema A. 2007. *A Place at the Multicultural Table: The Development of an American Hinduism.* New Brunswick, N.J.: Rutgers University Press.

Mahmood, Cynthia Keppley. 2005. "Sikhs in Canada: Identity and Commitment." In *Religion and Ethnicity in Canada,* edited by Paul Bramadat and David Seljak, 52–68. Toronto: Pearson Longman.

Narayanan, Vasudha. 1992. "Creating the South Indian 'Hindu' Experience in the United States." In *A Sacred Thread: Modern Transmission of Hindu Traditions in India and Abroad,* edited by Raymond Brady Williams, 147–76. Chambersburg, Penn.: Anima.

Pearson, Anne M. 1999. "Mothers and Daughters: The Transmission of Religious Practice and the Formation of Hindu Identity among Hindu Immigrant Women in Ontario." In *Hindu Diaspora: Global Perspectives,* edited by T. S. Rukmani, 427–42. Montreal: Chair in Hindu Studies, Department of Religion, Concordia University.

Pechilis, Karen, ed. 2004. *The Graceful Guru: Hindu Female Gurus in India and the United States.* New York: Oxford University Press.

Ṣekhar, Radhika. 1999. "Authenticity by Accident: Organizing, Decision making and the Construction of Hindu Identity." In *Hindu Diaspora: Global Perspectives,* edited by T. S. Rukmani, 307–48. Montreal: Chair in Hindu Studies, Department of Religion, Concordia University.

Singh, N. 1994. *Canadian Sikhs: History, Religion and Culture of Sikhs in North America.* Ottawa: Canadian Sikh Studies Institute.

Vertovec, Steven. 2000. *The Hindu Diaspora: Comparative Patterns.* London: Routledge.

Waghorne, Joanne Punzo. 2004. *Diaspora of the Gods: Modern Hindu Temples in an Urban Middle-Class World.* New York: Oxford University Press.

Williams, Raymond Brady. 1988. *Religions of Immigrants from India and Pakistan: New Threads in the American Tapestry.* New York: Cambridge University Press.

Younger, Paul. 1995. *The Home of Dancing Śivaṉ: The Traditions of the Hindu Temple in Citamparam.* New York: Oxford University Press.

——. 2002. *Playing Host to Deity: Festival Religion in the South Indian Tradition.* New York: Oxford University Press.

——. 2004. "Guyana Hinduism," *Religious Studies and Theology* 23.1.

——. 2010. *New Homelands: Hindu Communities in Mauritius, Guyana, Trinidad, South Africa, Fiji, and East Africa.* New York: Oxford University Press.

——. 2012. "Hindus." In *The Religions of Canadians,* edited by Jamie S. Scott, 219–60. Toronto: Toronto University Press.

PART 3

Reconsiderations

Context and Theory

The Accidental Ritualist

DAVID L. HABERMAN

There is renewed interest in ritual these days, especially within certain circles of European and American popular culture.[1] This growing interest seems to involve the assumption, and even hope, that ritual is a transformative experience affecting some kind of momentous change that might not occur in any other fashion. In my own study of academic theories about ritual, however, I have noted that this position is debatable. Some theorists do indeed support the contention that ritual is transformative. For example, in his famous statement on religion as a cultural system, Clifford Geertz writes: "Having ritually 'leapt' into the framework of meaning which religious conceptions define, and the ritual ended . . . a man is—unless, as sometimes happens, the experience fails to register—changed" (1973, 122). Other well-known theoretical statements about ritual, however, emphasize a more conservative view and suggest that rather than transform, ritual helps to maintain existing structures. Victor Turner, for example, in his most significant book on ritual, *The Ritual Process* (1977), suggests that ritual does not so much transform individuals as reduce social tensions and allow social structures to continue in a rejuvenated manner. According to him, with a ritual performance "the stage is then set for an ecstatic experience of communitas, followed by a sober return to a now purged and reanimated structure" (185). For Turner ritual functions like a steam valve on a pressure cooker that releases social tensions in a controlled manner. Within this tension-reducing model, ritual is not so much transformative as conservative, acting to preserve social structure.[2] Suffice it to say that the question of whether ritual is transformative or not is a contentious issue within the academic study of religion. Furthermore even among those who agree that ritual is transformative, there is still much that is debatable regarding the cause of change. If ritual is transformative, how is transformation accomplished? In other words the claim that ritual is transformative begs the further question: What is the key agent or mechanism of transformation?

Scholars of religious studies today are familiar with academic theories about the nature and function of rituals; we have our own ways of thinking and talking about ritual action. But what other perspectives on ritual outside the Western academy are available to us? Might there be indigenous views on ritual experience with which we can think productively? What kind of theorizing about ritual can be found in nonacademic literature, say even within sacred texts themselves? I propose that theorizing about ritual is indeed present in many primary texts, although, granted, this theorizing takes forms different from those we customarily see in academic studies on ritual theory. Here I am in agreement with Rob Campany, who, in an article titled "Xunzi and Durkheim as Theorists of Ritual Practice," sets out to deconstruct the dualistic supposition behind much past academic theorizing about ritual that assumes "we [Western academicians] had the theory, while what they [religious communities or the authors of primary ritual texts] could provide amounted only to 'raw' data; we theorized about their practices; we philosophized, they acted" (Campany 1996, 87). In contrast Campany insists that all practitioners of rituals have some self-understanding of why they do what they do, and he calls for "more studies of premodern and non-Western ritual theory" (98). I argue for the same; indeed this is a major objective of this essay. I propose to navigate the transgression of an academic boundary that divides those who promote and perform rituals from those who theorize about them while asking: What might indigenous theories embedded in religious texts have to say about the transformative process of ritual?

Hindu texts known as the Purāṇas—the term literally means "ancient"—are a collection of early texts that purport to tell of olden times and contain an ocean of information about a wide variety of subjects, such as creation, the ages of the world, and the genealogy of gods, kings, and sages. They are fluid and developing texts compiled by multiple authors over long periods of time (thus making them difficult to date) and reflecting oral and living traditions. The Purāṇas are the principal scriptures of theistic, temple-based Hinduism and are a treasure house for cultural practices that stretch over a period of some two thousand years. Ludo Rocher writes about them: "The Purāṇas are, first, important documents for the study and reconstruction of the history of Hindu India. In a more practical way, they have contributed to the continuity of Hinduism through the ages, and are indispensable for a correct understanding of Hinduism today. As a matter of fact, every Hindu is influenced by the Purāṇas, and his activities are guided by them" (Rocher 1986, 12–13). Important for our considerations, these texts are also filled with detailed descriptions of ritual performances and numerous accounts of the benefits to be gained by performing these rituals. Although the Purāṇas do not treat the subject of ritual theory explicitly, there is a rather common genre of story contained within them that I have come to regard as a kind of implicit theorizing about the efficacy of ritual experience. It is my intention to explore this genre by examining several examples and to investigate the way in which they might be read as theoretical speculations about ritual.

The Story of Guṇanidhi

I begin with a detailed summary of the story of Guṇanidhi, as it illustrates the genre I have in mind quite effectively. This story, which appears in the seventeenth and eighteenth chapters of the first section of the "Rudrasamhitā" of the Śiva Purāṇa, is told to the sage Nārada by Brahmā, god of creation (Singh 1981, 48–49).[3] In the city of Kāmpilya, there lived a great Vedic fire sacrificer named Yajñadatta. This Brahman was a very knowledgeable scholar and generous donor who stood as a model of virtue for his entire community. Yajñadatta had a son named Guṇanidhi (which means "a treasure house of virtues"). Guṇanidhi was handsome and well educated and, being the son of the learned Yajñadatta, had everything going for him. In his late adolescent years, however, unbeknownst to his father, he became addicted to gambling. This spelled the ruin of Guṇanidhi; he took money from his mother and squandered it all away on his gambling habit. Over time he fell away from his Brahman ways; he stopped his studies and began insulting the sacred texts. He kept a distance from his father and associated only with bad company. Although his loving mother strongly encouraged Guṇanidhi to emulate his virtuous father, she affectionately covered for him, allowing him to continue his bad conduct. Eventually Guṇanidhi's father discovered the truth and was so outraged that he threw Guṇanidhi out of the house. Guṇanidhi now had no choice but to live the life of a poor and homeless wanderer.

While a very hungry Guṇanidhi sat beneath a tree one evening at sunset, a devotee of Śiva walked past him. This happened to be the evening of Śivarātri, the annual night on which devotees of Śiva fast and remain awake while worshiping the deity with great ritual celebration. The devotee was therefore carrying a variety of sweet-smelling food offerings to be presented to Śiva in the form of a *liṅga*[4] in a nearby temple. Drawn by the delicious smells, the starving Guṇanidhi followed the devotee. He remained hidden outside the temple, waiting attentively for a chance to steal the food offerings for himself. Meanwhile he observed the worship being conducted in the temple and listened to the songs and prayers being sung. When the worshipers fell asleep, Guṇanidhi saw his opportunity and entered the inner sanctum of the temple to take the food offerings. Because it was dark inside the inner sanctum, he tore a piece of cloth from his lower garment and added it to the sacred lamp for extra light. Taking the food offerings with him, he exited the inner sanctum hastily, eager for his first meal in a long time. On his way out of the temple, however, Guṇanidhi tripped over a devotee and woke him. The devotee began to shout, and soon the night watchman on duty caught and killed Guṇanidhi, who never got a chance to eat the food he had stolen (which would have been a grave offense).

The attendants of Yama, god of death, soon appeared on the scene to drag Guṇanidhi off to hell for judgment and punishment. Just as they finished binding him, the attendants of Śiva arrived and ordered those of Yama to release him. The attendants of Yama were shocked by this request and demanded an explanation, arguing that surely Guṇanidhi's sinful conduct warranted punishment in a torturous hell. The attendants of Śiva responded by asserting that the ways of dharma are subtle (*sukṣma*). They insisted that they could detect an inner transformation in Guṇanidhi and went on to explain that on this auspicious night of Śivarātri, he had properly performed a number of ritual actions that had freed him from all his sins: (1) he listened to the names of Śiva being recited during the temple prayers; (2) he observed the worship being conducted; (3) he fasted and remained awake throughout the night; (4) he focused his mind in concentration on the activities around the Śiva *liṅga* within the temple; and (5) he added fuel to the lamp dedicated to Śiva just as it was about to go out. The attendants of Śiva acknowledged that Guṇanidhi performed all these sacred acts unintentionally and for the wrong reasons; nonetheless they insisted that the performance had transformed him and had made him eligible for residence in Śiva's abode, where he would enjoy great pleasures for some time. Moreover they announced that Guṇanidhi had become such a great favorite of Śiva that he would be reborn in the future as a favored king of Kalinga.

Significantly in this narrative Guṇanidhi undergoes personal ontological change. Surely this is a story about a tremendous transformation, one that is affected by ritual action. Since a major purpose of this text is to promote performance of the Śivarātri ritual, it is not surprising in any debate over the nature of ritual that this text would clearly side with those who view ritual as transformative. What is more significant for our considerations, however, is that this text identifies the agent or mechanism of transformation. More important than any other factor—such as intentionality, which is here implicitly denied as central—ritual action itself is identified as the transformative agent. The Śiva Purāṇa registers that Guṇanidhi's intention was to steal and that he fueled Śiva's lamp for his own gain. Nevertheless the power of ritual performance is affirmed, while physical action itself is highlighted as transformative. Yama instructs his attendants to leave alone any person who imitates the behavior of a worshiper of Śiva for any reason whatsoever. Here physical imitative action itself is clearly endorsed, regardless of knowledge or intention. Putting the body in the physical groove of ritual action is lifted up as foremost among the possible transformative elements.

Additional Purāṇic Śivarātri Stories

The story of Guṇanidhi is by no means unique; it is among a genre found throughout many of the Purāṇas. Another account of a wicked person transformed on the night of Śivarātri by an accidental ritual performance is present in the Garuḍa Purāṇa (1.124) in the form of a story about the Śivarātri *vrata* (ritual observance) that Śiva narrates to the goddess Gaurī (Bhattacharya 1964, 150–51).[5] Śiva begins his tale with a description of the Śivarātri *vrata* that is said to enable one to cross over and avoid hell (*naraka*). This text instructs the practitioner to keep awake all night and worship Śiva on the fourteenth day of the dark half of the month of Phālguna. To illustrate the power of this ritual, Śiva narrates the story of Sundara Senaka, the sinful king of Niṣādas. One day the king went hunting in the forest. After a long day without any success, the king became exhausted with hunger. He climbed a tree for safety and, because of his anxious condition, stayed awake all night. The tree happened to be a *bilva* tree (the tree most sacred to Śiva) and, unbeknownst to the king, beneath it stood a Śiva *liṅga*. As the king moved about in the tree, he accidentally knocked some leaves down on the *liṅga*. Later in the night, an arrow accidentally fell from the king's quiver, and he jumped down to retrieve it. Feeling around on the ground in the dark while searching for the arrow, he crawled up to the *liṅga* and touched it lightly with his right hand. Once he located the arrow and returned it to his quiver, the king took out a container of water he was carrying to wash the dust from his body. As he opened the container, some of the water accidentally splashed onto the *liṅga*. Thus, this text informs us, the wicked king accidentally performed all aspects of the Śivarātri worship: while staying awake all night, he bathed the Śiva *liṅga* with water, offered it sacred *bilva* leaves, prostrated before it, and touched it gently.

When Sundara Senaka died sometime later, Śiva informed Gaurī that Yama's attendants had caught him with a noose and had begun dragging him away. Śiva's attendants confronted those of Yama and forced them to release the king. Śiva's attendants then escorted Sundara Senaka to Śiva's abode, where he himself became an attendant of Śiva. Therefore, the text concludes, he achieved the benefits (*puṇya*) of the ritual even while performing it without knowledge *(ajñānataḥ)*. To be sure, the text does go on to explain that one who performs the ritual knowingly (*jñānāt*) will achieve eternal benefits (*akṣaya puṇya*). Intentionality, then, is not completely disregarded, but neither is it marked as necessary for ritual transformation. The story is obviously told to promote the intentional and knowledgeable performance of the Śivarātri ritual, but it is done in a manner that makes clear that the transformative benefit of the ritual is not derived primarily from any intention but rather from its physical performance.

A point of clarification is in order. The Purāṇas give expression to a theistic universe. This means that the ultimate power operative in the Śivarātri ritual is the power of the *liṅga,* and the power that originates from the *liṅga* clearly comes from Śiva himself. My argument here is not that the physical performance of ritual trumps the power of God (although in some ritual contexts, it may even accomplish this) but rather that the physical performance trumps both knowledge and intentionality in the ritual context of the genre of Purāṇic stories I work with in this essay. Śiva's power is supreme; however this power is not simply dispersed in some random fashion. Rather it flows to one who performs ritual interactions with the *liṅga*—whether intentionally or accidentally. I am highlighting in these stories the theoretical position that physical performance in ritual is more important than either intentionality or knowledge, not more important than the power of the deity.

Many similar stories about the performance of accidental rituals are contained within other Purāṇas. Another story of an accidental Śivarātri ritual performance is told in the "Uttarakhaṇḍa" of the Padma Purāṇa (154.8–53).[6] Here we meet Caṇḍa, a violent and cruel hunter who accidentally worshiped a Śiva *liṅga* on the night of Śivarātri by staying awake all night without eating and accidentally knocking *bilva* leaves onto the *liṅga* while trying to kill a boar. During the night Caṇḍa became greatly transformed by the performance of these acts; we are told that he was freed from all sins and his heart became pure. His alteration was so great that when his wife showed up the following morning with some meat to feed him, he protected a dog that his wife was about to beat for stealing the meat. Realizing the grievous mistakes of his previously wicked ways, Caṇḍa drew his sword to cut off his own head. At that moment the attendants of Śiva appeared and informed him that Śiva was now very pleased with him, since he had offered *bilva* leaves to Śiva in the form of a *liṅga* and had fasted and stayed awake all night on Śivarātri. As a result of these actions, he was taken away to Śiva's celestial abode.

Another such story is told in the fortieth chapter of the "Kotirudra Saṃhitā" of the Śiva Purāṇa, in a section titled "Śivarātri Māhātmya."[7] Here a group of sages specifically asks Sūta if the highest benefit (*phalam uttamam*) can be obtained from the ritual by one performing it without knowledge (*ajñānataḥ).* As an affirmative response, Sūta narrates the story of Gurudruha, a wicked thief and hunter, who was once caught in the forest on Śivarātri while hunting deer as night fell. Now following a familiar pattern, he climbs a *bilva* tree and accidentally worships a *liṅga* situated below the tree by spilling water and knocking *bilva* leaves on it four times while staying awake the entire night without any food. Once again the accidental performance of a ritual is declared to be transformative: Śiva himself appears before Gurudruha and makes him a privileged king. When he dies, he achieves the highest form of union (*sāyujya)* with Śiva. Sūta ends his tale by saying: "Even after performing this ritual in ignorance (*ajñātāt*) he attained union. What about those who are endowed with devotion? They will surely attain the highest end" (40.97). Once again knowledge and intentionality are not disregarded, but neither are they identified as the most important aspect of the transformative power of ritual. Physical performance of the ritual is credited for this.

Ajāmila's Shout

Such stories are not only found in the Śaivite context of Śaiva Purāṇas; many are also found in the Vaiṣṇava Purāṇas. Let me give one brief example before moving on with further analysis of these stories. In the sixth *skandha* of the Bhāgavata Purāṇa, we meet Ajāmila, an upright Brahman who is corrupted by his lust for a beautiful servant woman.[8] Ajāmila's attraction to this young woman causes him to abandon his legal wife and virtuous ways. Producing children with the servant woman, he supports his new family by gambling, stealing, and kidnapping for ransom. He even resorts to murder. Ajāmila is fond of his children, especially his youngest son, whom he named Nārāyaṇa (one of the names for Viṣṇu) and cares for with great personal attention. When the moment of death comes for Ajāmila and he sees the attendants of Yama approaching rapidly, he becomes frightened and shouts for Nārāyaṇa. Upon hearing the name of their master, the attendants of Viṣṇu rush to the scene to stop the attendants of Yama from dragging Ajāmila away for punishment. When the attendants of Yama demand justification for this intervention, the attendants of Viṣṇu explain that the act of uttering the name "Nārāyaṇa" freed Ajāmila from all sins. Indeed after calling out to Nārāyaṇa at his moment of death, Ajāmila is so transformed that he is restored to life and returns to his former virtuous ways; he spends the remainder of his years in devoted religious practice and upon death becomes an attendant of Viṣṇu.

The attendants of Viṣṇu directly acknowledge the intention behind Ajāmila's transformative action; they know he is calling out to his son in fear. Nonetheless they extol the efficacy of the act of uttering the name of Viṣṇu, a significant feature of Vaiṣṇava ritual practice. Regardless of his intentions, Ajāmila's act is profitable. Viṣṇu's attendants say: "Just as powerful medicine will produce its healing effects, even when taken accidentally (*yadṛcchayā*) by one unaware of its efficacy, so too the mantra consisting of Viṣṇu's name will produce its transformative effect, even when uttered accidentally by one unaware of its efficacy" (Bhāgavata Purāṇa 6.2.19). A similar statement might also be made about the ritual acts associated with Śivarātri in the previous stories. Here the power in Viṣṇu's name undoubtedly derives from Viṣṇu himself, but one accesses that power by the ritual act of uttering Viṣṇu's name, regardless of whether one does so intentionally or not.

Ritual Theory in the Purāṇas

What all these stories have in common is an accidental performance of a ritual with transformative results. This is curious. It is certainly possible to tell a *vrata* ritual story about an intentional, knowledgeable, and effective performance in a straightforward manner; indeed many such stories are also to be found in the Purāṇas. The Agni Purāṇa, for example, contains a description of the Śivarātri *vrata* that urges practitioners to engage in the Śivarātri ritual with full understanding and intention.[9] Why, then, tell a story of ritual performance in this way? Moreover, how might we read these stories as scholars of ritual and ritual theory? What do the Purāṇas contribute to our own consideration of ritual? Before turning to these questions, a preliminary matter must be addressed. The stories that I have retold from the Purāṇas, on the one hand, could be dismissed as mere religious propaganda; on the other hand, they might be accepted naively as explicit ritual theory. It seems to me that both extremes would be mistaken. Assuredly these stories are not explicit ritual theory; their primary function is to promote certain religious practices within a particular religious tradition. Nonetheless to reject outright consideration of these stories as kinds of ritual theory assumes that the authors of these texts share none of our speculative concerns about ritual or that their thoughts are so crude that they are not worthy for our thinking about ritual. Refusing to consider them, in my opinion, would mean an opportunity missed to think about the nature of ritual action cross-culturally with the aid of a fresh perspective of Purāṇic authors. I propose instead that they be read cautiously and critically as implicit theoretical speculations about ritual experience. And what do they teach us? They have much to say about intentionality and the efficacy of physical actions. I contend that narrating ritual stories in this way is significant, for it tells us something important about Purāṇic notions of ritual. Stories about effective but accidental ritual performances leave no doubt about the main transformative agent: physical performance is emphasized over knowledge and intentionality.

The texts from which I draw these stories do not completely ignore such issues as intentionality, knowledge, or sincerity. The Bhāgavata Purāṇa story of Ajāmila ends with the statement: "By calling out the name of Hari (another name for Nārāyaṇa/Viṣṇu) addressed to his son at the time of his death, even Ajāmila attained Viṣṇu's abode; how much more true would this be for one who does so with faith (*śraddhayā*)" (Bhāgavata Purāṇa 6.2.49). The Śiva Purāṇa story of Guṇanidhi counsels: "Thus even the smallest service rendered to Śiva bears fruit in time. Let all persons seeking happiness realize this and continue to worship Śiva" (Śiva Purāṇa 18.62). Although it is actually sincere and deliberate action that is being promoted in the Purāṇas, unintentional action is undoubtedly recognized as being efficacious. Another Purāṇic text filled with much detailed information and instruction about the performance of ritual worship is the Liṅga Purāṇa. Although its primary function is also to promote the intentional performance of such worship, it too states: "If even those who are devoid of devotion incidentally (*prasaṅgāt*) worship the Lord, he bestows fruits upon them."[10] The power of intentionality is acknowledged as being important in the Purāṇas, but it is clearly regarded as secondary to physical action; these are stories about transformation regardless of knowledge or motive.

The Efficacy of Physical Acts

How might we better understand the efficacy of physical actions disassociated from intentionality? Despite their aim, Guṇanidhi, Sundara Senaka, Caṇḍa, Gurudruha, and Ajāmila all performed actions identical to intentional ritualists. Although the motives differ between intentional ritualists and accidental ritualists, it is important to recognize that their actions are similar. In a previous work, I examined the relationship between what is called an *anubhāva* and *sādhana* in Indian religious culture (Haberman 1988). *Anubhāva* is a technical Sanskrit term drawn from the classical dramatic tradition; it means the natural expression of some inner state (*bhāva*). *Sādhana* is an intentional act designed to achieve a transformation of one's inner state, often understood as the imitation of the *anubhāvas* of some perfected being. Discussions of Rāgānugā Bhakti Sādhana, first articulated by Rūpa Gosvāmin in his *Bhaktirasāmṛtasindhu*—a work based primarily on Vaiṣṇava Purāṇas—and further elaborated upon by his nephew Jīva Gosvāmin and others, include examination of the intimate relationship between these two types of action and can serve as an example of one kind of thinking about the nature of ritual that exists within Indian thought rooted in the Purāṇas.

Rāgānugā Bhakti Sādhana is a form of practice that aims to achieve an ultimate religious world by intentionally imitating the behavior of perfected beings who inhabit that world. Specifically it is a *sādhana* that is designed to attain residence in Kṛṣṇa's blissful land of Vraja by imitating the *anubhāvas* of the perfected beings of that realm, the Vrajaloka, whose actions are available in Vaiṣṇava literature, especially the Bhāgavata Purāṇa. A common Hindu ritual adage is "Thus the gods did; thus men do."[11] In his commentary on the *Bhaktirasāmṛtasindhu*, Gosvāmin (1962, 1.3.1) indicates that the *anubhāva* and *sādhana* are two sides of the same coin; they differ in motive but have the same physical form.[12] That is, to the degree that it is successful, *sādhana* is action that conforms to the *anubhāva* form of action exhibited by the perfected Vrajaloka. Thus what is being expressed here is the idea that the way to religious perfection is through physical actions. Engaging one's body in disciplined imitative action is deemed to be transformative. Although he too promotes intentional action, Gosvāmin affirms the transformative power of physical action in his discussion of Rāgānugā Bhakti Sādhana by highlighting how the demoness Pūtanā achieved the highest goal by imitating (*anukāra*) a wet nurse for Kṛṣṇa (by suckling him at her breast, though her intention was to kill him with poison). Gosvāmin writes: "Scripture tells that a state similar to the state of those who possess Rāgātmikā Bhakti (the perfected ideal) may be obtained by means of mere imitation (*anukaraṇa*), even with bad intention. There is the case of Pūtanā's imitation of a wet nurse. How much more easily could this occur by conforming to a constant and complete *bhakti*" (1962, 322).[13]

While the main thrust of my argument is that taking seriously the theorizing about ritual within ritual texts augments our understanding of ritual, it is also expedient to recognize that implicit theories of ritual found in Western reflection on the nature of action may provide support to Purāṇic claims about ritual action. The effectiveness of physical acting has been insightfully explored in the West, for example, by the Russian theorist of dramatic acting, Constantin Stanislavski, who discovered intimate connections between internal mental states and external physical actions. Stanislavski defined the subconscious as the uncontrolled inner mental world and the conscious as the external world of controlled actions. Arguing in opposition to Freud, who stressed that the subconscious influences the conscious, Stanislavski asserted with the support of his friend Ivan Pavlov that the conscious can influence the subconscious or that external actions can influence inner mental states (Stanislavski 1946, 14–15). This was an extremely important breakthrough for Stanislavski, since his method of acting rests on the claim that an actor's success depends upon the ability to "turn on" inner mental states in such a way that they are in harmony with those of the character being portrayed. Perhaps Stanislavski's greatest contribution was his assertion that the inner world of the subconscious could be transformed through the external world of physical actions. "Thus physical actions are the 'key' that lets the actor penetrate the inner world of the character portrayed" (Simonov 1973, 41).

Stanislavski maintained that the inner world of human beings is expressed physically. This was also supported by the leading Russian scientists of his day. "The thesis of Stanislavski that the complex of human's psychological life—moods, desires, feelings, intentions, ambitions, for example—is expressed through simple physical actions has been confirmed by such scientists as Pavlov and I. M. Sechenov" (Moore 1965, 22). Thus access to the inner world of another, Stanislavski tells us, is through the other's external physical expressions; it is with the body that interior mental states are both expressed and accessed. Stanislavski informed his actors that the inner life of a character is approached by imitating the physical acts of that character. The anger of a particular character, for example, is realized by imitating the physical expressions of that particular character's anger, for example, pounding fists on the table. This he called the "Method of Physical Actions."

The goal of such intentional imitative action is to "live the role," that is, to take on the mental world of the character being imitated. "The very best that can happen is to have the actor completely carried away by the play" (Stanislavski 1946, 13). Stanislavski believed that through perfected acting technique an actor could totally identify with the disposition of the character being portrayed. This is the experience he called "re-incarnation." "An actor achieves re-incarnation when he achieves the truthful behavior of the character, when his actions are interwoven with words and thoughts, when he has searched for all the necessary traits of a given character, when he surrounds himself with its given circumstances and becomes so accustomed to them that he does not know where his own personality leaves off and that of the character begins" (Moore 1965, 22).

The whole of Stanislavski's research demonstrates that an actor can actually achieve the inner world of a character by imitating that character's physical actions. He asserted that inner experience is reproducible and that it is accessible through physical actions. Stanislavski considered the experience of reincarnation the height of the actor's art and argued that this experience has a tremendous effect on the life of an actor.[14] Although the Purāṇas are concerned with ontological transformations in addition to mental transformations, Stanislavski's insights lend themselves to supporting an understanding of how intentional physical imitative action might function in a transformative way. A similar notion seems to inform much Hindu *sādhana*. Physical acts are understood to have certain positive effects on one's inner mental state. A well-known teacher of yoga *sādhana* put it this way: "The relationship between mind and body is complete and so subtle that it is no wonder that certain physical training will induce certain mental transformations" (Sivananda 1978, 70). Ritual action, then, can be seen as a series of physical actions designed to guide the practitioner into a specific way of being.

Intentional and Unintentional Actions

This may be true for intentional imitative behavior, but what about unintentional or accidental action? The Purāṇas are filled with prolific discussion of the benefits of intentional ritual action, and those who discuss Rāgānugā Bhakti Sādhana articulate an Indian way of thinking about the effectiveness of intentional imitative behavior. While these discussions of *sādhana* are concerned with intentional imitative behavior, there is nothing in them that precludes the possible effectiveness of unintentional imitative action. What might stories such as those featuring Guṇanidhi, Sundara Senaka, Caṇḍa, Gurudruha, and Ajāmila add to a consideration of the effectiveness of ritual actions? It seems to me that being located among more abundant discussions about the effectiveness of intentional ritual action, these stories function to provide even more radical affirmation of the transformative power of physical action. By divorcing physical imitative action from intentionality, these stories serve to stress that physical action itself is the key to the transformative experience in ritual performance. Otherwise why assert that accidental rituals work? Getting the body in specific motion is what is most important. Yama instructs his deadly attendants in the Guṇanidhi story of the Śiva Purāṇa: "Do not bother those persons who imitate the behavior of a worshiper of Śiva. Never bring them here. Do not bother those persons who imitate the behavior of a worshiper of Śiva, even if they are faking it (*dambhenāpi*) or pretending (*chalenāpi*). Never bring them here" (Śiva Purāṇa 18.48–49). Physical imitative action itself is what is clearly endorsed, regardless of motive.

Within the Purāṇas, then, the exemplary expression of actions by perfected beings that serve as the models for much ritual action, the intentional imitation of these exemplary actions, and the accidental imitation of these exemplary actions are all connected. Although these three types of action differ in motive, they all result in the same action. If intentional ritual or imitative action has the ability to achieve the inner state of perfection, and if physical action is the agent of transformation, then accidental ritual action can also achieve an inner state of perfection. Stories about accidental ritualists, then, function to emphasize the point that physical action is the key to achieving the desired inner state in ritual performance.

Moving this into a more explicit theory of ritual, the Purāṇas seem to be asserting bodily action over thought (knowledge or intentionality) as the key transformative element in ritual. Many Western theories of ritual contend that ritual has a great deal to do with thought (for example, consciously imitating a myth), and although the Purāṇas support this contention to some extent, the stories I present here are about ritual performers who have no idea what they are doing. Yet still the rituals are said to succeed. Accounts of the success of intentional ritual performances might leave one in doubt regarding the transformative agent in ritual. Narrations of accidental ritualists, however, clearly distinguish physical action from intentionality and identify the former as the transformative agent. The emphasis on physical action over thought affirms an understanding of Hinduism as being more concerned with orthopraxy than orthodoxy. If this is the case, then the theory of ritual operative in the Purāṇas is continuous with Vedic ritual concerns and notions about the proper performance of the sacrifice, in which accurate ritual performance was assumed to yield a tremendous power on its own—a power that could even control the gods. Regardless of what one thinks, it is what one *does* that determines the success of ritual performance.

Conclusion

The Purāṇas, then, appear to be in agreement with Catherine Bell, who follows Pierre Bourdieu in arguing that "we can speak of the natural logic of ritual, a logic embodied in the physical movements of the body and thereby lodged beyond the grasp of consciousness and articulation. . . . In other words, the molding of the body within a highly structured environment does not simply express inner states. Rather, it primarily acts to restructure bodies in the very doing of the acts themselves. Hence, required kneeling does not only merely communicate subordination to the kneeler. For all intents and purposes, kneeling produces a subordinated kneeler in and through the act itself" (Bell 1992, 99–100). These Purāṇic accounts add to Bell's point by placing a weighty emphasis on the fortuitous and, by so doing, laying even greater emphasis on the physical performance of rituals and causing us to ponder the efficacy of bodily acts completely divorced from any intention. The Purāṇas assert—in narrative form—that ritual is indeed transformative and, beyond that, go on to identify the key agent of ritual transformation to be physical action itself. Accidental ritualists may be lost with regard to knowledge and intentionality, but in the Purāṇas they achieve the desired goal nonetheless, and in so doing give us much to think about when considering the nature of ritual performance.

Notes

1. I have in mind recent experiments with ritual construction in contemporary eco-spirituality, neo-paganism, and some forms of Christianity. See, for example, discussion of the Council of All Beings in Seed et al. 1988; various books by Starhawk, including *The Earth Path* (2004) and her most popular book, *The Spiral Dance* (1999); and Fox 1991.

2. Although the nature of the tension is understood differently, others also affirm a tension-reducing view of ritual. Jonathan Smith has contributed relevant statements about ritual along these lines. In his study of the Ainu bear ritual, he asserts that ritual functions to reduce the ideological tension between the way things are and the way things ought to be. "Ritual is a means of performing the way things ought to be in conscious tension to the way things are" (1982, 63). For Smith, like Turner, ritual functions to reduce tensions, although in this case the tensions are ideological rather than social. The Ainu bear ritual does not change anything, according to Smith; instead it provides an aid to acknowledging that ideal change is not possible in the real world. One might add to this discussion Freud's view of ritual as being a form of obsessive neurosis that functions to reduce psychological tensions associated with certain kinds of anxiety caused by unconscious factors. Far from being transformative, ritual for Freud is actually entrenching. See Freud 1950.

3. For an English translation, see Shastri 1970, part 1, 255–65.

4. This is the aniconic stone form in which Śiva is most typically worshiped in a temple.

5. For an English translation, see Tagare 1970, part 1, 375–77.

6. For an English translation, see Deshpande 1991, part 8, 2874–76.

7. For an English translation, see Shastri 1991, part 3, 1431–39.

8. The story of Ajāmila is found in the first two chapters of the sixth book of the Bhāgavata Purāṇa.

9. See chapter 193. An English translation of the description of this ritual is found in Gangadharan 1985, part 1, 517–18.

10. *Liṅga Purāṇa* 1973, part 1, 389.

11. Eliade's (1954, 21) citation of the Taittirīya Brāhmaṇa.

12. See Haberman 1998, 69.

13. For further discussion see Haberman 1998, 78.

14. This contention has subsequently been substantiated by numerous actors. See, for example, the interviews with Method actors in Funke and Booth 1961.

References

Bell, Catherine. 1992. *Ritual Theory, Ritual Practice.* New York: Oxford University Press.

Bhattacharya, Ramshankar, ed. 1964. *Garuḍapurāṇa.* Varanasi: Chowkhamba Sanskrit Series Office.

Campany, Robert F. 1996. "Xunzi and Durkheim as Theorists of Ritual Practice." In *Readings in Ritual Studies,* edited by Ronald L. Grimes, 86–103. Upper Saddle River, N.J.: Prentice Hall.

Deshpande, N. A., trans. 1991. *Padma Purāṇa.* Delhi: Motilal Banarsidass.

Eliade, Mircea. 1954. *The Myth of the Eternal Return.* Princeton: Princeton University Press.

Fox, Matthew. 1991. *Creation Spirituality: Liberating Gifts for the People of the Earth.* San Francisco: Harper.

Freud, Sigmund. 1950. "Obsessive Acts and Religious Practices." In *Collected Papers,* vol. 2, translated by Alix and James Strachey, 25–35. London: Hogarth.

Funke, Lewis, and John E. Booth, eds. 1961. *Actors Talk about Acting.* New York: Random House.

Gangadharan, N., trans. 1985. *Agni Purāṇa.* Delhi: Motilal Banarsidass.

Geertz, Clifford. 1973. *The Interpretation of Cultures: Selected Essays.* New York: Basic Books.

Gosvāmin, Jīva. 1962. *Bhakti Sandarbha.* Edited with Bengali translation by Rādhāraman Gosvāmī Vedāntabhīṣan and Kṛṣṇagopāla Gosvāmī. Calcutta: University of Calcutta.

Haberman, David L. 1988. *Acting as a Way of Salvation: A Study of Rāgānugā Bhakti Sādhana.* New York: Oxford University Press.

Liṅga Purāṇa. 1973. Translated by a board of scholars. Delhi: Motilal Banarsidass.

Moore, Sonia. 1965. *The Stanislavski System.* New York: Penguin Books.

Rocher, Ludo. 1986. *The Purāṇas.* Edited by Jan Gonda. Vol. 2 of *A History of Indian Literature.* Wiesbaden: Harrassowitz.

Seed, John, Joanna Macy, Pat Fleming, and Arne Naess. 1988. *Thinking Like a Mountain: Towards a Council of All Beings.* Philadelphia: New Society Press.

Shastri, J. L., trans. 1970. *Śiva Purāṇa.* Delhi: Motilal Banarsidass.

Simonov, P. V. 1973. "The Method of K. S. Stanislavski and the Physiology of Emotion." In *Stanislavski Today,* edited by Sonia Moore, 34–43. New York: American Center for Stanislavski Theatre Art.

Singh, Nag Sharan, ed. 1981. *The Śiva Mahāpurāṇa.* Delhi: Nag.

Sivananda, Swami. 1978. *Practical Lessons in Yoga.* Rishikesh: Divine Life Society.

Smith, Jonathan Z. 1982. *Imagining Religion: From Babylon to Jonestown.* Chicago: University of Chicago Press.

Stanislavski, Constantin. 1946. *An Actor Prepares.* Trans. Elizabeth R. Hapgood. New York: Theatre Arts.

Starhawk. 1999. *The Spiral Dance.* San Francisco: Harper.

——. 2004. *The Earth Path.* San Francisco: Harper.

Tagare, G. V., trans. 1970. *Garuḍa Purāṇa.* Vols. 12–14 of *Ancient Indian Tradition and Mythology.* Delhi: Motilal Banarsidass.

Turner, Victor W. 1977. *The Ritual Process: Structure and Anti-structure.* Ithaca: Cornell University Press.

Ritual as Dharma

The Narrowing and Widening of a Key Term

ALF HILTEBEITEL

In the early 1980s, while I was preparing an article for publication, it was suggested to me that I was perhaps a little too eager to run several rituals through one processual scheme.[1] In this essay I try to do something that looks to be more or less the opposite: that is, question a scheme through which others have run a number of rituals. There are differences in the generative sources of these schemes. The one I was using came from the anthropologist Victor Turner, then at the University of Chicago, from his book *Dramas, Fields, and Metaphors* (1974, 23–155, esp. 37–42), and involved interpreting ritual through a pattern of breach, crisis, redressive action, and resolution (Hiltebeitel 1982); the one I wish to address here comes from India and has to do with interpreting dharma as ritual action. In Turner's scheme the "root metaphor" of social drama provides a model for interpreting ritual; in the scheme I wish to address in this essay, ritual is the model invoked for interpreting dharma. But as we shall see, dharma itself, in certain aspects, might be interpreted as a root metaphor and even as something akin to Turner's four-phase model. I thus do not intend these comments to suggest dissatisfaction with theoretical models. But whether ritual is the model or the modeled, the need to think carefully about the schemas we use to interpret it is always a good caution.

I begin with the equation often made between dharma and karma as ritual action and argue that it is misleading to derive this equation from the earliest uses of the term *dhárman*, from which the concept and word *dharma* derive. I then call attention to three much ignored or overlooked splits in the ways that activities are ascribed to different castes and personages within them. One split models the assignment of *svakarmas* ("their own jobs") to Brahmans while other classes are assigned *svadharmas* ("their own laws" or "duties"), thereby reserving priestly offices for Brahmans. A second split applies within the Kṣatriya or warrior class between the *svadharmas* of warriors and those of kings, whereby a self-sacrificial ideology is prescribed mainly for the former around the idea of "desireless action." And a third split is found between the usages of the term *karmayoga* in the

Bhagavad Gītā and the Laws of Manu: the Gītā to describe this "desireless action" of the self-sacrificing Kṣatriya; the Laws of Manu to describe Vedic "ritual usage" as inevitably including desire. I attempt to bring this discussion together by tracing these threads to the point where, I hope, they confer some new and differential light on the roles of Brahmans, kings, and Kṣatriyas in the ritualization of war and violence.

The "First Foundations" of Ritual

In a 2004 essay in a *Journal of Indian Philosophy* double issue dedicated to the subject of dharma, Joel Brereton attempts to set the terms for a "reevaluation of the history of *dharma*" around an interpretation of Ṛgvedic usages of *dhárman* as meaning "foundation." This is a root metaphor if there ever was one, since the hymns refer to *dhárman* not only as a "foundation" below but also a celestial "foundation" above or in thought (for example, Ṛgveda [ṚV] 3.38.2; 5.15.2; 5.63.1; 5.69.1; 9.86.8–9; 9.97.12). If one considers that the universe is conceived of in Bhagavad Gītā 15.1–3 as an inverted tree with roots above and that this image itself has Upaniṣadic precedent (Kaṭha Upaniṣad 6.1), one might relate such an enigmatic understanding of *dhárman* to the Mahābhārata allegory that compares "Duryodhana made of wrath (*manyumayo*)" and "Yudhiṣṭhira made of dharma (*dharmamayo*)" as each a "great tree," with others on their sides as each tree's crotch, branches, flowers, and roots (Mahābhārata [Mbh] 1.1.65–66). The Duryodhana tree is rooted in Duryodhana's blind and wavering father, Dhṛtarāṣṭra; the Yudhiṣṭhira tree is rooted in Kṛṣṇa, *brahman,* and Brahmans. For the Mahābhārata, and one could say for the Bhagavad Gītā, the dharma embodied in Yudhiṣṭhira has its foundation and roots in this transcendent source.

Brereton begins with several important observations. "Since *dhárman* is a developing term in *Rigveda,* its meaning reflects directly its etymology and form. And, happily, the formation of *dhárman* is transparent. It is derived from √*dhṛ* 'uphold, support, give foundation to' and a *-man* suffix. Therefore, it denotes a thing that upholds or supports, or, more simply, a 'foundation.' The word *dharmán,* a noun of agent, then designates an 'upholder' or 'foundation-giver'" (Brereton 2004, 450). Sixty-three usages of *dhárman* and four of *dharmán* is "not a small number," but "this relatively modest frequency of *dhárman* nonetheless implies that it was not a central term in the Rigvedic lexicon or in Indian culture of the Rigvedic period" (449). Yet even if not central, "*dhárman* is thoroughly established in the text, since the word is attested in all its chronological levels," with "increasing frequency in the younger layers" (450). Moreover, unlike Ṛgvedic *ṛta* (truth) and *vratá* (commandment), which *are* "central" and, with their Avestan cognates, point back to "significant roles in the old Indo-Iranian religious vocabulary," *dhárman,* at least in its Ṛgvedic meanings, does not have such a prehistory.

For Brereton this means that in contrast to the other two terms, "the discussion of *dhárman* can reasonably begin with the *Rigveda*" (449). Indeed, setting the old cognate *firmus* aside, it would seem that we could also suspect that *dhárman* could be a Ṛgvedic coinage.

Brereton's interpretation is thoroughgoing, new, and productive. I do not wish to illustrate it here with many of the passages he treats. But one is crucial: ṚV 10.90.16, the last verse of the famous "Puruṣasūkta," or hymn to Puruṣa, which attributes the creation of the universe to the sacrifice and dismemberment of this cosmic "Male." This is a late Ṛgvedic hymn, one that is transitional for being what Michael Witzel has called "the first constitution of India," defining "Kuru orthopraxy" for the late Vedic Kuru state that combined the completion of the Ṛgveda Saṃhitā with the early collection of the other three Vedas during the post-Ṛgveda "mantra period" (Witzel 1997, 36, 51).

Now it can be noticed that verses mentioning *dhárman* often occur at the beginning and/or the end of hymns. Its placement in the last verse of ṚV 10.90 can hardly be accidental. The same exact verse also occurs as the fifty-second of fifty-four verses in the much more rambling ṚV 1.164 (the riddle-laced "Asya vāmasya" hymn), from which 10.90 probably lifts it into its much more memorably structured slot (Houben 2000, 524–25; Horsch 2004, 444n20). ṚV 10.90's earlier verses can thus be reviewed from the standpoint of the "foundations" proclaimed at its end: "With the sacrifice the gods sacrificed the sacrifice: these were the first foundations (*dhármāṇi*), / and those, its greatnesses, follow to heaven's vault, where exist the ancient ones who are to be attained, the gods" (ṚV 10.90.16; trans. Brereton 2004, 460).

Brereton takes this verse as emblematic of the poets' concern not only that *dhárman* be a foundation for heaven and earth and the gods, but also "that the ritual itself have a foundation" (2004, 459–60). Thus "the 'first *dhárman*s' are the model sacrifice instituted by the gods and replicated in human performance, and as such, they are the 'foundations' for the ritual performance" (460)—itself described in the verse's paradoxical first line that uses three derivatives of ✓*yaj* to suggest that Puruṣa is both the sacrificial victim and the means by which the sacrificial process of the gods who sacrificed him is set in motion (although Brereton says it might also just mean that the gods "sacrificed again and again" [460; cf. Horsch 2004, 428]).

Brereton's translation of *dhárman* as "foundations" is especially lucid here, and preferable, as he notes, to "ordinances," "institutes," or "laws"; for as Brereton says, in the Ṛgveda "the ritual was varied and fluid" (467). This makes the translation "foundations" especially preferable to "ritual laws"—Wendy Doniger O'Flaherty's translation (1981, 31), which has misled Rupert Gethin's attempt to link the famous Buddhist meaning of dharmas in the plural (meaning phenomena, mental events, or regularities in that context) back to this verse (2004, 531). Among the "first foundations" that ṚV 10.90 sets is "the 'official' establishment of the four social classes (*varṇa*)" of the Brahman or priest from Puruṣa's mouth, the Rājanya or nobility from his arms, the Vaiśya or people from his thighs, and the Śūdra or serving class from his feet (verse 12). It thus comes to serve as a charter for "increasing social stratification," with cooperation between the armed nobility and a Brahman class that now cuts across and unifies the older clans of poet-priests; the "joint power" of these two upper classes over the Vaiśya; and further internal *varṇa* division between Ārya and Śūdra (Witzel 1997, 267).

Moreover ṚV 10.90 says nothing that would either ground kingship itself in the "first foundations" or the "first *dhármans*" in kingship. It just mentions the nobility as a class from which kings would presumably come and shows its subordination to the Brahman class not only by asserting the Rājanyas' second position but also by saying in verse 13 that Indra and Agni come from the mouth of Puruṣa just after the Brahman came from Puruṣa's mouth in verse 12. (One wants to say the *same* mouth, but Puruṣa has a thousand heads.) This priority might suggest that even if Indra and possibly Agni participate as divine kings (which is not clear) in implementing the sacrificial "first foundations," they would do so on the precedent of the sacred speech that the prior birth of the Brahman makes possible, and Indra in particular would do so by association with the purifying ritual fire.

We may thus say that Ṛgvedic *dhárman* does not refer to "law" or "laws," or "ritual laws," but is a term by which the Ṛgvedic poets describe "foundations," including but not limited to the foundations of sacrificial ritual. Nor does it refer to ritually instituted acts. But we can see the possibility of smuggling later notions of ritual action into readings of the Vedic *dhárman,* especially in this hymn where it could be taken to imply the "ritual laws" or "institutes" of the four classes. William Mahoney (as one example among many) extends such a back-reading to other *earlier* Ṛgvedic verses. He argues, "In early Vedic texts *dharman* refers to an established or proper mode of conduct that supports or helps maintain the continuing health of the world. According to one such visionary [referring to the poet of ṚV 6.70.1], for example, it was through Varuṇa's *performance of his dharman* that the sky was raised above the land. . . . The Vedic idea of *dharman* stands as precedent for the later idea of *dharma* as *responsible, proper activity that supports the world*" (Mahoney 1998, 107; emphasis added). Similarly Mahoney translates *dhárman* as "support, proper conduct" (49–50) and as "established rites" in 5.26.6 and "proper ritual performance" in 8.43.24 and considers it "closely associated with" *karman* (108).

Surely these nuances are projected back into the Ṛgveda, probably from the Bhagavad Gītā: "performance of his *dharman*" looks like a transparent back-reading of the Gītā's notion of *svadharma,* one's "own duty," meaning nothing else—as we shall see—than the duties pertinent to one's social class (*varṇa*). Along with the whole first sentence, "responsible, proper activity that supports the world," which is supposed to gloss the early Vedic meaning, is a restatement of the Gītā's notion of *lokasaṃgraha*, action (*karman*) done "for the welfare of the world" (Bhagavad Gītā [BhG] 3.20). This is said by Kṛṣṇa both to gloss his prior Gītā teaching of dharma as *svadharma* (2.31 and 33) and to set things up for his famous pronouncement to the great warrior-prince Arjuna: "Better one's own duty (*svadharma*), (tho) imperfect, than another's duty (*paradharma*) well performed; better death in (doing) one's own duty, another's duty brings danger" (3.35; trans. Edgerton 1952, 39). The inappropriateness of such a reading of Ṛgvedic verses should be apparent. Rather than importing notions like this into the Vedic past, it behooves us to see how new classical concepts construct dharma as ritual on this fluid Vedic foundation.

Svadharma and *Svakarma*

The compound *svadharman* has one occurrence in the Ṛgveda at ṚV 3.21.2b, where it would seem (following Brereton's translation of *dhárman*) to ask that Agni from "his own foundation"—no doubt fire itself—bestow (✓*dhā*) what is best "for us" that is acceptable to the gods. In the Śrautasūtras, according to Patrick Olivelle, *svadharma* has a specialized meaning when it refers to instances where "a particular rite has its own ritual details (*dharmas*) specific to it and not taken over from or extended to other rites" (Olivelle 2004a, 502). The ground may thus be set for *svadharma* as "own ritual details" to be applied in later Brahmanic texts to the personal "duties particular to" groups and individuals.[2] This Śrautasūtra usage of *svadharma* is probably pre-Buddhist. Meanwhile early Buddhists—perhaps wary of the implications of *self* and *ownership* in such terms—do not use the term. As Richard Gombrich says of Buddhist criticism of this "Hindu notion," "Buddhists do not even have the term *svadharma* (Pali **sadhamma*)" (1985, 436). Indeed its one appearance in Aśvaghoṣa's Buddhacarita puts the term into the mouth of the devil when Māra, fingering an arrow (Buddhacarita 13.8), starts challenging the Bodhisattva's right to sit beneath the *bodhi* tree: "9. Up, up, Sir Kṣatriya, afraid of death. Follow your own *dharma* (*cara svadharmam*), give up the *dharma* of liberation (*tyaja mokṣadharmam*). Subdue the world with both arrows and sacrifices, and from the world obtain the world of Vāsava" (trans. Johnston 2004, 189–90).[3] Aśvaghoṣa's usage of *svadharma* would seem to parody Kṛṣṇa's promptings of Arjuna in the Bhagavad Gītā (see Hiltebeitel 2006, 273).

As far as I can see, then, the term *svadharma* gets its first workout, together with *svakarma*, in the Dharmasūtras, where a kind of semantic drift between the two terms is set in motion; and the two are then further developed as governing paradigms in the Laws of Manu (henceforth Manu) and the Mahābhārata, where they are sometimes harnessed to varying notions of *karmayoga*. In the Dharmasūtras we may begin to notice a pattern that Manu and the Mahābhārata only reinforce. The Brahman authors of the three earliest Dharmasūtras (Āpastamba Dharmasūtra, hereafter Ā; Baudhāyana Dharmasūtra, hereafter B; Gautama Dharmasūtra, hereafter G) use the term *svadharma* mainly to prescribe or "legislate," as it were, what is generally appropriate and to be enforced (by the king or the karmic mechanism of reincarnation) for all the social classes and *āśramas* (life stages or patterns).[4] But their particular targets in prescribing *svadharma* are the classes below the Brahman (Ā 1.18.3)—especially the Kṣatriya and still more singularly the king.

This looks fairly straightforward, but it is less so than it appears. When the same Brahman authors speak specifically of themselves and the privileges and occupations reserved for them, they do not use the term *svadharma*. Rather they prefer the term *svakarma*, thereby speaking of their "own actions" or "activities" or "own occupations" rather than their "own dharma." And when they speak of other classes' "appropriate actions" or "occupations" (*svakarmas*) instead of their *svadharma*, they seem to do so where the activities of such others would impact directly upon Brahmans, as with what Brahmans can eat that others might offer (G 17.1; B 1.3.17–18) or where occupations reserved for Brahmans set the paradigm for what other classes may and may not do. Thus Āpastamba, before its author lists the occupations of the two Ārya castes below the Brahman (in Ā 2.10.6–7), defines those reserved for the Brahman. "The occupations specific to a Brahman (*svakarma brāhmaṇasya*) are studying, teaching, sacrificing, officiating at sacrifices, giving gifts, receiving gifts, inheriting, and gleaning, as well as appropriating things that do not belong to anybody" (4–5). While the last three of these nine "occupations specific to a Brahman" are idiosyncratic to Āpastamba, the other six become standard and are set off in pairs that distinguish the second of each pair (teaching, officiating at sacrifices, and receiving gifts [referring to honoraria at sacrifices]) as reserved only for Brahmans, while the first members of each pair (studying, sacrificing, and giving gifts) are suitable for all three twice-born or Ārya classes and thus for Kṣatriyas and Vaiśyas as well.[5] The overall implication, as I see it, is that the *svakarma* of Brahmans defines the "archetype" or default position of dharma, usually without mentioning the term *dharma*, for all Āryas, with only the unremunerative half of their "own actions" or "occupations" being appropriate for Kṣatriyas and Vaiśyas. Meanwhile in this passage from Āpastamba, "the Śūdra is purely and simply eliminated, or perhaps there is nothing new to say as regards *varṇa* concerning him" (Biardeau 2002, 1, 77). Oddly enough, Biardeau says the passage concerns itself with "a Brahman's *dharma*," but surprisingly that term is not even used with regard to Brahmans (1, 77).

Yet the Brahmans' *svakarma* does of course provide those below them with an archetype that models the *svadharma* of Kṣatriyas above all, and others below them, on sacrificial ritual. And among Kṣatriyas the pivotal figure for whom and through whom the Dharmasūtra authors begin to legislate dharma is the king. Gautama Dharmasūtra has a fine passage on this subject, out from which Manu and the Mahābhārata might be said to build:

> The king rules over all except Brahmans. He should be correct in his actions and speech and trained in the triple Veda and logic (*ānvīkṣikī*). Let him be upright [or pure, clean (*śuci*)] [cf. G 9.2, 9.12], keep his senses under control, surround himself with men of quality [have companions who possess *guṇas*: *guṇavat sahāya*], and adopt sound policies (*upāya-sampannaḥ*). He should be impartial to all his subjects and work for their welfare. As he sits on a high seat, all except Brahmans should pay him homage seated at a lower level, and even Brahmans should honor him. He should watch over (*abhirakṣet*) the social classes and the orders of life in conformity with their rules (*nyāyatas*), and those who stray (*calatas*) he should guide back to their respective duties [that is, to their *svadharma*, singular], "for the king," it is stated, "takes a share of their merits (*dharma*)." He should appoint as his personal priest a Brahman who is learned, born in a good family, eloquent, handsome, mature, and virtuous (*śīlasampannam*); who lives according to the rules (*nyāyavṛttam*); and who is austere. He should undertake rites (*karmāṇi*) only with his support, "for a Kṣatriya, when he is supported by a Brahman," it is said, "prospers and never falters." (G 11.1–14)

On the one hand, the king should keep his own senses under control, implying the mastery of virtues that have come by the time of the late Upaniṣads to be associated with yoga, and he should reap the "merit" (*dharma*) that comes from seeing to it that the social classes and orders of life do not stray from their *svadharma*. It is, of course, thereby implied that all the classes and life stages have their *svadharma*, but the focus is on the king's reaping that "cumulative *svadharma*" as merit for himself. There is nothing more precise on the king's dharma than that it concerns what he earns by watching over others and himself, which implicitly includes letting Brahmans advise him and do his rites (*karmāṇi*).

This role of the king in dealing with those who "stray" (✓*cal*) is presented even more starkly in Manu, where it is a question specifically of the king's need to apply punishment or "the rod of force" (*daṇḍa*) (which Gautama deals with subjacently) (11.28–32). "It is the fear of him that makes all beings, both the mobile and the immobile, accede to being used (*bhogāya kalpante:* literally, being enjoyed, eaten) and to not deviate (✓*cal*) from the Law proper to them (*svadharmāt:* from their *svadharma*)" (Manu 7.15). On the other hand, the Brahmans with whom he should surround himself as advisers have more innately defined "qualities," or *guṇas*, which entitle them to their *svakarma*. In so far as Brahmans have an implied or largely unstated dharma or *svadharma*, it is to be "qualified" innately.[6]

Indeed Manu exerts considerable energy in showing through six widening iterations how *guas* correlate with reincarnation and the "fruits of action" (12.24–50). (Kṛṣṇa, as will be noted, will override such a distinction between attained and innate qualities by defining *svadharma* as *svabhāva*.)

I cannot treat here the considerable number of passages where Manu follows suit in speaking mainly of Brahman karma and *svakarma* around the issue of jobs and of dharma and *svadharma* as legislated mainly for others, particularly Kṣatriyas and kings.[7] In contrast there are only a few scattered passages where the texts speak of Brahman *svadharma* (Manu 4.2–4; Mbh 13.131.8). And I find very little, despite what has been written on these subjects, to clarify any further the *svadharma* of kings or to suggest that women have a *svadharma* other than their *strīdharma* to marry, be faithful, and have children.[8] There is even less to suggest that there is a *svadharma* of demons or of the gods who oversee the cosmic processes of creation, maintenance, and destruction (see O'Flaherty 1976, 68; Hill 2001, 104–6). And most telling, there is nothing at all about *svadharmas* for mixed classes or for those outside the system, such as the heterodox naysayers or *nāstikas* (actually, as we have seen, the Buddhists seem to have preferred to do without the concept) and the barbarians or *mlecchas*.

The Laws of Manu and the Bhagavad Gītā: Two Kinds of *Karmayoga*

This brings us to a concept used in both Manu and the Mahābhārata. *Karmayoga* has a single usage in the Dharmasūtras, where, in Olivelle's translation, it means "ritual use" when Āpastamba says, "The suspension of vedic recitation laid down in the vedic texts refers to vedic recitation and not the *ritual use* of vedic formulas (*na karmayoge mantrāṇām*)" (1.12.9). Otherwise, as far as I can see, if *svadharma* and *svakarma* get their first workouts together in the Dharmasūtras and are then more fully developed as governing paradigms in Manu and the Mahābhārata, *karmayoga* is a term that gets its first real workout in Manu and the Mahābhārata as a concept by which each of these texts ties these paradigms to certain (but by no means all) formulations of their higher purpose. In Manu these formulations are concentrated in its final and most "philosophical" chapter, the twelfth, on the fruits of action and the process of reincarnation. In the Mahābhārata they are concentrated almost exclusively in the Bhagavad Gītā, while the Rāmāyaṇa has one curious instance describing Hanumān as *svakarmayogaṃ ca vidhāya*, which Goldman and Goldman (1996, 241) translate as "settling into his own plan of action" (Rāmāyaṇa [Rām] 5.45.30).

To read just translations of these texts, one would never gather that they are rendering the same term. Although Manu certainly does have a distinctive take on *karmayoga*, it almost seems that its translators have rendered the term in ways that would avoid suspicion that they were contaminating Manu by a Gītā reading.

But clearly it is the same term, and I think the usages in the two texts probably have some kind of relation to each other in the pivotal ways they position the concept. (I favor the slight priority of the Mahābhārata.) In both texts one can easily tie in the usages of *karmayoga* with those of *svadharma* and *svakarma* as they relate to theories of ritual and ideologies of sacrifice centered on the Brahman, the Kṣatriya, or the king; but the theory and ideology differ in each text. In each case *karmayoga* is clustered with a different range of concepts, about which I have to be somewhat brief.

In the Gītā, as is well known, *karmayoga* is taught by a Kṣatriya deity of an emergent *bhakti* tradition. As far as the text is concerned, Kṛṣṇa is God himself as the ultimate *karmayogin,* and he imparts the Gītā to another Kṣatriya.[9] Here *karmayoga* is arrayed with the two other yogas or "disciplines" of *jñānayoga* and *bhaktiyoga. Karmayoga* involves *niṣkāma-karma,* or "action without the desire for its fruits," that is, "unattached (*asakta*) action or karma" that is "devoid of the intention (*saṃkalpa*)"—a key term in both texts—to achieve a ritually defined "desire." And *svadharma* and *svakarma* are explained against this background but compounded by the additional concept of *svabhāva,* "inherent nature." That is, according to Kṛṣṇa, doing one's duty and occupations properly springs ultimately from one's "intrinsic," "innate," or "inherent nature."

Moreover, of all the places in the Mahābhārata that present extensive mixed discussions of *svadharma* with *svakarma,*[10] the Gītā presents the only case where these terms are compounded by this additional "inherent" grounding, which is ultimately a grounding in Kṛṣṇa's lower nature or *prakṛti.* In the key passage (BhG 18.41–47), Kṛṣṇa teaches that confusion among classes is to be avoided by not abandoning one's "own dharma" (*svadharma*), which, he says, "springs from" each class's "intrinsic nature" (*svabhāva*). Kṛṣṇa begins, "Of Brahmans, warriors, and artisans, and of serfs, scorcher of the foe, the actions are distinguished according to the strands that spring from their innate nature (*svabhāva*)." And after Kṛṣṇa has detailed the natural-born (*svabhāva-ja*) karma of each social class that should guide the performance of its appropriate tasks, he ends, "Better one's own duty (*svadharma*), (even) imperfect, than another's duty (*paradharma*) well performed. Performing action pertaining to his own intrinsic nature (*svabhāva*), he incurs no guilt." Note that the first line repeats the first line of Gītā 3.35 but differs in the second. In 3.35 the second line begins with *svadharma* rather than *svabhāva.* "Better death in (doing) one's own duty (*svadharma*); another's duty brings danger" (3.38–39). Here Kṛṣṇa finally straightens out the "confusion of social classes" (*varṇasaṃkara*) that defined "lawlessness" (*adharma*) for Arjuna (1.38–44) and paralyzed him to his "very being" (*svabhāva*) (2.7) at the Gītā's beginning. Moreover, Kṛṣṇa finally tells Arjuna that, by "abandoning all dharmas" (*sarvadharmān parityajya*), he can come to Kṛṣṇa released from all sins (18.66), apparently because every "intrinsic nature" (*svabhāva*) has come from "the oversoul" (*adhyātma*), meaning Kṛṣṇa, in the first place (3.30, 7.29, 8.3).[11]

As Simon Brodbeck points out, if we are to understand the Gītā as having any impact on Arjuna, "the notion of *svabhāva* used here must logically be specific to individual people rather than to individual *varṇas*. We would even want to go further and describe *svabhāva* as variable within one lifetime" (2004, 90); it must be "a continuously varying quality" (99) if it is to have any bearing on the change Arjuna undergoes from the Gītā's beginning to its end. Moreover this manner of acting that Kṛṣṇa teaches Arjuna is presented as having "universal applicability" that extends rhetorically to "the text's audience," which does not exclude modern scholars (81–82), a number of whom have taken *karmayoga* as a key to interpreting specific passages elsewhere over the Mahābhārata as a whole. Arti Dhand (2004, 50–51), for instance, provides a curious and perhaps successful example—there is really very little to go on—in her discussion of the Śūdra maidservant's easy manner in having a proxy union (*niyoga*) with the smelly ascetic author Vyāsa.

But one must be careful in reading *karmayoga* into the Mahābhārata, whether piece by piece or as a whole. As Brodbeck nicely shows, "the availability of nonattachment in action functions as a narrative fiction to explain, on the conventional level, how Arjuna can satisfactorily be persuaded to fight"; "the universal applicability of Kṛṣṇa's technique is a conceit of the way in which the text reports Arjuna's changing his mind" (2004, 100). Indeed there is nothing to indicate how or whether Arjuna actually understood or benefited from Kṛṣṇa's *karmayoga* teaching and plenty of later evidence that it could not have touched him very deeply. Moreover we may note that when Kṛṣṇa first speaks to Arjuna about *karmayoga* in Gītā 3.3, he responds to a question by Arjuna, if at all, only by deflection. "If more important than action the mental attitude is held of thee, Janārdana, then why to violent action (*karmāṇi ghore*) dost thou enjoin me, Keśava?" (trans. Edgerton 1952, 33; slightly modified). As Brodbeck says, "There is no getting around it: the extent of Kṛṣṇa's 'rational assessment of the situation,' at least as far as ethics is concerned, is that Arjuna is a kṣatriya and so must—and will—fight" (2004, 98). That is, Kṛṣṇa's teaching of *karmayoga* is tailor-made for the consummate warrior Kṣatriya and not for the king.

Warrior *Svadharma* and Royal Ritual

As I have tried to show elsewhere, "a clear epic-long pattern is that while the deity and author work together, the god deals primarily with Arjuna and the author with Yudhiṣṭhira," who, unlike Arjuna, is a king (Hiltebeitel 2001, 90). As Nicholas Sutton (2000, 318) demonstrates, Yudhiṣṭhira shows a "repeated insistence on placing moral ethics above those of *svadharma*"—in particular Kṣatriya *svadharma* as preached by Kṛṣṇa to Arjuna in the Gītā (Sutton 2000, 296, cf. 301;

Sinha 1991, 383). Particularly in the aftermath of the war and near the beginning of epic's twelfth book, the Śāntiparvan, Kṛṣṇa leaves it to his co-ordainer, Vyāsa ("the author"), to deliver an authoritative statement on the implications of the Gītā's teachings for Yudhiṣṭhira.[12]

Vyāsa speaks sternly of law (*dharma*), assuring Yudhiṣṭhira that what he has done through war falls within it, and when Yudhiṣṭhira protests his guilt for so many deaths, Vyāsa offers four perspectives on what accounts for action: the Lord, man, chance, and karma (32.11). Focusing on the king's use of the *daṇḍa*, or rod of punishment, Vyāsa says Yudhiṣṭhira is blameless from each perspective but gives the greatest attention to the first and his own, the fourth. On the Lord, he begins, "When men who have been enjoined by the Lord (*īśvareṇa niyuktāḥ*) do a good or bad deed, the consequences of that deed go to the Lord. For obviously if a man were to chop down a tree in the forest with an axe, the evil would belong to the man doing the chopping and not at all to the axe" (Fitzgerald 2004, 241–42; 32.12–13). As in Gītā 11.33d, a king using the *daṇḍa*, like Arjuna taking up his weapons, would, like the ax, be the "mere instrument" (*nimittamātram*) of the Lord. Vyāsa concludes that from this standpoint "it would not be right, son of Kuntī, that one should acquire consequences effected by another. Therefore assign it to the Lord (*tasmāc ca īśvare tan niveśaya*)" (Fitzgerald 2004, 242; 12.32.15).

Here, as applied to a king's use of the *daṇḍa*, one may detect echoes of the Gītā's *bhaktiyoga* such as Kṛṣṇa details it soon after telling Arjuna to "be a mere instrument": "But those who, all actions (*karmāṇi*) casting on Me, intent on Me, with utterly unswerving discipline meditating on Me, revere Me, for them I am the Savior from the sea of the round of deaths become right soon, son of Pṛthā, when they have made their thoughts enter into Me. Fix thy thought-organ on Me alone. Make thy consciousness enter into Me (*mayi buddhiṃ niveśaya*); and thou shalt come to dwell even in Me hereafter; there is no doubt of this" (BhG 12.6–8). In each case one has the imperative *niveśaya* plus a locative construction applied to casting one's karma on God. But whereas Kṛṣṇa recommends this to Arjuna as a *bhaktiyoga* technique, Vyāsa leaves it as a theoretical option for Yudhiṣṭhira's "intellect" to ponder and, with Kṛṣṇa standing by, soon gets to his own recommendation.

What Vyāsa believes, he says, is that since karma always has good or bad consequences, Yudhiṣṭhira should do his own dharma (*svadharma*) and take advantage of "expiatory measures" (*prāyaścittāni*), "or you will roast when you die" (*pretya taptāsi*) (Fitzgerald 2004, 242; 12.32.20–24). Note that Yudhiṣṭhira's *svadharma* involves doing something that sounds a little unusual as *svadharma:* expiation, which will require of him the services of Brahmans. It is rather different from Arjuna's Kṣatriya *svadharma* that requires a good or just war (BhG 2.31). Indeed it is a kind of redressive action after a breach and crisis on the way to some resolution.

Victor Turner's schema survives the test of twenty-five years and is close enough to the Mahābhārata's own structure and terms to look comfortably native.

Yudhiṣṭhira eventually does as the author advises, but it takes a long conversation. Upon first getting this message from Vyāsa, he envisions falling "headfirst into hell" (33.11cd), much as Vyāsa had just warned him. But rather than expiatory measures, he says he wants to free himself by fierce austerities or *tapas*, closing with a curious line: "Grandfather, tell me about some especially good hermitages/stages of life" (Fitzgerald 2004, 243; 33.12cd). Yudhiṣṭhira can hardly expect Vyāsa to tell him about lovely forest retreats or further stages of life. (Both meanings of *āśrama* would be possible.) But it is not a throwaway line, since upon hearing it Vyāsa marks something significant, perhaps seeing an opening, since *tapas* and acts of penance are not irreconcilable. Says the narrator, Vaiśampāyana, beginning the next chapter *(adhyāya)*, "After listening to what Yudhiṣṭhira said, the seer Dvaipāyana [Vyāsa], who had made a shrewd assessment (*samīkṣya nipuṇam buddhyā*)" of him, responds with what Fitzgerald rightly flags as "an intricate and important sermon" (2004, 209), which he summarizes nicely but mentions only this much of what I now discuss: "Invoking the kṣatriya Law and Time (Time in its lordly form uses beings to slay beings), he tells Yudhiṣṭhira that those killed were villains with wicked intentions, while Yudhiṣṭhira is still virtuous since he was compelled to do what he did" (209).

If we examine Vyāsa's words more closely, we see that he makes these connections by building upon matters first aired in the Gītā that reconcile the first and fourth options while also mentioning the third, chance, which he just presented in his previous speech.[13] "You were not their killer (*na tvaṃ hantā*), nor was Bhīma, nor Arjuna, nor the twins. Time, in its characteristic revolution (*kālaḥ paryāyadharmeṇa*), took the life of those embodied ones (*dehinām*). They were destroyed by Time, Time who has no father or mother, who treats no one kindly, who is the witness of creatures' deeds. This [war] has merely been the instrument of Time (*hetumātram . . . kālasya*) (cf. BhG 11.32a, 33d); when it slays beings by means of other beings, that is its form as Lord (*tad asmai rūpam aiśvaram*). Realize that Time has deeds for its bodily form (*karmamūrtyātmakaṃ viddhi*)—it is witness to deeds good and bad, and it yields its fruit later in Time, giving rise to pleasant and unpleasant things" (Fitzgerald 2004, 243; 12.34.4–7). In effect with all these allusions to the Gītā, Vyāsa is clearly reinforcing that text's earlier prominence. But rather than reasserting Kṛṣṇa's revelation, Vyāsa offers a selective rereading of the Gītā—even with Kṛṣṇa standing by—that is more palatable and pertinent to a ritually (and, one could add, philosophically) inclined king. Continuing to offer this depersonalized Gītā theology in the deity's presence, Vyāsa turns to what Yudhiṣṭhira should derive from it. "Consider your own good character, your vows, and your special observances; yet you were made to act and approach such deeds as these by rule (*vidhinā*).[14] Just as an apparatus (*yantra*) fashioned by a carpenter is in the control of the one who holds it, so the universe is driven by action that is yoked to Time [cf. BhG 18.61]. . . . But now since falsehood snares your mind on this, king, you are therefore commanded: 'Perform expiation (*prāyaścittam*) now'" (Fitzgerald 2004, 243–44; 34.9–10, 12). As Fitzgerald nicely observes, "As they have all failed to persuade Yudhiṣṭhira that he is not guilty of wrongdoing, Vyāsa reluctantly tells him he must perform the expiation" (2004, 709). Note, however, what Vyāsa does not and cannot tell him: to act (or better, the impossible—to have acted) without desire for the fruits of his actions. It is precisely because that course is closed off to Yudhiṣṭhira that *prāyaścitta* is required.

Typically Vyāsa has made his authorial "command" coincide with what is divinely "ruled" or "ordained," on which he offers a story as divine precedent. Demonstrating from this tale that "the wise man must realize that there is Right (*dharma*) with the appearance of Wrong (*adharma*)" and urging that as "an educated man (*śrutavān*)"—which implies a Vedic education—Yudhiṣṭhira should realize he is not going to hell, he says, "Cheer (*āśvāsaya*) your brothers and your friends" (34.13–22). Now making his point that Yudhiṣṭhira is one whose karma was done "unwillingly (*anicchamānaḥ*)" and with regret, he says the Aśvamedha or horse sacrifice is the right expiation (34.23–26). He concludes on the note of Yudhiṣṭhira's current worries about hell. "Perform your Law, son of Kuntī, and what you experience after death will be better" (Fitzgerald 2004, 245; 34.36). Vyāsa thus offers a traditional ritualist solution that could reflect the association made between the early Dharmasūtras and the Śrautasūtras, the ritual texts on Vedic sacrifices such as the Aśvamedha that precede the Dharmasūtras in the ritual manuals (Kalpasūtras) of certain Vedic schools. What is right (*dharma*) for Yudhiṣṭhira is to find the right ritual of atonement. Vyāsa leaves the Mahābhārata's discourse on *karmayoga* pretty much to Kṛṣṇa and, more specifically, Kṛṣṇa's instruction of Arjuna.

Vyāsa thus acknowledges that Yudhiṣṭhira is a different kind of character than is Arjuna and that he must be addressed with different solutions to his problems—not only because it is after the war rather than before it, but also because Yudhiṣṭhira is a king and not simply a paragon warrior. Indeed before Vyāsa chimes in, Kṛṣṇa himself recognized this earlier in this postwar cheering up of Yudhiṣṭhira, and his cheerfully shrewd intervention offers no Gītā reiterations even though it comes after Arjuna has repeatedly berated Yudhiṣṭhira with calls to Kṣatriya dharma, which echo what Kṛṣṇa told him in the Gītā (see Hiltebeitel 2005, 249–56). It is thus, I believe, unsatisfactory to interpret Kṣatriya *svadharma* as though it holds the key to the dharma of kings (*rājadharma*), which is Yudhiṣṭhira's first concern (Mbh 12.38.1–2) when Vyāsa, following up Kṛṣṇa's intervention, turns Yudhiṣṭhira's ongoing postwar instruction over to Bhīṣma in the first of the three "anthologies" (see Fitzgerald 2004, 142–64) of instructions of the Śāntiparvan (see Hiltebeitel 2005, 259). On this point I must thus take issue with Madeleine Biardeau, who has attempted to make Kṣatriya *svadharma* fit that lock a bit too exactly.

Biardeau offers a brilliant synthesis that is, however, possible only because she takes Arjuna as the epic's ideal king, sidesteps Yudhiṣṭhira, and imposes the Gītā's *svadharma* on the king's dharma. The first consequence is to make the violence of war as justifiable as any killing performed within a sacrificial rite: it cannot be called *hiṃsā* if this violence is not for the sake of killing but intended as sacrifice.

> But Kṛṣṇa's teaching goes one step further. Even though the war should result in kingship being restored to the Pāṇḍavas, kingship is not its aim, but dharma and the welfare of the world. . . . The sacrificer thus becomes also the true renouncer, the true saṃnyāsin. Keeping his sacrificial fires burning, lighting the fires of war, he never has his self-interest in view but devotes himself to God and acts as his duplicate or his representative on earth. As such a Kshatriya can be a true yogin when performing the sacrifice of war. The idea, of course, gives the svadharma of kings a new content and links with salvation. The specific Kshatriya way to salvation is also their specific saṃnyāsa and sacrifice. Kings have not to renounce ultimate values when they remain kings. . . .
>
> . . . If the practice of svadharma, which has for its aim the maintenance of universal dharma, is now linked with the attainment of mokṣa, the word dharma acquires a new meaning by which it encompasses all goals including mokṣa. (Biardeau 1981, 93–94)

This is all apt and indeed elegant for Arjuna, and perhaps for some medieval and neo-Hindu notions of kingship that have taken the Gītā to heart. But it is not apt for Yudhiṣṭhira, who can only agonize after the war over such an idea that it was all for dharma and the welfare of the world. Indeed the encompassment of *mokṣa* by this meaning of dharma is not at all what interests Yudhiṣṭhira or Bhīṣma when they get to the pluralistic topic of *mokṣadharma* (the laws of salvation) as the third anthology, after those on *rājadharma* (the laws of kings) and *āpaddharma* (the laws for times of distress) of the Śāntiparvan. If it was all for dharma and the welfare of the world, the idea has to sink in slowly, if it does so at all. It has no quick traction in Yudhiṣṭhira as it does with Arjuna.

Desireless Action versus *Karmayoga* in Manu

Manu, on the contrary, is first of all addressed primarily to Brahmans and, where it is addressed to Kṣatriyas and the king, the king is to be addressed through Brahmans. Moreover in Manu's very first usage of *karmayoga* (2.2), Manu explicitly rejects the idea of desireless action:

> To be motivated by desire is not commended, but it is impossible here to be free from desire (*akāmatā*); for it is desire that prompts vedic study and the performance of vedic rites (*karmayogaś ca vaidikaḥ*). Intention (*saṃkalpa*) is the root of desire; intention is the wellspring of sacrifice and intention triggers every religious observance and every rule of restraint—so the tradition declares. Nowhere in this world do we see any activity done by a man free from desire (*akāmasya*), for whatever at all that a man may do, it is the work of someone who desired it. By engaging in it properly, a man obtains the world of the immortals and, in this world, obtains all his desires just as he intended. (Manu 2.2–5; trans. Olivelle 2004b, 94; slightly modified)

As Brodbeck notes of this passage from Manu, marking the contrast with the Gītā but without addressing the Gītā's usages of *karmayoga* directly, the "performance of vedic rites" or, as he translates it, the "'engagement in Vedic action,' may also be translated . . . Vedic *karmayoga*'" (2004, 85). Moreover whereas Manu compounds *karmayoga* primarily with ritual rules (and thus implicitly with both *svadharma* and *svakarma*), he never relates these concepts to any usage of *svabhāva*, which he keeps to two usages: one to describe the "natural range" of the black buck (2.23) and the other to assert that "the very nature of women" is "to corrupt men" (2.212; Olivelle 2005, 103).

Manu's other uses of *karmayoga* are enough to indicate that they are not late afterthoughts to the text, and Olivelle includes only the first one, just cited, among what he calls "excurses" (2004b, 94), by which he suggests interpolations. At Manu 2.68 Olivelle translates the term *karmayoga* as "the activities connected with" the *upanayana*, or sacred thread ceremony, and this is in a transitional verse with what Olivelle regards as Manu's signature transition marker, *nibodhata*, "listen" (2005, 7–11). At 6.86, in another transitional verse with *nibodhata*, Olivelle translates *karmayoga* as "the ritual discipline of vedic retirees" (*vedasaṃyāsins*). At 10.115, among the seven means of acquiring wealth, it surely means more than just "work"—Olivelle's translation; Doniger offers "working" (Doniger and Smith 1991) and Bühler "the performance of work" ([1886] 1969). At 12.2, in something like the transitional verses, there is a return to the frame, where the great seers are told, "Listen to the determination with respect to the engagement in action (*karmayoga*)." Finally, in chapter 12, where Manu unfolds "Vedic *karmayoga*" most fully, he does so in relation to ideas of *pravṛtti* and *nivṛtti* that bear especially on reincarnation and *mokṣa*.

> One should understand that acts prescribed by the Veda (*karma vaidakam*) are always a more effective means of securing the highest good both here and in the hereafter than the above six activities (Vedic recitation, *tapas*, knowledge,

controlling the senses, noninjury, and service of the teacher) (Manu 12.83). All these activities without exception are included within the scheme of the acts prescribed by the Veda (*vaidike karmayoge*), each in the proper order within the rules of a corresponding act (*kriyāvidhau*). Acts prescribed by the Veda are of two kinds: advancing (*pravṛttam*), which procures the enhancement of happiness; and arresting (*nivṛttam*), which procures the supreme good. An action performed to obtain a desire here or in the hereafter is called an "advancing act" (*pravṛttaṃ karma*), whereas an action performed without desire (*niṣkāmam*) and prompted by knowledge is said to be an "arresting act" (*nivṛttam*). By engaging in advancing acts, a man attains equality with the gods; by engaging in arresting acts, on the other hand, he transcends the five elements (Manu 12.86–90; trans. Olivelle 2005, 234). Again, "the scheme of the acts prescribed by the Veda (*vaidike karmayoge*)" could be translated "Vedic *karmayoga*."

One thing is definite: Manu does not subordinate "Vedic *karmayoga*" to *bhaktiyoga* or to any ideas about "inherent natures" that underlie karmic or dharmic actions. As Biardeau puts it, whereas the Mahābhārata marks a *bhakti* "swerve" (*écart*) in the Brahmanic tradition, Manu refuses to "budge" in his allegiance to the Veda (2002, 1, 85, 87, 96). Yet it is not clear how one is to reconcile Manu's earlier statements that no action was ever done "without desire" (*akāma*) with this allowance for *nivṛtta* actions to be *niṣkāma*. Perhaps it is an allowance for what the Gītā would call the *jñānayoga*, differentiating it from "Vedic *karmayoga*" rather than correlating the two. Whatever the reason, whereas Manu allows that the desires of Brahmans are ambiguous, the Gītā wants the desires of Kṣatriyas to be self-sacrificial.

Conclusion

It thus takes tracing several threads to see how the ritualization of war and violence is tied together in these largely complementary texts. Out of the nexus of Kṛṣṇa's teachings to Arjuna, many wondrous things stand out in making him forget his lingering question, "Then why to violent action?" I leave aside the idea that warriors who die in battle go to heaven, which Kṛṣṇa delivers as part of his shock treatment before he gets to any yogas and about which everybody (or at least Manu 7.89) seems to agree, with the notable exception of the Buddha. When pressed on the question by martial types of "headmen" (*gamaṇi*), the Buddha revealed with great reluctance that a soldier who dies in battle does not go to heaven but to the "Battle-Slain Hell," since he dies with "his mind already low, depraved" and "misdirected" toward killing others (see Schmithausen 1999, 48; Bodhi 2000, 1334–36). Manu also declares that one should never kill an animal out of desire. "Killing in sacrifice is not killing": when plants and animals die in sacrifice they earn superior births, and "when killing is sanctioned by the Veda it should definitely be regarded as non-killing" (5.37–44)—all of which Brian K. Smith assigns to the "fog machine" (Doniger and Smith 1991, xlii).

Recently I read an outstanding dissertation on the "inner jihad" and remarked to its author, Waleed El-Ansary (2006), that it sounded like *karmayoga*, by which of course I meant the Gītā's *karmayoga,* with which he enthusiastically agreed. Like "inner jihad," Arjuna's inner struggle is one thing and deserving of our respect, but arguments to kill others in God's name are another and are an agony of our times—and obviously, as the Buddhist response suggests, not our times alone. So I turn to Yudhiṣṭhira's dilemma as one that is more to my taste, at least for its rejection of such easy solutions. Of the cluster of ideas that Kṛṣṇa assembles in the Gītā to get Arjuna to fight, it is not *svadharma* that must be singled out. Yudhiṣṭhira too is concerned to figure out what his ritualist postwar *svadharma* might be that Vyāsa has posed for him, and I suppose anybody could profitably follow a *svadharma* line of thought other than a depersonalizing Buddhist. It is Kṛṣṇa's particular grounding of *karmayoga* in the "inherent nature" of the warrior that gets the warrior the same prize—heaven being just a favorable rebirth—as the sacrificial goat.

Notes

1. This good advice came after a presentation at a conference on religion in South Asia from Fred Clothey, who ultimately accepted the article in question for inclusion in his edited volume *Images of Man* (1982).

2. Among the few Gṛhyasūtra usages of dharma that Olivelle notes (2004a, 502–3), that of *dhārmika* for the Veda student (Baudhāyanagṛhyasūtra 3.3.31) could be said to point in this direction.

3. 13.9. *uttiṣṭha bhoḥ kṣatriya mṛtyubhīta/cara svadharmaṃ tyaja mokṣadharmam// bāṇaiś ca yajñaiś ca vinīya lokam/lokāt padam prāpnuhi vāsavasya.*

4. See Ā 2.2.2; Ā 2.6.5; G 11.29; and B 10.17.4, which mentions an allowance that a man may undertake renunciation (*saṃnyāsa*) after he has "settled his children in their respective duties."

5. See Manu 10.74–75; Mbh 5.29.26; 7.168.22–23; 12.297.15; 13.129.7–8.

6. See Malamoud 1982, 49. "What provides the foundation for Brahman superiority is the fact that their svadharma is of the same nature as dharma in general. Their specialty in the code is to hold the keys to the code; they watch over and judge the whole of the svadharma. This peculiar affinity that the Brahmans have for dharma is derived from their alone being *qualified* to teach vedic texts which are the ultimate source of dharma" (emphasis added).

7. See 1.53; 1.107; 2.183; 4.03; 4.155–61; 10.1–3. Cf. 2.8; 3.3; 3.235; 4.3; 4.155; 5.2; 6.91–93; 6.97; 7.36; 8.41–42; 8.390–91; 9.251; 10.95–97; 11.84.

8. Leslie 1989, 273–74, takes the idea to be axiomatic, but it is nonexistent in the Dharmasūtras and Manu and rare and surprisingly anomalous in the epics; see Hiltebeitel 2011, 495–98, 532–34.

9. See Van Buitenen 1981, 12, 18–20; Brodbeck 2004; Hill 2001, 331–34, 342, 351; Woods 2001, 71–76, 143, 172, 182; and Sutton 2000, 65, 126, 137, 330.

10. Found in Hanumān's encounter with Bhīma (3.148.17; 149.25–50); the "Colloquy of the Brahman and the Hunter" (3.198.25–38; 199.14–15, 34); and the "Instruction of Śuka" (12.309.46–90). Cf. 2.50.6–7; 12.67.30–31; 12.107.14–16.

11. As with the usages of *svabhāva* in the Gītā, however one translates *adhyātma,* there is no good reason to translate its Gītā usages differently, as, for example, Van Buitenen (1981) does in these and other instances.

12. For a fuller treatment of this section, see Hiltebeitel 2005, 249–58.

13. On the third option, chance, see Bhavagad Gītā 2.32 and 4.22, where Kṛṣṇa mentions it twice.

14. Fitzgerald's translation has "fate" here for *vidhi* (2004, 243), which is no doubt also, if not even primarily, meant. But it is worth bringing out *vidhi*'s meaning of "ritual rule" here, since it is contextually appropriate to what precedes and follows in Vyāsa's recommendation and fits what Matilal (2002, 34) has called Yudhiṣṭhira's predilection for rules.

References

Biardeau, Madeleine. 1981. "The Salvation of the King in the *Mahābhārata.*" *Contributions to Indian Sociology* n.s. 15, nos. 1 & 2: 75–97.

——. 2002. *Le Mahābhārata: Un récit fondateur du brahmanisme et son interprétation.* 2 vols. Paris: Seuil.

Bodhi, Bhikkhu, trans. 2000. *The Connected Discourses of the Buddha: A Translation of the Sayutta Nikāya.* The Teachings of the Buddha. Boston: Wisdom.

Brereton, Joel P. 2004. "*Dhárman* in the *gveda.*" *Journal of Indian Philosophy* 32, no. 5–6: 449–89.

Brodbeck, Simon. 2004. "Calling Ka's Bluff: Non-attached Action in the *Bhagavadgītā.*" *Journal of Indian Philosophy* 32: 81–103.

Bühler, Georg, trans. [1886] 1969. *The Laws of Manu.* New York: Dover.

Clothey, Fred W., ed. 1982. *Images of Man: Religion and Historical Process in South Asia.* Madras: New Era.

Dhand, Arti. 2004. "The Subversive Nature of Virtue in the *Mahābhārata:* A Tale about Women, Smelly Ascetics and God." *Journal of the American Academy of Religion* 72, no. 1: 33–58.

Doniger, Wendy, with Brian K. Smith, trans. 1991. *The Laws of Manu.* London: Penguin.

Edgerton, Franklin, trans. 1952. *The Bhagavad Gītā.* Part 1. Harvard Oriental Series 38. Cambridge, Mass.: Harvard University Press.

El-Ansary, Waleed. 2006. "The Spiritual Significance of *Jihād* in the Islamic Approach to Markets and the Environment." Ph.D. diss., George Washington University.

Fitzgerald, James Leo, trans. and ed. 2004. *Book 11, The Book of the Women. Book 12, The Book of Peace, Part One.* Vol. 7 of *The Mahābhārata.* Chicago: University of Chicago Press.

Gethin, Rupert. 2004. "He Who Sees Dhamma Sees Dhammas." *Journal of Indian Philosophy* 32, no. 5–6: 513–42.

Goldman, Robert P., and Sally J. Sutherland Goldman, trans. 1996. *Sundarakāa*. Vol. 5 of *The Rāmāyaa of Vālmīki*. Princeton: Princeton University Press.

Gombrich, Richard. 1985. "The Vessantara Jātaka, the Rāmāyaa and the Dasaratha Jātaka." In "Indological Studies Dedicated to Daniel H. H. Ingalls," special issue, edited by Ernest Bender. *Journal of the American Oriental Society* 105, no. 3: 427–37.

Hill, Peter. 2001. *Fate, Predestination and Human Action in the Mahābhārata: A Study in the History of Ideas*. New Delhi: Munshiram Manoharlal.

Hiltebeitel, Alf. 1982. "Sexuality and Sacrifice: Convergent Subcurrents in the Firewalking Cult of Draupadī." In *Images of Man: Religion and Historical Process in South Asia*, edited by Fred W. Clothey, 72–111. Madras: New Era.

——. 2001. *Rethinking the Mahābhārata: A Reader's Guide to the Education of the Dharma King*. Chicago: University of Chicago Press.

——. 2005. "On Reading Fitzgerald's Vyāsa." *Journal of the American Oriental Society* 125, no. 2: 241–61.

——. 2006. "Aśvaghosa's *Buddhacarita:* The First Known Close and Critical Reading of the Brahmanical Sanskrit Epics." *Journal of Indian Philosophy* 34: 229–86.

——. 2011. *Dharma: Its Early History in Law, Religion, and Narrative*. South Asia Research Series. New York: Oxford University Press.

Horsch, Paul. 2004. "From Creation Myth to World Law: The Early History of *Dharma*." Translated by Jarrod L. Whitaker. *Journal of Indian Philosophy* 32, no. 5–6: 423–48.

Houben, Jan. 2000. "The Ritual Pragmatics of a Vedic Hymn: The 'Riddle Hymn' and the Pravargya Ritual." *Journal of the American Oriental Society* 120, no. 4: 499–536.

Johnston, E. H., trans. 2004. *Aśvaghosa's Buddhacarita or Acts of the Buddha: Part 1, Sanskrit Text, Sargas 1–14; Part 2, Introduction and Translation; Part 3, Translation of Cantos 15–28 from Tibetan and Chinese Versions*. Delhi: Motilal Banarsidass.

Leslie, Julia, ed. 1989. *The Perfect Wife: The Orthodox Hindu Woman according to the Strīdharmapaddhati of Tryambakayajvan*. Oxford University South Asian Studies Series. Delhi: Oxford University Press.

Mahoney, William. 1998. *The Artful Universe*. Albany: State University of New York Press.

Malamoud, Charles. 1982. "On the Rhetoric and Semantics of the Puruārthas." In *Way of Life: King, Householder, Renouncer: Essays in Honor of Louis Dumont*, edited by T. N. Madan, 32–54. New Delhi: Motilal Banarsidass.

Matilal, Bimal Krishna. 2002. *Ethics and Epics: The Collected Essays of Bimal Krishna Matilal*. Edited by Jonardon Ganeri. New Delhi: Oxford University Press.

O'Flaherty, Wendy Doniger. 1976. *The Origins of Evil in Hindu Mythology*. Berkeley: University of California Press.

——, trans. 1981. *The Rig Veda*. London: Penguin.

Olivelle, Patrick, trans. 1999. *Dharmasūtras: The Law Codes of Ancient India*. Oxford: Oxford University Press.

——. 2004a. "The Semantic History of Dharma: The Middle and Late Vedic Periods." *Journal of Indian Philosophy* 32, no. 5–6: 491–511.

——, trans. 2004b. *The Law Code of Manu.* Oxford: Oxford University Press.

Schmithausen, Lambert. 1999. "Aspects of the Buddhist Attitude towards War." In *Violence Denied: Violence, Non-Violence and the Rationalization of Violence in South Asian Cultural History,* edited by Jan E. M. Houben and Karel R. Van Kooij, 45–67. Leiden: Brill.

Sinha, Braj. 1991. "Arthaśāstra Categories in the *Mahābhārata:* From *Daanīti* to *Rāja—dharma.*" In *Essays on the Mahābhārata,* edited by Arvind Sharma, 369–83. Leiden: Brill.

Sutton, Nicholas. 2000. *Religious Doctrines in the Mahābhārata.* Delhi: Motilal Banarsidass.

Turner, Victor. 1974. *Dramas, Fields, and Metaphors: Symbolic Action in Human Society.* Ithaca: Cornell University Press.

Van Buitenen, J. A. B. 1981. *The Bhagavadgītā in the Mahābhārata: A Bilingual Translation.* Chicago: University of Chicago Press.

Witzel, Michael. 1997. "Early Sanskritization: Origins and Development of the Kuru State." In *Recht, Staat und Verwaltung im klassischen Indien. The State, the Law, and Administration in Classical India,* edited by Bernhard Kölver, 27–52. Munich: Oldenbourg.

Woods, Julian F. 2001. *Destiny and Human Initiative in the Mahābhārata.* Albany: State University of New York Press.

From Diaspora to (Global) Civil Society

Global Gurus and the Processes of De-ritualization and De-ethnization in Singapore

JOANNE PUNZO WAGHORNE

> There are a number of Indians (including South Indians) who raise questions about this form of ritualized Hinduism [performed in temples]. A number of them agree that it is a form of religion that is more emulative than innovative, more pietistic than ethically explicit; more the product of an era of kingship than of a "democratic" society, more ethnic than global.
>
> *Fred W. Clothey (1983, 136)*

The benevolent faces of mobile gurus stare out from the great hoarding (billboards) of contemporary Chennai advertising upcoming lectures alongside other huge images of new refrigerators and automobiles, the ever-increasing choices available to a once-controlled economy in India. The massive structures may deface the city, but they do not hide key changes in the cultural and religious life of this great global center in the southern state of Tamilnadu. Across the Indian Ocean and through the straits, the more controlled skyline of Singapore abjures such displays, but the increasing importance of "spirituality" and "religion" made headlines in the *Straits Times* under the sky-blue headline "GOD and US" (July 16, 2005). While the accompanying article discussed a return to organized religions, subheadings included "Choices Galore" and "God? YES Religion? NO" interspersed with advisements for movies and a multicolumn blackened square with "Liberating" in white letters above a radiant silver car. All of these signs mark changes in the multireligious milieu of this former British colonial port city, where migrants from India (mostly from Tamilnadu) and China settled along with Malays. Alongside of the temples, mosques, and churches, new religious movements—many Hindu-derived and guru-centered—thrive.

Thus I write now not about the rise of temple culture with its concomitant for renewed rituals (see also Waghorne 2004) but about its shadow, the rapid growth of guru-centered movements among the largely Tamil Indian diaspora in multiethnic Singapore. These formal and informal groups openly replace "religion" with "spirituality" and substitute the construction of ethno-religious identity with the search for widely applicable values and practices that burst the bounds of Indian and Hindu self-identification. With their gurus based mostly in South India, these movements nonetheless remain global in outlook as they seek to move their rhetoric of inclusiveness into practice by openly seeking members from the more numerous Chinese. In this process of restructuring religiosity, "ritual" becomes suspect as part of the traditional Hindu world, perhaps still useful for those from a strong Hindu heritage but ineffective as a source either for personal spiritual growth or for facilitating the growth of a multiethnic constituency. Fred Clothey noticed the rise of this kind of consciousness in the Indian community amid the intense re-creation of temple rituals in Singapore in the late 1980s. I saw this trend in Singapore in the summers of 2005, 2006, 2010, 2011, and 2012 and for an entire year in 2007–2008. Karen Pechilis describes parallel movements among the Indian diaspora in the United States:

> It seems that currently gurus and Indian-style Hindu temples have marked off very different spaces in the United States. The guru path tends toward inclusivity, with its emphasis on self-power in relationship to the guru's guidance, acceptance of participants from all ethnic and religious backgrounds, congregational modality of worship, and a tendency to disassociate itself with organized religion. As such, the guru path in the United States displays characteristics of the globalization of Hinduism. In contrast, the Indian-style Hindu temples tend toward specificity, with an emphasis on the ritual worship of a distinctive and often sectarian-defined God, ethnic Indian clientele, priestly modalities of worship, and explicitly Hindu self-identification. (Pechilis 2004, 36)

Pechilis's references to the different spaces of temple and guru organizations ended her insightful introduction to *The Graceful Guru*, but the issue of differing religious space should begin any discussion of current trends toward the formation of globalized, guru-centered associations in contradiction, as well as confluence, with the continuing formations of Hindu ethno-religious identities. Most important for a discussion of contemporary trends in Hindu-based movements, this process of conscious "de-ethnization" seems deeply linked to another process, "de-ritualization."

While the intense construction of new temples in the diaspora reestablishes Āgama-based (orthodox) ritual reaffirming the need for qualified priests and established practices, guru-centered organizations eschew "religion"—often rejecting or devaluating received "ritual" and redirecting bodily engagement to other practices called the *kriya.* Such organizations relocate their activities from ethnic spaces into global spaces and reform their rhetoric into assertions of universality and global values. "De-ritualization" appears implicated in the globalization of Hindu-based organizations as "ritual" becomes associated with ethnic specificity. For ritual studies this may force a consideration of when and in what kind of spaces a concern for "ritual" recedes or disappears. So this essay offers an alternative to discussions of the rise of ritualization described by Clothey's earlier work in Singapore: a consideration of emerging spaces where new movements perceive "ritual" to be literally out of place. In Singapore, as global guru movements pointedly shun the designation *religion* out of preference for the term *spiritual*, many avoid meeting in temples—often situating themselves in or amid commercial offices and retail buildings near major shopping areas in these cities. Thus the processes of de-ethnization and de-ritualization seem inseparable for a very contemporary form of secularization or, following the alliteration, de-sacralization.

Clearly these shifts in key terminology introduce a dialogue between what the fields of ritual studies and religious studies, mainly situated in North America and the United Kingdom, would ordinarily classify as "ritual" and what these Asia-based organizations understand by the terms. But keep in mind that these shifts in terminology occur now within a common milieu: we are all speaking the same language, global English, reading the same popular literature, and often sharing very similar educational backgrounds. As these spiritual organizations shift their venues to the ordinary spaces of daily middle-class life, the daily worlds of the observer and the observed move closer, but the nuances of seemingly common English terminology, vestiges from differing histories, step farther apart.

"Religion" and "Spirituality" in New Global Spaces

Just at the moment when guru movements enter global spaces equipped with a new de-ethicized outlook and de-ritualized practices, they are not only positioned amid the commercial world but also quickly implicated in economic globalization and worldwide commodity cultures. The broad field of religious studies has taken Hindu gurus and their multiethnic followers seriously in recent years (Forsthoefel and Humes 2005; Pechilis 2004; S. Srinivas 2008; T. Srinivas 2004). Likewise fine-tuned discussions of the closely related cultural shift from religion to spirituality abound (Heelas and Woodhead 2005; Roof 1999; Wuthnow 1998). Considerations of this trend toward spirituality, however, often meld choice with commodity culture in such titles as *The Spiritual Marketplace* (Roof 1999), *Selling Spirituality* (Carrette and King 2005), and *New Age Capitalism* (Lau 2000). Sometimes the talk of trends and trajectories is alarmed about an insidious move away from organized religion to a new "privatised" mishmash of spiritualized materialism (Carrette and King 2005, 38). A particularly telling example appeared in a special thematic issue of the *Journal of the American Academy of Religion*, "The Future of Religion in the

Academy." In his invited essay, Graham Ward sharply and sadly demarcates spiritualism from faith as the last of three major "trajectories" of the future "of religion and religious studies" (2006, 184–85). His understanding of spiritualism clearly includes the sensibilities that mark guru-centered associations: eclecticism, healing, and self-help. Echoing an all too common critique, he melds this culture of choice with the twin evils of commodity culture and the ubiquitous popular media, which cannot live in anything but polar opposition to faith. Ward predicts "an increasing polarization between those who talk of spirituality and those who talk of faith":

> As religion becomes more culturally pervasive, the more it becomes commodified and the more it becomes in Taylor's term post-Durkheimian. That is, rather than functioning as an integrating factor in the life of a society, religion will develop forms of hyper-individualism, self-help as self-grooming, custom-made eclecticism that proffer a pop transcendence and pamper to the need for "good vibrations." By means of this "spiritualism"—that is sensation hungry and the counterpart to extreme sports—a collection of religious people will emerge (are already emerging) who are unable to tell the difference between orgasm, an adrenalin rush and an encounter with God. (2006, 185)

Ward worries about the fate of democracy in this world of "personal satisfaction" and sees all of this resulting in increasingly conservative boundaries around "faith communities." Here he indicts this all too loose "spiritualism" as an accessory to the coterminous loss of public consciousness and the rise of tightly bounded communities and, hence, fundamentalism.

In spite of all of this academic rhetoric of hyper-individualism and privatization, guru-centered movements function as organizations at the same time that they openly adopt the language of spirituality, eclecticism, and inclusivity. Their websites may offer everything from photos of the guru to CDs, books, and T-shirts, but they also include long lists of the hospitals, schools, and dispensaries built by their gurus as well as relief work and services offered by their communities of devotees. In Singapore the same groups offer numerous social services as part of the government-sponsored development of community self-help organizations in the island nation. Thus the guru-centered organizations join other public service associations in a newly emerging image of a unified secular world that enfolds all such volunteer organizations, including those more often classified by scholars as religious. Sociologists and philosophers of political life name the public space inhabited by these organizations as *civil society,* and some use the more overarching term *global civil society.*

But why place Hindu-based religious organizations into conversation with the ubiquitous but often unwieldy concept of civil society or the evermore debated notion of global civil society? For those of us engaging in the comparative study of religion, the almost breathless references made by policy experts and political theorists to an emerging set of normative values, a new form of worldwide interconnectivity that transcends older universalisms, and new organizational structures that communicate fluently in innovative media cannot be ignored (Walzer 1995; Chambers and Kymlicka 2002). Political philosopher John Keane speaks cautiously but effectively of "global civil society" as "an unfinished project that consists of sometimes thick, sometimes thinly stretched networks, pyramids and hub-and-spoke clusters of socio-economic institutions and actors who organise themselves across borders, with the deliberate aim of drawing the world together in new ways" (2003, 8). In Keane's description of this "new world-view radically different from any that has existed before," he adopts terms with a religious valence, such as *cosmology,* and considers the role of traditional religious worldviews in the older universalizing visions. However when he outlines the rising "normative ideal" of global civil society, religion recedes as a dominant factor in creating and sustaining these norms.

As a self-confessed historian of religions with an empirical bent, I remain intrigued by Keane's careful description of this seemingly new form of associational life but also take seriously his disassociation of religion from newly emerging global values. Earlier I would have rejected this idea outright; now I see a connection between his almost natural assumption that religion is not the defining factor in the new cultural canopy as well as the shaky concern of religion scholars such as Ward that somehow religion is failing as *the* integrating factor in society in this so-called post-Durkheimian era. Paul Heelas, in his recent rich refutation of scholars such as Graham Ward, renames these movements "Spiritualities of Life." He argues that for such movements, especially in contemporary Britain, "the sacred is located within the depths of the shared life" and generates "an ethic of humanity" (Heelas 2008, 127).

Certainly within Hindu circles, the lack of church structures, once considered a liability, and the long history of religious movements outside and between the social constructions of the Hindu way of life now ironically open the door for the current upsurge of guru-centered organizations speaking of spirituality. Once suspect as not quite genuine, now in their new global attire as nongovernmental organizations, they command networks of charities, hospitals, and medical colleges that—in cases such as Mata Amritanandamayi, Satya Sai Baba, and the Ramakrishna Missions as well as the newer Art of Living founded by Sri Sri Ravi Shankar and the Isha Yoga Foundation of Sadhguru Jaggi Vasudev[1]—rival many mainstream institutions in India and abroad. On the national level, established religious institutions still have a prominent voice, but on the immediate micro and macro levels, independently administered spiritual organizations—loosely networked with each other but also with other NGOs—are beginning to dominate globally well beyond the network of diasporic Hindus.

More important, I would argue that these Hindu-based, guru-centered organizations may be more capable of shaping as well as mediating the rising normative values carried by the concept of global civil society in a way that ostensibly mainstream Hindu institutions—traditional monasteries (*maṭha*) and temples—cannot. This is because their organizational structure parallels other actors within this widely acknowledged but loosely organized sphere that includes social, cultural, and economically centered groups. But as "spiritual" organizations, these groups lay claim to effective bodily techniques, "tools to rejuvenate," "to liberate human beings to reach an unbounded state," as the Isha Foundation declares on its website. So while their websites list the many social service projects in which they engage, emphasis always falls on techniques of self-transformation that lead to a widening consciousness of others and the world.

Never naming their bodily practices as rituals, these spiritual organizations offer their practices to the general public as educational courses; instructors teach the *kriya* as ancient practices compatible with and even proven by contemporary science for verifiable bodily and mental healing. The Art of Living presents its courses as helping practitioners to discover the rhythmic breathing in their bodies and to use "this link between our breath and our emotions to come closer to the rhythm of our natural Being," as the website puts it. Members who undergo these courses pledge to keep the details of the practices confidential, as must I, but all *kriyas* involve a combination of yoga *āsanas* (postures), special breathing techniques, chanting, and mediation. Members of these spiritual organizations ideally perform the *kriya* daily but also come together weekly or monthly for *satsang*, where the group performs the *kriya* together, sometimes combining this with personal testaments of deep transformation and listening to talks by the guru in person, on DVD, or via a video link to the main ashram where the guru resides. So by recentering bodily activity from traditional "ritual" actions to the *kriya*, spiritual movements indeed refocus bodily participation within the individual but in such a way as to relink the person to an emerging community of fellow practitioners and to the world at large.

The recognition of such spiritual groups as moving well beyond privatized experience to a role within civil society could radically shift our understanding of them from proffering cleverly disguised indifferent individualism and crass materialism to offering their members a technique as well as a platform for entering into an evolving global cultural framework that emphasizes belonging but as a function of choice. Spirituality manifests now, as in the past, within growing organizational structures—a welcome point emphasized by Robert Wuthnow (1998, 17)—as many specific studies of devotees and their gurus confirm (Warrier 2005,

59–60; Bryant and Ekstrand 2004) and Max Weber made central to his sociology of religion.

Welcome to Singapore, Inc.

Singapore, Inc., as many residents call it, facilitates rapid work in any field. During my initial research in the summers of 2005 and 2006, with welcome help from Prof. Vineeta Sinha, her graduate advisee Nagah Devi Ramasamy, and other faculty at the National University of Singapore, I discovered numerous organizations and met many officials and devotees of guru-oriented religious movements. I attended a prayer session of one Satya Sai Baba center, discussed charities at another, and met with the directors of their major social services centers. In all, Singapore accommodates fourteen Satya Sai Baba centers in different parts of this city-state of 266 square miles. At the old Arya Samaj building, I witnessed a simplified *homa* (fire ritual) that marks this early reform movement, a once powerful voice of the Hindu community now in decline. At the simple Amritanandeewari Society Building, I sang along with Singapore devotees of Mata Amritanandamayi at their weekly devotional meeting. The head monk of the firmly established Ramakrishna Mission—housed in a large bungalow-style building with offices, a meditation hall, and quarters for resident monks—took time in his busy day to describe the various activities and charities that the mission administers. In a much less expected space, Sinha took me to meet the couple who founded a recently registered society, the Samayapuram Mariamman Pillaigal (Samayapuram Māriyammaṉ Piḷḷaikaḷ, "children of Samayapuram Māriyammaṉ"), which functions out of their large high-rise condominium at the top of one of the many government-built "estates." A *vimāna* or large shrine to the goddess Māriyammaṉ fills much of their living room, and an assortment of goddesses, including Kuan-yin (the Buddhist goddess of mercy), sits atop the long credenza near the television.

When I returned to Singapore associated with the excellent Asia Research Institute of the National University of Singapore in 2007–2008, I found that many new organizations had gained popularity. I began to chart numerous guru-centered organizations meeting in business school classrooms, private flats (condominiums), rented cultural halls, and in some cases newly purchased floors within larger commercial complexes, as well as the community centers attached to temples, mostly Hindu but sometimes Buddhist as well. The case of the Māriyammaṉ shrine within a high-rise flat began to seem unremarkable for this globalized city. The high-rise temple inside a living room in many ways typifies the complexities of places accommodating such organizations in Singapore. I witnessed members of another informal group build a mini *homa* inside a patio-sized hibachi on the seventh-story apartment of another housing complex. In a single-family terrace house in an upscale neighborhood, I joined a group of friends of both Indian and Chinese ethnicity at an informal workshop learning to draw and understand the *chakra* (mystic diagram). A German woman, a disciple of the rising guru Sri Kaleshwar, instructed us on how to attract and hold the presence of the goddess as Śakti, the powerful creative and healing forces in the universe, within the *chakra*. In addition I attended the basic multiday course for the Art of Living and Isha Yoga, many mediation sessions for a group dedicated to Shivarudra Balayogi, as well as numerous *satsangs*. Toward the end of my research, I encountered the new Rajayoga Power Transcendental Meditation group in Singapore and crossed into Johor Bahru in Malaysia to attend the "100th Kundalini Awakening" session conducted in person by Yoga Jnana Sitthar Om Sri Rajayoga Guru Saranam, usually called H.D.G. (His Divine Grace).

In all of these cases, some form of ritual seemed to be occurring, but it was understood as a means of self-help and self-development in the context of these newly formed groups, which included people of multiple ethnic and even multi-religious heritages meetings weekly or monthly usually within the commercial and residential spaces of Singapore. The confluence between these groups and everyday life permeated their locations and their practices. While in many cases

Ornate alcove for His Divine Grace Jnana Sitthar in the Singapore center of Rajayoga Power Transcendental Meditation. Photograph by the author with kind permission of H.D.G.

organizations openly chose commercial locations, government policy also ironically pushed spiritual "societies," inadvertently or consciously, toward secular spaces and, as we will see, toward civil spaces and civil society as well.

The current government inherited and confirmed the practice of the British to keep Hindu temples under government auspices through the Hindu Endowment Board, which continued from the former British administration. No new temples can be built without its approval, which a member of the board explained was now very unlikely because of the acute shortage and expense of land in this small state (also see Sinha 2005a, 31–38). In addition almost all of the land in Singapore is owned by the government and is now leased—as in many parts of the United Kingdom—usually for thirty-year terms, which is too short a time to warrant the major investment that new temple construction would require. So in effect the construction of new temples, which occupies the energy of so many other Hindu communities in the diaspora, remains nearly impossible in Singapore, although many have found ways to reuse and rededicate existing structures (Sinha 2005a, 107–18).

The government regulates not only temples but also all voluntary organizations. My conversations with faculty at the National University of Singapore and administrators of charities began to reveal both the structure and consequences of these policies. While freedom of religion is guaranteed by the constitution, religious organizations are regulated. A Singaporean citizen may worship in any way he or she wants within the privacy of the home. Public religious meetings, door-to-door collections of funds, and processions, however, all require that an organization be officially registered as a "society" with a government agency called the Registry of Societies (ROSES), which until recently was under the Ministry of Community Development, Youth, and Sports, or MCDYS for short. Equally interesting is that, while formal religious organizations such as the temples administered by the Hindu Endowment Board continue under the MCDYS, the Registry of Societies now falls under the Home Ministry, whose major function is the "safety and security" of this city-state. Much of this information is openly available on the massive website of the Singapore government.

In Singapore a prudent self-censoring tends to limit public criticism of the government, which technically is not forbidden except interestingly in connection with religion. A leading member of one charity organization spoke with amazement about the fiery style of preaching he had heard in an African American church in Atlanta, where the president of the United States was openly criticized. This does not happen in Singapore. Thus the familiar mix of political and social critique from the pulpit or *minbar* does not appear in Singapore, apparently by design. The Maintenance of Religious Harmony Act of 1990 openly constrains "any leader, official or member of any religious group or institution, who causes ill-feelings between different religious groups or who promotes a political cause or carries out subversive activities or who excites disaffection against the President or Government under the guise of propagating or practicing any religious belief," as a pamphlet from the Ministry of Information and the Arts announced (1992, 1). Recently the Declaration on Religious Harmony, "which is a product of a bottom-up consultation process involving all major stakeholders," was posted on the official government website in the form of a pledge of mutual respect and common recognition of "the secular nature of our state" to "thereby ensure that religion will not be abused to create conflict and disharmony in Singapore." With such curbs on religiously inspired political critique, Singapore may paradoxically foster the kind of spirituality that characterizes transnational guru-centered movements rather than official faith organizations. While I was at the National University of Singapore, I attended a lecture by a professor at the National Institute of Education who argued for an alternative to the usual factual presentation of religious traditions in the public schools. She advocated "Spiritual Education (SE) which aims to help students acquire insights into their personal existence which are of enduring worth, attribute meaning to their life experiences, and values a non-material and transcendental dimension to life" (Tan 2007).

Just prior to passing the religious harmony legislation in 1990, the government commissioned a series of studies by the Institute of Policy Studies associated with the National University of Singapore, which surveyed the contours of religion in Singapore, especially changes in religious affiliations. One survey reported the obvious—a "substantial increase in the number of Christians" as well as "persons claiming to have no religious beliefs"—and concluded that young, middle-class, educated persons accounted for both of these trends. The report worried that "if religious belief is seen to be inherently valuable for the moral strength of society, which is a controversial proposition in itself, then this trend of secularization deserves some concern." At the same time, the rise in conversion to Christianity also elicited the following conclusion: "Compared to other religions, Christianity is unique in its active fellowship and activities not directly relating to religion, including social and community service" (Kuo and Quah 1988, 66–71). Research out of Australia during the same period tackled this phenomenon of "religious switching" but concluded that the most significant "switch was among the young Chinese who moved out of their parents' amorphous mass of beliefs and practices" to listing "none" as their religious identity. Hindus and Muslims rarely switched religions, because among the Malay, who are all Muslim, and the Indians, who are largely Hindu, "religion is an integral part of their ethnic or national identities . . . and the costs of religious switching are high" (Tamney and Hassan 1987, 41). Clearly by the late 1980s religious affiliations were enough in flux to concern the government. At one level the parliament acted to insure that any associated political turmoil—and of course political criticisms—would be checked. But at another level, the "threat" may have shifted the subtle governmental understanding of the nature of mainstream religion as part of community solidity to religions as having a strong potential for civil disruption.

Documenting the changes in government policy and attitudes toward religious organizations would require far more space than is available here (see Sinha 2011). Suffice it to say that any mention of religion, and even specific religions, remains safely buried in an assortment of significant euphemisms on the website of the Ministry of Community Development, Youth, and Sports, which in reality regulates all religious institutions associated with formal religion in the state. Of particular interest is the Social Cohesion subministry, under which is the Registry of Co-operative Societies, whose webpage goes on to outline a distinction between "Co-operative Society and a Society registered under the Societies Act." This difference is not immediately clear except to say that cooperative societies "promote the economic interest of their members," while societies function more like a club or partnership of the type that must now be registered under the Societies Act under the Home Ministry.

Such bureaucratese not so subtly hides an ever-lurking fear of ethno-religious conflict and the loss of secularism—here understood not as a cultural phenomenon but as the cipher for a religiously neutral state system that sharply differentiates this fragile island from the Malaysian mainland just a river's width away. The categories of community relations and cooperative societies interestingly mirror the same descriptive binaries that began this essay: tradition-based identities that—especially in diaspora—equate with ethnic identities and the guru-centered spiritual movements. In Singapore, as in surrounding Malaysia and Indonesia, tradition-based divisions continue to equate with ethno-religious identities, which Sir Thomas Raffles, the founder of modern Singapore, literally designed into the architectural plan of the city. To this day there is a Little India, a Malay quarter, and a Chinatown. All Malays are Muslim, and the state makes conversion out of Islam difficult. Most Indians are Hindu, with a small minority of Muslims. The Chinese, as in many parts of the world, have eclectic temples incorporating Taoist, Confucian, and Buddhist elements. Many Chinese are Christian. The wild cards for many Singaporeans are the spiritual-based, de-ethnicized new religious movements; the government tucks them nicely into societies, which can be religious but are classified like clubs rather than temples.

The Culture of Consumption

An overarching secular but nonetheless value-laden ideology of harmonious, albeit distinct, ethno-religious communities (*communities* appears always in the plural) touting abundant volunteerism and charity with vigorous youth and happy elders shines like the sun in all official websites meant for internal and external consumption. Seeing Singapore after more than a three-decade interval, I confess my own astonishment at how closely this ideal comes to my experience of this refashioned metropolis. The realization of this ideal rests within a "culture of consumption," as sociologist Chua Beng Huat argues in *Life Is Not Complete without Shopping* (2003)—a motto close to my heart and my favorite form of participant observation with Singaporeans most Saturdays in the many spectacular malls. Moreover an entire essay could be devoted to these malls as "sacred spaces" to parallel Ira G. Zepp's study of shopping malls as ceremonial centers in America. However for this essay the position of shopping as something more than a national pastime even for the government points to consumerism as a culture in its own right and with its own rites. A direct connection between shopping and the bodily practices of new guru-centered movements becomes too shadowy to prove. However testimonies during *satsangs* and declarations on the websites and in the gurus' sermons especially for Art of Living and Isha assert that the performance of the *kriya* ensures health, better performance at work, and, by inference, worldly as well as spiritual success. For a new group, Rajayoga Power Transcendental Meditation, the connections are explicit even to the point of teaching visualization techniques to imagine moving up to a better automobile

Saturday shoppers crowd the stunning ION center on Orchard Road.
Photograph by Dick Waghorne.

and a better house. In this case the meditations do not promise the car but rather to "awaken the power in you," as Yoga Jnana Sitthar, His Divine Grace, explained ("Kundalini Awakening" session, May 4, 2008). The practices transform the practitioner's mental and energy to enable such success.

Chua takes the phrase "Life is not complete without shopping" from a 1996 National Day Rally speech of the prime minister. "The People's Action Party (PAP) that governed Singapore without break since 1959 is driven by pursuit of national economic growth. And the record has been nothing short of impressive. This is its 'performance' principle and singular claim to legitimacy to rule. It will go to all lengths, including curtailing conventional democratic rights and practices, to 'deliver the goods' to the people. In this sense, the PAP is singularly motivated to improve the material life of Singaporeans through the expansion of material consumption" (2003, 3). In an earlier study, *Communitarian Ideology and Democracy in Singapore,* Chua outlined the government's foray into and subsequent failure at social engineering through "Confucianisation," which would seem a return to religious sensibilities. However, according to Chua, the People's Action Party repackaged the same unrelenting model of strong economic development under the widely held theory that Confucianism was the locus "of ascendancy of Asian capitalism" (1995, 151). This idea accords with a number of American communitarians who noted a similar phenomenon during the rapid rise of the "little tigers" of Taiwan and Singapore in the 1980s and later by theorists of alternative visions of civil society (see, for example, Madsen 2002). The current, cheerful website of the MCDYS appears to be a de-Confucianized version of those reworked "Confucian" values. An official teacher's guide to Confucian ethics published during the Confucianizing campaign in the mid-1980s listed as instructional objectives "To show pupils how the Confucian cultural tradition can help to promote harmony and stability" and "To show students how the Confucian cultural tradition can contribute towards the economic, political, and cultural development of Singapore" (Curriculum Development Institute 1986, 95). So when the government gave up social engineering via a Confucian model, they turned to more neutral secular language but retained a Singaporean cultural ethos in which, as the prime minister's speech so clearly implied, shopping is the secular rite of Singapore and material success its creed.

There are some interesting curves in the case of Singapore that deserve attention, lest we travel a straight path from faith to self-indulgent spiritualism. Singapore's state policies position guru movements in the almost classic language of "civil society," while the much-used American term "faith communities" translates more readily into family, ethnicity, and bounded communities that must be tamed into useful self-help organizations. As such the latter are only tangentially part of civil society, since, unlike the classic definition, these do not meet the assumption of voluntary membership always connected with associational life. Once outside the bounds of American religious sensibilities and American political history, a citizen's primary religious connection no longer equates with choice. *Faith* as a code word for *religion* becomes an exceptionally inadequate term. This is mirrored even in Christian conversions, since the most successful churches are independent evangelical associations that resemble the organizational structure of new religious movements rather than that of mainstream churches (Wolffe 2002). Returning a moment to Ward's essay mentioned above, outside the United States—and I am not willing to cede the inside so easily—the building of new service-oriented, humanity-centered communities belongs not to the birthright ethno-religious traditions (or "faiths") but to many spirituality-touting, guru-adoring, this-worldly new religious organizations.

The processes of de-ethnization in the guru-centered organization, then, mirror the cultural and governmental logic of Singapore: religion equals bounded ethnic communities into which citizens are born, while spirituality opens into a voluntary associational life, which Singaporeans freely choose to join. Individuals join associations as free agents but are then reoriented via the *kriya* to openness to and success in the larger secular sphere but also to concern for the greater good. I heard constant references to the inner life, to the personal act of choosing, to openness to all, and to service to society as a natural consequence of service to the divine guru or to a deeply held sense of the unity of the world. Swami Muktirupananda, president of the long-established Ramakrishna Mission, eloquently articulated the interconnection of inner spirituality, service, and the unity of humankind. When I asked about the mission's service activities, he began with the orphanage and school. While these serve the Indian community, the mission's yoga classes draw widely from all sections of Singapore society. I asked why yoga was so popular and brought so many different peoples together. Muktirupananda responded that yoga offers "mastery of your own self." The mind and body are connected, and yoga can bring "rest for the mind" because "the mind is made up of matter." When I asked about God, he answered, "Leave God aside. The goal of humans is happiness and peace of mind. Everything is inside us and us only. . . . When the mind is transparent, you understand your own being. . . . Religion means within us." I asked about current attempts to define Hinduism within Indian ethnicity. He denied that the mission was for Hindus only. "Human beings everywhere in the world are important to us." He emphasized in his terms that Vivekananda (1863–1902), who founded the mission in 1897, "was a universalist" and went on to say that there are now more than a thousand monks around the world, many of whom are Jews or Muslims and Christians by birth, "so we cannot discriminate." Finally I also asked about ritual. "Ritual only creates the mood but it is not the end. It's just like toys for a child" (personal interview, July 15, 2005).

Note the string of connections in Swami Muktirupananda's explanations: he relegated both ethnicity and ritual to a less advanced understanding of the religious-spiritual impulse. I found the same set of associations in a series of intense encounters and interviews with leaders of the Art of Living that brought into sharp focus the issues of self-centeredness, group consciousness, service, and the subtleties of de-ritualization in the context of de-ethnization. Indian followers of Sri Sri Ravi Shankar (usually called "Guruji" by his followers) registered Art of Living (AOL) as a society with the government in the mid-1990s. The society grew in popularity in 2008 especially among newer émigrés from India to Singapore and Singaporean Chinese, who likewise were mainly professionals. The Indian high-tech city of Bangalore houses the main AOL ashram for the globally popular Guruji, who recently celebrated the silver anniversary of the Art of Living. In downtown Singapore I completed the basic course in Art of Living with four other people: a young ex-pat American, an Australian of Thai-Chinese heritage, a German woman married to a Malay Muslim, and an Indian engineer who had studied AOL in India. Our teacher, Vijay, a Singaporean lawyer of Indian ethnicity, introduced this diverse group to Guruji's special form of yoga, breathing exercises, and practical teachings by using Hindu-derived terms intertwined with psychological and ethical discourse. This downtown center of AOL, a large room occupying a floor in a characterless commercial building across the street from a fashionable shopping center, had a small photo of Guruji but no other marks of sacrality. Signs for follow-up sessions were posted on the walls in English and Chinese. A large poster announced the special birthday celebrations for Guruji to be held the following week.

Now duly initiated into Sudarshan Kriya, the main yogic practice of AOL, I was able to attend and participate fully in the birthday celebrations of Sri Sri Ravi Shankar and was kindly given permission to photograph. Held at the auditorium of the Chinese Chamber of Commerce, this exuberant celebration included a group session of the *kriya* with more than one hundred people participating in the yoga and breathing practices together. Devotional songs followed, a birthday cake and balloons appeared, and some happy dancing erupted among the Chinese and Indian followers. A large garlanded photo of Guruji sat at the end of the stage flanked by bronze images of female guardians with flower vases in front, burning josh sticks, and baskets of coconuts and fruit. At the end of the celebration, some came to this seeming altar to receive flowers and fruit from the woman in charge of the event. To my eye these activities gave the appearance of ritual with the offerings and then the receiving of seemingly sanctified food. However I now realize that these activities did not conform to traditional ritual in the sense that this spiritual movement understands the term: no proper priest officiated, only a volunteer. All events, moreover, happened as the faces of numerous successful

Woman takes *prashad* (sanctified food) at the end of a birthday celebration for Sri Sri Ravi Shankar. Photograph by the author.

Chinese business-oriented families gazed out from huge photos on the back wall of this chamber of commerce.

The following week I met with Shail, one of the founding members of AOL, at another Art of Living center on the third floor of a business complex. Anxious to ask questions about the implicit ritual in AOL as well as the reason for the emphasis on group *kriya*, I noticed that an altar was set up on the demonstration platform in this sparse, industrial-sized room and immediately concluded that this was Shail's doing. I was wrong. During the interview, as we discussed the ritual elements in AOL, she mentioned that some of the Chinese members had set up this altar, and she hated to hurt their feelings by taking it down, although she felt that such rituals can turn many people away from the meditations—she spoke of Christians, especially Protestants, being uncomfortable with such displays. These days she sees fewer Muslims at her center and especially worries about their reactions, since most people take the yoga course for "peace of mind and health" and not for *jñāna* (philosophical knowledge) or even *bhakti* (devotion). When I looked at the altar more closely, she was right: someone had garlanded the picture of Guruji, placed the framed picture on a small white eyelet cloth, and added a golden bowl filled with grapes and a candle in front of it—mixing Indian, Chinese, and English styles.

I learned much from Shail, especially about who came to Art of Living and under what conditions. According to her, her chapter of AOL does not attract many Singaporean Indians but rather a lot of Singaporean Chinese. Those Indians active in AOL are mostly professional "ex-pats," in her words, while the Chinese come from all classes and seem to enjoy the meditation and regularly attend follow-up sessions. She felt that the long-settled Singaporean Indians, mostly Tamil, were "ritualistic" and tended to confine their religious practice to temples. We talked about such migrants being "stuck" in the time that they left India, while the ex-pat Indians are far more "modern." She remained concerned that AOL did not foist Hindu ritual practices on those who came for mediation and advises other teachers to be sensitive to the religious backgrounds of those who come. Because of her own education in Catholic schools, she admitted that she always feels secure when communicating with Christians in her classes. However when a group of Hindu followers wanted to offer a special guru *pūjā* (devotional ritual) for Sri Sri Ravi Shankar immediately preceding his general birthday celebrations, she was concerned that only those who were comfortable with this kind of ritual be invited. In the end she also invited some Chinese whom she knew would be comfortable with these rituals. She invited "only those who are interested in it, who believe in it," because everyone identifies his or her guru in different forms. Shail personally does *pūjā* daily at home and attends temples but understands her AOL practices to strike another chord. For her separating rituals from meditation means opening the practice beyond those who identify as Hindus.

In a series of e-mail conversations with my instructor, Vijay, I pressed this issue of the relationship between ritual and Art of Living. Her answers were even more pointed than were Shail's, but she cautioned that these were her opinions only and not official Art of Living pronouncements. Vijay understood the practice of Sudarshan Kriya as distinct from temple rituals in important ways. The *kriya* "is a rhythmic breathing technique that cleanses the system of negative emotions—long buried emotions—depending on which religion a person subscribes to—even seeds of past karma. In addition we are bombarded with negative emotions . . . stress at work, people telling me their problems, economic stress—what is happening to the world with its political turmoil, economic slowdown and natural disaster—how do we get rid of it?" Vijay went on to argue that, to take care of this residue of troubles, many people either go to a temple and let the priest intercede with God or, as in her case,

> some people do rituals in the temple . . . and believe that performing these rituals gets rid of the negative energy that is affecting them. When I do the *kriya* I find my own strength to overcome the obstacles in life, and I have faith that whatever is happening—good or bad—is happening for my growth. . . . I believe in this power called God, but somehow I feel that he wants me to chart my own

> path in life—he will be there for me, will give me strength but he won't do things for me—spoon-feeding—he does not do that. Temple rituals may not give people the strength that the *kriya* gives because I feel that it makes people think that once they have done the ritual, God takes care of things and they just sit back and relax. But believe me, the faith I have in God now is much stronger than before, and I'm beginning to understand my own religion better; and if I want to take time to understand rituals performed, I can, but it's just that they are not as important now. (personal interview, May 27, 2008)

Although Shail and Vijay place different values on temple rituals, they both distinguish between the functions and effect of the *kriya* and of rituals, locating each in a different domain. *Kriya* creates a space of peace and well-being, of stress-free living, of personal involvement and empowerment. For Vijay ritual was the province of priests in traditional temples, while Shail included her own daily *pūjā* at home. For both, moreover, the *kriya* is a generally available practice outside of specific religious identities. For Shail mixing in too many Hindu-style or even Chinese-style rituals could lead to turning away sincere practitioners who either want meditation without any religious sentiment or who do not wish to have any clash between their religious commitments and these practices. For her Sudarshan Kriya operates outside of these identities and in another space.

But for all of their language about self, both of these Art of Living leaders emphasize that *kriya* practices were far more powerful when done in a group. AOL practice enjoins members to come together once a week for the "Long Kriya" and schedules these sessions on different days throughout their centers in Singapore. Vijay explained: "The Long Kriya cleanses not only the body, but also the environment—it releases positive ions into the environment. Hence when done collectively, it releases positive energy into the environment. It's like the concept of meditation—when a religious group wants to do meditation for things like world peace, etc., the larger the group the better, because the positive energy created is much higher than when one or two individuals do the meditation. Same principle applies—just that [in AOL] we do it every week" (personal interview, May 27, 2008). So for Vijay the Long Kriya becomes a personal, social, and cosmic event with very real benefits for both the practitioners and the world.

Conclusion

One major lesson that Singapore teaches is that, along with the careful, consciously constructed space of this global city, pluralism as a (supposedly enlightened) recognition of discrete faiths was part of its initial design, but it was never associated with the overall cultural framework of the whole. As in the pre-European traces of the city, the common framework and overarching worldview, the "canopied civilizational identity" (Hefner 2001, 42), was never associated with any single religion—or with religion at all, since commonality flowed from shared lifestyles, language, and "permeable ethnicity" (Hefner 2001, 13). The government of Singapore has made forays into this kind of social engineering through the "Confucianisation" that Chua describes, but in the end the overarching values retain a strong nationalism coupled with a relentless pursuit of economic growth, which continue to be linked to the values of close cooperation of communities and families in this joint enterprise. Singapore as a state seems to act seriously on near textbook models of religion and religions. The government assumes bounded ethnic identities closely connected to religious affiliation—at least in the case of the minority communities of Malays and Indians. In Singapore, and in the entire region, religion remains so embedded in ethnicity that Robert Hefner (2001) uses the term *ethnoreligion* throughout his insightful introduction to "the politics of multiculturalism" in the region. The government also assumes that ethnoreligious identities are tinderboxes unless carefully circumscribed in the language of communities. To return to the MCDYS website, the online application to register as a society includes a final page that is telling. The proposed society must attest to several conditions, among which is that the society "is not intended to represent, promote any cause or interest of, or discuss any issue relating to, any religion, ethnic group, clan, nationality, or class of person by reference to their sexual orientation" and "is not intended to represent persons who advocate, promote, or discuss any issue relating to any civil or political rights (including humans rights, environmental right and animal rights)" (see "Registry of Societies: Step-by-step Guidelines for Online Registration of a New Society"). Spiritual organizations may indeed parallel many of the markers of civil society organization in their volunteerism and their inclusivity but not as organized citizens voicing grievances on religious or indeed any other grounds. The state becomes the umbrella—the canopy—under which all else operates. This may be one of the more relentlessly secular visions in the world, yet at the same time, good order, moral behavior, and a caring community are enveloped in its vision.

Singapore remains heir to these ethno-religious borders and ironically works within them with caution. Religion does not now, nor indeed ever did, provide the cultural canopy that oriented this society. Whatever overarching values hold citizens together, they must remain secular—which in Singapore comes very close to the sense of spiritual values that many guru-centered movements enjoin. In Singapore these movements complement the formation of a new "sacred canopy" presented in the rhetoric of secularity not religion. Moreover Singapore's spiritual movements (in their openly global connections, they are all transnational groups) flow with the emerging nature of global civil society. In a suggestive description of "the sacred canopy of Global Civil Society," this theme of a moral economy as the umbrella culture appears.

> World culture thus is a rational, moral project of value attainment, a "modern" project over which there is much conflict. It is millennial in the sense that the groups involved are oriented to a future good society. It is this-worldly or naturalistic because ultimate authority is located in humanity (the individual and society), not in God or the super-empirical. This project is not neutral vis-à-vis religions even as religions are practiced within it and must engage it. Because it has a diffuse moral nature, world culture competes with religions for providing the moral ground to public and private life, and thus much conflict takes religious forms. (Thomas 2001, 517)

In this region of the world, then, religion guarantees neither public order nor public cohesion beyond the bounded forms usually closely associated with ethnic groups. In this context rituals also are circumscribed with boundaries. Indians belonging to new spiritual groups in Singapore may continue to perform ritual, but only as a Hindu practice embedded within their heritage. Shail may do *pūjā* and the *kriya,* each in its prescribed form daily, but she, and many others, would never apply the term *ritual* to the latter practice. Ritual is religion, the *kriya* is spirituality; the former is for Hindus, the latter for the world.[2] Thus de-ethnization requires de-ritualization. And for ritual studies this means that the field must listen to these important tones in terminology, for they signal the rise of global secular values within which actions we would call ritual are understood as scientific, universal, and therefore widely applicable to daily human problems—the stress and competition of a rapidly consumer-driven, technology-centered globalizing world. The new "sacred canopy" may indeed compete with religions, but most of the new spiritual movements of Singapore sit comfortably under its shade, adding a spoke here and a patch there and perhaps ultimately redesigning its very structure.

Notes

1. In Singapore there are four official languages, but English remains the language of business, education, and most public discourse. For proper names diacritics are rarely used. In this essay I have maintained the spelling of persons, organizations, and place names as they appear in published English works in Singapore. For the names of deities and other Tamil or Sanskritic terms, I revert to the standard transliteration.

2. I received an email announcing "Bhairagini Maa from the Linga Bhairavi temple in Isha Yoga Centre, to conduct a Devi Darshan process here in Singapore" (May 15, 2014). Sadhguru Jaggi Vasudev built a major temple complex at his ashram in Coimbatore and now has offered new rituals to his Ishas, often of his own creation. In the last year, other guru-centered organizations have also re-ritualized, which I will discuss in forthcoming work.

References

Bryant, Edwin F., and Maria L. Ekstrand. 2004. *The Hare Krishna Movement: The Post-charismatic Fate of a Religious Transplant.* New York: Columbia University Press.

Carrette, Jeremy, and Richard King. 2005. *Selling Spirituality: The Silent Takeover of Religion.* London & New York: Routledge.

Chambers, Simone, and Will Kymlicka, eds. 2002. *Alternative Conceptions of Civil Society.* Princeton: Princeton University Press.

Chua, Beng Huat. 1995. *Communitarian Ideology and Democracy in Singapore.* London & New York: Routledge.

——. 2003. *Life Is Not Complete without Shopping: Consumption Culture in Singapore.* Singapore: Singapore University Press.

Clothey, Fred W. 1983. *Rhythm and Intent: Ritual Studies from South India.* Madras: Blackie.

Curriculum Development Institute. 1986. *Confucian Ethics: Teacher's Guide, Secondary Four.* Singapore: Educational Publications.

Forsthoefel, Thomas A., and Cynthia Ann Humes, eds. 2005. *Gurus in America.* Albany: State University of New York Press.

Heelas, Paul 2008. *Spirituality of Life: New Age Romanticism and Consumptive Capitalism.* Oxford: Blackwell.

Heelas, Paul, and Linda Woodhead. 2005. *Spiritual Revolution: Why Religion Is Giving Way to Spirituality.* Hoboken, N.J.: Wiley.

Hefner, Robert W., ed. 2001. *The Politics of Multiculturalism: Pluralism and Citizenship in Malaysia, Singapore, and Indonesia.* Honolulu: University of Hawai'i Press.

Keane, John. 2003. *Global Civil Society?* Cambridge: Cambridge University Press.

Kuo, Eddie C. Y., and Jon S. T. Quah. 1988. *Religion in Singapore: Report of a National Survey.* Singapore: Ministry of Community Development.

Lau, Kimberly J. 2000. *New Age Capitalism: Making Money East of Eden.* Philadelphia: University of Pennsylvania Press.

Madsen, Richard. 2002. "Confucian Conceptions of Civil Society." In *Alternate Conceptions of Civil Society,* edited by Simone Chambers and Will Kymlicka, 190–204. Princeton: Princeton University Press.

Ministry of Information and the Arts. 1992. *The Need for the Maintenance of Religious Harmony Act.* Singapore: Resource Centre, Publicity Division, Ministry of Information and the Arts.

Pechilis, Karen, ed. 2004. *The Graceful Guru: Hindu Female Gurus in India and in the United States.* New York: Oxford University Press.

Roof, Wade Clark. 1999. *Spiritual Marketplace: Baby Boomers and the Remaking of American Religion.* Princeton: Princeton University Press.

Sinha, Vineeta. 2005a. *A New God in the Diaspora?—Muneeswaran.* Singapore: National University of Singapore Press.

——. 2005b. "Theorising Talk about Religious Pluralism and Religious Harmony in Singapore." *Journal of Contemporary Religion* 20, no. 1: 25–40.

——. 2006. "Constructing and Contesting 'Singaporean Hinduism.'" In *Race, Ethnicity and the State in Malaysia and Singapore*, edited by Lian Kwen Fee, 145–68. Leiden: Brill.

——. 2011. *Religion-State Encounters in Hindu Domains: From the Straits Settlements to Singapore.* Dordrecht & New York: Springer.

Srinivas, Smriti. 2008. *In the Presence of Sai Baba: Body, City, and Memory in a Global Religious Movement.* Leiden: Brill.

Srinivas, Tulasi. 2004. "Sacred Webs: Rethinking Globalization and Religion through the Transnational Satya Sai Movement." Paper presented at the Annual Meeting of the American Academy of Religion, San Antonio, Texas, November 20–23.

Tamney, Joseph B., and Raiz Hassan. 1987. *Religious Switching in Singapore: A Study of Religious Mobility.* Singapore: Select Books.

Tan Hwee Phio, Charlene. 2007. "Religious Education in Singapore: Exploring the Options." Lecture (with published abstract) presented at the Asia Research Institute, National University of Singapore, August 29, 2007.

Thomas, George M. 2001. "Religions in Global Civil Society." *Sociology of Religion* 62, no. 4: 515–33.

Waghorne, Joanne Punzo. 2004. *The Diaspora of the Gods: Modern Hindu Temples in an Urban Middle-Class World.* New York: Oxford University Press.

Walzer, Michael, ed. 1995. *Toward a Global Civil Society.* New York & Oxford: Berghahn Books.

Ward, Graham. 2006. "The Future of Religion." *Journal of the American Academy of Religion* 74, no. 1: 179–86.

Warrier, Maya. 2003. "Processes of Secularization in Contemporary India: Guru Faith in the Mata Amritanandamayi Mission." *Modern Asian Studies* 37, no. 1: 213–52.

——. 2005. *Hindu Selves in a Modern World: Guru Faith in the Mata Amritanandamayi Mission.* London: Routledge.

Wolffe, John, ed. 2002. *Global Religious Movements in Regional Contexts.* Aldershot: Ashgate.

Wuthnow, Robert. 1998. *After Heaven: Spirituality in America since the 1950s.* Berkeley: University of California Press.

Zepp, Ira G. 1997. *New Image of Urban America: The Shopping Mall as Ceremonial Center.* 2nd ed. Boulder: University of Colorado Press.

CONTRIBUTORS

Elizabeth Fuller Collins is professor of Southeast Asian studies in the Department of Classics and World Religions at Ohio University. She is the author of *Pierced by Murugan's Lance: Ritual, Power, and Moral Redemption among Malaysian Hindus* (1997), *Indonesia Betrayed: How Development Fails* (2007), and articles on Islamic movements in Indonesia. She is currently working on a book titled "Ritual and Rule: Religion in Southeast Asia," a historical overview of the religious traditions that have played a major role in shaping the political institutions and societies of the region.

Corinne Dempsey is associate professor of religious studies at Nazareth College. Her research interests include Hindu-Christian popular exchange in South India and Hinduism in North America, featured in her books *Kerala Christian Sainthood: Collisions of Culture and Worldview in South India* (2001) and *The Goddess Lives in Upstate New York: Making Home and Breaking Convention at a North American Hindu Temple* (2006). With Selva Raj she has edited three volumes on South Asian traditions that focus on popular Christianity, conceptions of the miraculous, and ritual levity. Her most recent work, *Bringing the Sacred down to Earth: Adventures in Comparative Religion* (2012), compares Hindu and Christian strategies for accessing the sacred.

David L. Haberman is professor of religious studies at Indiana University Bloomington. He is author of *Acting as a Way of Salvation: A Study of Raganuga Bhakti Sadhana* (1988), *Journey through the Twelve Forests: An Encounter with Krishna* (1994), *River of Love in an Age of Pollution: The Yamuna River of Northern India* (2006), and *People Trees: Worship of Trees in Northern India* (2013). His work, which has focused on the rituals and aesthetics of the temple traditions of medieval and modern northern India, combines both textual research and ethnographic fieldwork. He continues to be interested in issues related to religion and nature and is conducting research on the worship of sacred mountains in India.

Alf Hiltebeitel is Columbian Professor of Religion, History, and Human Sciences at the George Washington University. His research focuses on the Mahābhārata and related texts, most notably the Rāmāyaṇa, as well as Tamil Mahābhārata "folk" traditions. He is the author of dozens of articles and book chapters, as well as a number of monographs, four edited volumes, and several translations. His most recent publications include *Dharma* (2010), *Reading the Fifth Veda: Studies in the Mahābhārata* (2011), *When the Goddess Was a Woman: Mahābhārata Ethnographies* (2011), and *Dharma: Its Early History in Law, Religion, and Narrative* (2011).

Philip Lutgendorf is professor of Hindi and modern Indian studies in the Department of Asian and Slavic Languages and Literature at the University of Iowa. His book on the performance of the Rāṃāyaṇa, *The Life of a Text* (1991), won the A. K. Coomaraswamy Prize of the Association for Asian Studies. He received a Guggenheim Fellowship in 2002–3 for his research on the popular Hindu "monkey-god" Hanuman, which was published as *Hanuman's Tale: The Messages of a Divine Monkey* (2007). His interests include epic performance, folklore and popular culture, and mass media, and he maintains a website devoted to Indian popular cinema, a.k.a. "Bollywood" (http://www.uiowa.edu/~incinema). He is currently working on a social history of the beverage chai and on a new translation of the Rāmcaritmānas for the Murty Classical Library of India and Harvard University Press. He serves as president of the American Institute of Indian Studies.

Leslie C. Orr is professor of religion at Concordia University in Montreal. In addition to her book *Donors, Devotees and Daughters of God: Temple Women in Medieval Tamilnadu* (2000), she is the author of a number of articles, including "Words for Worship: Tamil and Sanskrit in Medieval Temple Inscriptions" (in *Bilingual Discourse and Cross-Cultural Fertilisation: Sanskrit and Tamil in Mediaeval India,* edited by Whitney Cox and Vincenzo Vergiani, 2012) and "Orientalists, Missionaries and Jains: The South Indian Story" (in *The Madras School of Orientalism: Producing Knowledge in Colonial South India,* edited by Thomas R. Trautmann, 2009). Her current research project is titled "Renovation, Replication, Recovery, and Revival: Building Temples and Building Histories in South India."

Linda Penkower is associate professor of religious studies at the University of Pittsburgh and a former colleague of Fred W. Clothey, who inspired this volume. She has published on the historical, social, institutional, and doctrinal aspects of East Asian Buddhism, especially the Chinese Tiantai tradition. Previously supported by Fulbright-Hays and National Endowment for the Humanities Fellowships, she is currently completing two monographs: "Tiantai Buddhism and the Construction of Lineage during the Tang" and "Shared Sacrality," an annotated translation of the *Jin'gangbei* (The Diamond Scalpel), the eighth-century Chinese locus classicus for the idea of insentient buddha-nature.

Tracy Pintchman is professor of Hindu studies and director of international studies at Loyola University Chicago. She teaches courses on Hinduism, ethnography of religion, and other religious studies topics. Her research interests include Hindu goddess traditions, women and religion, and transnational Hinduism. Her scholarly publications include about two dozen articles and book chapters as well as five books: two monographs, *The Rise of the Goddess in the Hindu Tradition* (1994) and *Guests at God's Wedding: Celebrating Kartik among the Women of Benares* (2005); two edited volumes, *Seeking Mahādevī: Constructing the Identities of the Hindu Great Goddess* (2001) and *Women's Rituals, Women's Lives in the Hindu Tradition: Domesticity and Beyond* (2007); and one coedited volume (with Rita D. Sherma), *Goddess and Woman in Hinduism: Reinterpretations and Re-envisionings* (2011).

K. Ramanathan is associate professor in the School of Distance Education at the University Sains Malaysia in Penang. He has published articles on Hindu religious practice and the challenges it faces in the multiethnic society of Malaysia. His books on political science are used as textbooks and as reference material in Malaysia. He received his Ph.D. degree from the University of Amsterdam. His dissertation, "Hindu Religion in an Islamic State: The Case of Malaysia," examined the formation of and challenges faced by Hindu religious institutions and temples in Malaysia.

Joanne Punzo Waghorne is professor of religion at Syracuse University, where she researches issues of changing religious organizations, practices, and self-understanding in the present era of urbanization, globalization, and transnational migration. Her *Diaspora of the Gods: Modern Hindu Temples in an Urban Middle-Class World* (2004) was recognized for "Excellence in the Study of Religion" by the American Academy of Religion in 2005. An earlier work, *The Raja's Magic Clothes: Re-visioning Kingship and Divinity in England's India* (1994), was revived in an invited contribution titled "The Power of Public Splendour" in *Maharaja: The Splendour of India's Royal Courts* (edited by Anna Jackson and Amin Jaffer, 2009), which accompanied a major exhibition at the Victoria and Albert Museum. A Fulbright-Hays Fellowship in 2007–8 supported her recent work on global guru-centered movements in Singapore and Chennai. "Global Gurus and the Third Stream of American Religiosity" (in *Political Hinduism,* edited by Vinay Lal, 2010), reflects this new work.

Paul Younger is professor emeritus of religious studies at McMaster University in Hamilton, Ontario. He is the author of numerous articles and books, including *The Home of Dancing Sivan: The Traditions of the Hindu Temple in Citamparam* (1995), *Playing Host to Deity: Festival Religion in the South Indian Tradition* (2002), and *New Homelands: Hindu Communities in Mauritius, Guyana, Trinidad, South Africa, Fiji, and East Africa* (2010). His most recent publications include "Learning about Hindu Practice: Fighting Late-Colonial Attitudes and Discovering Temples and Festivals" (in *Studying Hinduism in Practice,* edited by Hillary P. Rodriques, 2011), "Hindus" (in *The Religions of Canadians,* edited by Jamie S. Scott, 2012), and "M. K. Gandhi: A Post-Colonial Voice" (in *Teaching Religion and Violence,* edited by Brian K. Pennington, 2012). He is currently conducting research on Hindus in Canada.

INDEX

Brahmanic Hinduism, 181; Brahmanization, 44; in Canada, 129–36, 140–41; Murukaṉ in, 10, 12, 35, 83, 89; Śrīvidyā tradition, 107, 111, 115, 116, 118, 121–22; texts, 170
Brahman priests: in diasporic temples, 107, 111, 134, 141; in Malaysian temples, 84, 95; at marriage rituals, 48, 49, 68
Brahmans: Ajāmila, 157–59, 161, 164n8; *dhárman* and, 169; Laws of Manu and, 179, 181; Subrahmaṇya worship and, 28; *svabhāva* and, 174; *svadharma* and, 15, 176, 182n6; *svakarmas* and, 166–67, 171–73; Yajñadatta, 153. *See also* Śrīvidyā Tantric tradition
Braj, Uttar Pradesh (India), 55n5
breathing exercises, 191, 200
Brereton, Joel, 167–68, 170
Britain, 127; British High Commission, 99; British scholarship, 2; spiritual movements in, 190
British colonization: in Canada, 126–27; in Malaya, 84, 86–87, 89, 99, 186, 194
British Columbia, 127
Brodbeck, Simon, 175, 180
Brooks, Douglas, 116, 121
Buddha, 181
Buddhism, 168–70, 173, 182; Kuan-yin, 192
Bühler, Georg, 180
Burma, 90
Burnham, Forbes, 128

California, United States, 146n3
Campany, Rob, 152
Canada, 13–14, 126–46; Ati Para Sakti Temple in, 141–43; Ayyappan Temple in, 140–41; Canadian Council of Hindus, 145; Canadian National Exhibition grounds, 138; ethnic communities in, 136–39, 145; Ganesha Temple in, 133–36, 140; Hindu Samaj in, 14, 129–31, 136, 144; immigration to, 127–28; Sikhs in, 127–29, 138, 144, 146nn2–4; storefront temples in, 140–43, 145; temple traditions in, 145; Vaiṣṇo Devī Temple in, 136–37; Vishnu Mandir in, 131–33, 136, 141
Caṇḍa ("Uttarakhaṇḍa"), 156, 159, 161
Caṅkam literature, 23, 30, 34–35
capparam chariots, 109–11. *See also* chariots
Caribbean, 133
caste system: in Canada, 144; Hindi film and, 57, 71; householders, renouncers, and, 43–44, 54; Indian identity and, 72, 84; Maha Mariamman Temple and, 87; at Rush temple, 111, 112; of Tamil Hindus in Malaysia, 12, 83–90, 92, 97, 98, 100. *See also* untouchables; *varṇa* (social classes)
caturmāsa (monsoon period), 42, 46
Caudhurī, Siddhārth (character), 66–67
caves: Batu Caves, 89, 99, 100, 101; images of Murukaṉ in, 22, 25, 29
celibacy, of Rāmānandi renunciants, 53, 55n7
Ceylon. *See* Sri Lanka
Chaitanyananda, Sri. *See* Aiya (Sri Chaitanyananda)
chakra (mystic diagram), 193
changes. *See* transformation
chanting, 132; of *bhajans*, 74; in *Hum Aapke Hain Koun*, 68; in *Jai Santoshi Maa*, 63, 77; in *kriyas*, 191; at Rush temple, 115, 118; of Sanskrit verses, 51
chariots, 134–35; *capparam*, 109–11; at Tai Pūcam, 86–87, 93, 96
charities, 190, 192, 194, 196–97
Chennai, Tamilnadu, 141–42; advertising in, 186
Chettinad (Tamilnadu), 84, 101n2
Chetti Pusam (celebration), 86, 88
Chettiyar chariot procession, 86
Chettiyars, 92, 101n2; description of, 84; in Independent Malaysia, 90; Nattukottai Chettiar Temple, 84, 86; origin of Chetti Pusam and, 86–87; ritual performance and, 85; Tai Pūcam and, 88; worship of Murukaṉ by, 12, 83, 89
chief of Sambuvaraya, 39n9

CPSIA information can be obtained at www.ICGtesting.com
Printed in the USA
LVOW10*2341220914

405353LV00002B/3/P

9 781611 173895

Due Date	Date Returned
	APR 1 4 2015
	JAN 07 2015
MAR 2 3 2015	MAR 0 7 2017
MAR 1 3 2017	

RECEIVED

JAN 2 2 2015

GUELPH HUMBER LIBRARY
205 Humber College Blvd
Toronto, ON M9W 5L7

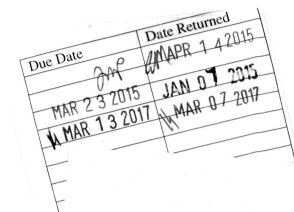